"If you are a leader, and if you desire to help develop other leaders for both today and tomorrow, this is a must read! The biblical principles unfolded by Carson, along with his vast experience, will prove to be a fantastic aid to your own growth and effectiveness, not to mention the growth of your colleagues, team, and those in whom you are able to invest. Carson will sharpen the arrow of your own life and leadership and help you make sure you are on target for leading a life worth sharing!"

Bob Reccord, president, North American Mission Board

"If you have never had a mentor—but, always wanted one—get this book and read it word for word and cover to cover. A book cannot be a mentor, but this one comes from a mentor's heart with a mentor's style. Then use the book as a guide as you begin the exciting process of mentoring others."

Bobb Biehl, president, MasterplanningGroup.com

"Carson Pue's *Mentoring Leaders* is not only the source of sound, practical help for mentoring future Christian leaders, but what stands out for me is that, unlike several other books on this topic I have seen, it is thoroughly biblical and theologically sound. It focuses on the character, calling, and spiritual development of the leader, not just his or her competence. I also like the fact that it is 'inclusive'—a much needed corrective in our chauvinistic world."

Archibald D. Hart, Ph.D., senior professor of psychology and dean emeritus, Graduate School of Psychology, Fuller Theological Seminary

"I know no one better prepared to think and write on the topic of mentoring than Carson Pue. Gladly I commend this book, because to Carson Pue mentoring has evangelistic impact. A mentored leader with a heart for the lost will move thousands toward the kingdom."

Lon Allison, director, Billy Graham Center, Wheaton College

"This book is filled with truth that can ripple down the generations until Jesus comes. The information on self-awareness alone is worth more than you have paid to read it. It is a book that can change you. But better yet, God can use the insight and inspiration in these pages to change others through you! Can you think of anything better than that?"

Rich Stevenson, director, The Expansion Network

"Carson Pue understands that developing men and women for leadership is more than passing on skill-based information. In seeking to shape another person's heart, Carson, throughout these pages, gives you his own heart."

Graham Johnston, pastor, Subiaco Church, Perth, Western Australia; author of *Preaching to a Postmodern World*

"The world today, and the church in particular, face a crisis of leadership. This is why Carson Pue's new book is so important. Leaders are needed in all walks of life, but few people have taken as much effort as Pue to think through the complex issue of mentoring the next generation. I heartily recommend this book"

Irving Hexham, Ph.D., professor of religious studies, University of Calgary

"*Mentoring Leaders* is one of the more insightful books on mentoring emerging leaders. Since intentional mentoring is the key, Carson's purposeful mentoring model makes a significant contribution."

Martin Sanders, founder and president, Global Leadership, Inc.

"I read a sign outside a garden center: 'The best time to plant a tree was twenty-five years ago; the second best time is today.' I wish I had read Carson's book twenty-five years ago when I started in the ministry, but thank God I read it today. It has planted so many sacred seeds into my mind and heart that can only produce good fruit."

J. John, director, The Philo Trust

"Carson Pue is one of the most thoughtful advocates of mentoring for Christian leaders. He does it well. And he has a pulse on what it takes to equip others for the task. Please read his book."

Susan Perlman, associate executive director, Jews for Jesus

"Read this slowly with a pen and journal at your side. The concepts are invigorating and practical, this is the best of instruction for leaders on the job."

Lorna Dueck, executive producer, Listen Up TV/Media Voice Generation

"I've had only one regret knowing Carson Pue: that I don't know him better. And I've had only one disappointment spending time with him: that I couldn't spend more. Carson is a leader's leader and a mentor's mentor, and now—finally—he's captured on paper, available to all, his insights in both areas. This book unfolds like a season of long chats with a man of great grace and deep wisdom."

Mark Buchanan, author of *The Holy Wild* and *The Rest of God*

"Drawing on years of mentoring work with well-known global leaders and emerging leaders alike, Carson Pue writes insightfully about the practical and spiritual matters that all Christian leaders need to consider. Carson anchors it all in the importance of a life of personal devotion and prayer, paired with a relentless desire to pursue God's vision and enhance the gifts he has invested in you."

Dave Toycen, president, World Vision Canada

MENTORING
LEADERS

# MENTORING
# LEADERS

WISDOM FOR DEVELOPING CHARACTER,
CALLING, AND COMPETENCY

## CARSON PUE

BakerBooks
Grand Rapids, Michigan

© 2005 by Carson Pue

Published by Baker Books
a division of Baker Publishing Group
P.O. Box 6287, Grand Rapids, MI 49516-6287
www.bakerbooks.com

Printed in the United States of America

Library of Congress Cataloging-in-Publication Data

Pue, Carson
   Mentoring leaders : wisdom for developing character, calling, and competency / Carson Pue.
      p.    cm.
   Includes bibliographical references.
   ISBN 0-8010-9187-X (pbk.)
   1. Christian leadership. 2. Mentoring in church work. 3. Leadership—Religious aspects—Christianity. I. Title.
   BV652.1.P84 2005
   253—dc22
                                                2005018707

Arrow Leadership Program is a service mark of Arrow Leadership International Ministries.

# Contents

PHASE FIVE:
## Sustaining

# Foreword

A recent visitor noticed the thousands of books in my office and politely asked if I had read them all. After I admitted that I had not, my friend asked how I choose which ones to read and which ones to discard.

Upon reflection, I realized that there are three critical elements that make a book appealing to me.

First, *the messenger must be trustworthy.* For me, that means the author must be a person of integrity. In practical terms, such authors are experts on their subject matter, approach the topic from a reasonable perspective, and draw insights from both experience and instruction.

Second, *the message must be trustworthy.* The information provided must fit the known facts. The argument presented should be clear and articulate. The message must have the potential to bear fruit in or through me. I do not have to completely agree with the argument, but I must understand it and believe it to be a valid representation of a realistic point of view.

Third, *the message must be helpful to the reader.* Time is too short to waste on useless information or inapplicable theories. The message should therefore be timely, practical, and beneficial.

I recognize that not everyone looks at books through such a lens, but given my background and goals, this filter serves me well.

That is one of the reasons I have so enjoyed Carson Pue's book on mentoring. Not only is he addressing a topic about which I am passionate (leadership) and a facet that is often overlooked (mentoring), but Carson's book is three for three in reference to my criteria. Having known and served with him for over a decade, I know him to be a man of great integrity and wisdom. I trust him. Having been intimately involved in leadership development for many years, I recognize the veracity of many principles and conditions described by Carson throughout this labor of love. I have seen Carson use these principles in his work with leaders. I trust his message. And as someone who often struggles with how to more effectively mentor people—especially the very young leaders with whom I work—I found this book as one that offers real-world solutions to the real-world challenges I face in helping young leaders grow. I have been helped by this message.

The research I have conducted regarding leadership shows that mentoring is one of those areas that people value but are ignorant of. Too few leaders have had a good mentor. Surprisingly few constructive books have been written on the matter. Most leadership courses extol the virtues of mentoring but provide little in the way of hands-on, proven assistance. Consequently, Carson's life experience and careful guidance are a welcome addition to the voluminous body of literature regarding leadership development.

It is my hope that you find this book to be just the wisdom you need as you mentor leaders to greater productivity and impact.

George Barna
The Barna Group
Ventura, California

# Acknowledgments

I wish to acknowledge the input of all the mentors in my life and the wisdom they have shared so openhandedly. Without your investment from near and far, my ability to minister for the kingdom of God would have been greatly diminished. Mentoring is loving—and I know that I am loved, so thank you.

Speaking of love . . . Brenda, you have shown more love to this leader than can be measured. Your sacrifice of time and relationship due to writing was greater than either of us anticipated. Your amazing gifts combine with your prayer life to make you one incredible leader.

Speaking of sacrificing time and relationship . . . Jason and Kristin, Jeremy and Jonathan, thanks for being so supportive and ministry minded while Dad locked himself away to write. Jason, your contributions are included within. Jon, your words of encouragement and shoulder rubs kept me going. Jer, your music buoyed me, and Connor (our Wheaton Terrier), you kept my feet warm. Kristin—you bring a smile to my face by the love you have brought into our family.

Speaking of being supportive . . . thanks to the team at Arrow: Aklilu Mulat, Steve Brown, Tarra Wellings, Michele Yackel, Jeremy Tjosvold, Justin Reid, Shelaine Chu, Shari Bouleau, Jane Omelaniac, and Ofelia Comandao. Let me also add Miller and Terri Alloway, Laurie and Jane Barber, Gregg and Cathy Becker, Jacqueline Bland, Roger and Lori Kemp, Doug and Gayle Moffat, and Gary and Lynne Schmidt, for all you have given and continue to give to the Arrow board. Your love for God, your investment in his leaders has inspired and influenced thousands.

# A Note on Personal Pronouns and People's Names

## This Book on Leadership Is Written for Both Women and Men

Arrow Leadership International Ministries has from its inception valued women in leadership. The number of top-level leadership positions held by women in the Christian ministry world is still much smaller than that held by men. Yet, I was birthed and raised by a woman who was a leader, and I am married to one—Brenda. We minister side by side at Arrow.

I desire to be clearly nonsexist in this book, and tried using "he/she," and then tried alternating masculine pronouns in one chapter with feminine pronouns in the next. Both methods proved distracting and confusing.

I have chosen to stay with traditional forms, understanding that the masculine pronouns are used generically, not sexually. You will note my intentional inclusion of women leaders along with men as illustrations. Until such time as we develop non–gender-related pronouns, please hear my heart on this issue.

## This Book on Leadership Protects and Lifts Up Leaders

There are several stories told out of personal mentoring experience with leaders. I did not feel it was necessary, nor appropriate, to use their actual names or the names of their ministries for the point of the illustrations. Whenever the use of an illustration would cause personal concern to leaders or their ministries, alternate names and contexts were used. However, several leaders have participated willingly, and the references to their ministry websites are included in endnotes.

# The Process of Mentoring

## THE HISTORY AND BACKGROUND

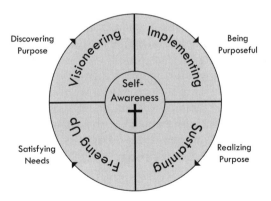

## Developing Leaders: Jesus Didn't Do It in a Weekend

My love and passion for the development of leaders has only grown through the years through my experiences with mentors and other leaders and the undeniable spiritual call in my life to be engaged in assisting the Lord's anointed ones.

Bookstore shelves today are lined with volumes on the subject of leadership. They are addressing an important need—or perhaps better, a desperate need. The post–World War II Christian leaders who emerged on the international scene with such vision and energy in the 1950s have largely moved off the stage today. Yet they have built denominations, parachurch organizations, and other ministries that require a high degree of leadership competency. There are not many young leaders rising up to take their place. Why is that?

Few are actually called to be leaders. Those who are must be nurtured and developed one person at a time. To develop—really develop—transformational leaders, the process must be highly personalized. The long-term results of large leadership or motivational events and seminars show little depth in the developing of anointed leaders. Jesus did not do it in a weekend! I am convinced that their leadership will take the right mix of calling, character, and competency.

New emerging leaders breathe expectancy. They seek out their mission field in every corner of the world, including their own backyard. Moreover, they desire to build the kingdom of God for his glory, not to build empires for themselves. The heart of Jesus's leadership was putting his Spirit in his disciples by mentoring and teaching, and then setting them free to pursue vision, for God.

We live in the crucible of a most extraordinary moment in time. Never before have we faced the vast ethical and leadership challenges that lie before us today. Those leaders who guided the moral fabric of society up to this point are coming to the end of their leadership careers. New leaders must be empowered to take their place. Who will share the vision of emerging leaders?

*Mentoring Leaders* is an ongoing expression of my calling to both mentor leaders and develop more mentors who will commit to the one-on-one practice of developing godly leaders. Although filled with wisdom for leaders, it also contains sidebars with instructions, questions, and tips on how to mentor leaders. I pray that one or two nuggets may fall from these pages and encourage you as a leader to get a mentor, and be a mentor.

## Emerging Leaders

Arrow exists to prepare the next generation of Christian leaders. With passionate commitment, top leaders of today are training a generation of new leaders to deal with the challenges before them. These men and women, carefully selected to represent the finest young leaders in the world, are being equipped to lead us into tomorrow. I invite you, through *Mentor-*

*ing Leaders*, to gain a behind-the-scenes look at this exciting process of shaping the future leaders for the challenges ahead.

## What Do You See?

It's a question Jesus asked his leaders in the making. And with good reason! Vision, the ability to see beyond the immediate to God's desired future, is what leadership is all about. If the vision is clear, the leader can communicate. However, if the vision is fuzzy, people will not be moved to follow.

It was vision that shaped the ministries of Billy Graham, John Perkins, Bob Pierce, Ted Engstrom, Bill Bright, Leighton Ford, Anne Graham Lotz, Bob Reccord, Stuart and Jill Briscoe, Gib Martin, and modern visionaries like Peter Chao, Mark Buchanan, Karen Souffrant, J. John, Lorna Dueck, Graham Johnston, Joyce Meyers, and Lon Allison. Yet there is much more behind the success of their ministries than vision alone.

Older mentors guided these Christian leaders through their vision. A process of accountability kept them on track. In addition, they relied on dedicated peers to build character. They were kept on course through mentoring.

Today, thousands of young leaders are equally passionate about their vision for ministry. But to turn those dreams into reality, they need to be challenged to be clear. They need to be exposed to needs and opportunities. They need to be encouraged to be prayerful and reflective until their vision sharpens. They need to study models of integrity, to go through experiences that stretch character and build commitment. And they need to spend quality time with seasoned mentors. These are the ways Arrow helps shape young leaders. Together, we believe that we can help build their future ministries. The next Billy Graham, Henrietta Mears, or Dawson Trotman can spring from one of the young men or women now being trained for leadership.

Arrow was founded on the belief that there are young people in the world today with the vision and strength and skill to take the reins of leadership. Beginning with the vision of one man—Leighton Ford—the ministry of developing younger leaders has impacted millions through the ripple effect of each young leader affecting his circle of influence.

Even as a teenager, Leighton demonstrated his abilities as a leader, organizing and preaching at evangelistic youth rallies. Because of Leighton's height, Evon Hedley encouraged him to step into a leadership role without even knowing how young he was at the time. Personally mentored by Billy Graham, Leighton was an associate evangelist and vice president with the Billy Graham Evangelistic Association.

After three decades of ministry, a personal tragedy helped give Leighton direction. Shortly after his twenty-first birthday, the Ford's oldest son, Sandy, went running with his roommate and arrhythmia struck. He died on an operating table a few days later. Out of this loss, Leighton gained a heart's desire to help emerging communicators of the gospel. He took his idea to "The Point Group," a group of committed younger leaders he had assembled, and asked for their contribution to this vision. Out of that desire and meeting emerged the Arrow Leadership Program.[SM] Unique in structure and focus, Arrow is a carefully crafted, intensive development program aimed at already gifted young leaders. It has been referred to as a Christian executive MBA program, and even as the Christian leadership equivalent to special forces training, like the Navy SEALs, the Army Rangers, or the Air Force's Delta Force receive.

The men and women selected for participation continue in their own ministries while taking part in the two-year program. Participants commit to attend four weeklong seminars, to join in ministry outings, to meet regularly with mentors, to gather quarterly with peers for accountability and encouragement, to complete extensive assignments, and to immerse themselves in a transparent, in-depth assessment of their capabilities and characteristics.

Participants set goals to build on their strengths and to minimize their weaknesses—all toward the larger goals of being led more by Jesus, leading more like Jesus, and leading more to Jesus.

The aim is to see young Christian leaders develop powerful, long-term ministries as they develop personal character, spirituality, and professional leadership skills. It's not enough to do the right thing; it is vital that ministry leaders are right people—reflecting the very heart of Jesus Christ.

The leadership development process focuses on four primary elements:

1. Character
2. Leadership
3. Evangelism
4. Kingdom Seeking

Although there are residential seminars—weeklong group meetings with featured speakers—that provide valuable content, the leadership development approach at Arrow is focused on the individual. Faculty, made up of some of the world's top leadership specialists, act more as personal consultants to the participants than as lecturers. It is not uncommon for class sessions to extend well into the night as participants seek out practical advice and counsel from the instructors. Learning takes place in "real time." Topics are no longer theory but applicable to the specific issues faced in each participant's personal ministry context.

Arrow uses a unique competency model to measure the progress of leaders in the program. This emphasis on spiritual maturity, character, values, attitude, and skills of participants allows the organization to build their leadership and management capacity from a strong foundation, leading to strong, mature leaders.

Progress is evaluated in a number of ways, utilizing comprehensive 360-degree feedback and on-site mentoring. Each participant is teamed with a mentor, who provides valuable advice and godly counsel. In addition, fellow classmates give honest feedback and accountability in an atmosphere of grace. This peer feedback often continues for decades as graduates keep in touch with one another through Arrow's global network. The aim is to track long-term results in these young leaders to help build ministries that impact lives for generations to come.

## Elements of Leadership Development

Because this process is regarded as the premier leadership development process among Christian leaders, it will be helpful to understand why it works so effectively. Many people look at one or two aspects of the Arrow experience and miss the process. I have come to see how the Lord works through this systematic and spiritual experience. The Arrow Leadership Program has matured since 1992 into a comprehensive, proven leadership training system, and although we have changed some of the modules, we maintain the following elements:

### Leadership Assessment

As the program begins, a battery of evaluation tests is given each leader, ranging from leadership style to emotional stability. Some results are shared as a cohort, building a strong level of transparency among participants. That leads to humility and openness. From there, the younger leader, his mentor, and the Arrow team help shape a personalized development plan.

### Leadership Development Plan

This custom-tailored plan includes specific areas that will be strengthened over the course of twenty-four months and beyond. Progress toward this plan is evaluated every six months by the young leader's leadership partner and also encouraged by his local mentor.

### Residential Seminars

Intensive, weeklong seminars bring all the participants together to learn and interact with some of the leading Christian thinkers and activists involved in ministry today.

### Mentoring

Each participant is teamed with a senior mentor. The mentor and young leader meet monthly during the two-year program to interact over assignments and ministry or personal challenges. With permission, Arrow shares a summary of the assessment evaluation with the mentor, who then assists the young leader and guides him in his development.

### Leadership Cluster

Each leader becomes part of a smaller group, which meets quarterly for prayer, accountability, and the pooling of wisdom on successes and failures. In addition, leadership clusters are encouraged to find ways to work together during the leader's time of development.

### Assignments

Regular readings and videotapes add to the knowledge base for young leaders. Each participant is also encouraged to keep a journal of prayer and progress. Assignments are tied to the content of the residential seminars and are often interfaced practically with the young leader's place of specific ministry.

### Structured Experiences

Field assignments are offered through the course work. These may consist of urban evangelism and cross-cultural ministry ventures in community outreaches. The purpose is to practice real-world evangelism in the presence of other leaders, building Christlike character and passion for the lost.

## Why Share Faith?

At my core, evangelism fuels me. I get emotional when people come into a relationship with Jesus. This is really what being a follower of Jesus is all about—living a life that so fully proclaims God's love and Spirit within you that others are drawn into a saving relationship with Christ. We live in a season right now where, as Eddie Gibbs quips, "The church needs to become *infiltrational* rather than *invitational*" (emphasis added).

I determined long ago that if I am personally going to give any time or energy to developing leaders, it must be centered in our calling to share Jesus with others. I have a passion for raising up an army of infiltrators of the gospel. Now, I understand that not all who picked up this book as another tome on leadership will be comfortable with this—but please, get over it and read on!

Jesus would ask his chosen leaders to face situations that stretch their level of comfort or competency. Leadership by its very nature takes faith—a readiness to be shaped by God in new and uncharted ways.

God has to be fully involved in this process of developing leaders, and that is why I have tried to emphasize the spiritual dimension of the process throughout *Mentoring Leaders*. The truth is that we cannot identify future leaders, with certainty. We can spot talent. We can see potential. But you and I really don't know who will press on to see fruitful ministries—only God knows this. But what we can do is provide some spiritual "venture capital," empowering these young leaders to realize fully their potential for the kingdom of God. That support requires others—mentors and other senior leaders—committed to the same vision. Are you ready to share the venture, and the rewards, with some of tomorrow's great leaders?

If so, *Mentoring Leaders* will teach you the principles of a proven mentoring process that has been highly effective in the development of leaders. If you are willing to take up the meaningful ministry of mentoring leaders, this book will provide you with a practical framework for developing leaders gained over our years of experience. On the other hand, if you are a leader longing for a mentor, then allow this text to be a guide on your own personal journey and begin the self-learning necessary to establish a great mentoring relationship.

## Five Phases of the Mentoring Matrix

There is a pattern and flow of developing leaders in a transformational manner that we describe as a mentoring matrix.

A few years ago we hosted a residential seminar for Arrow leaders in the beautiful setting of Cedar Springs in Washington State. It was near the end of a very productive day, and we decided to take the last few minutes for a question and answer time. On this particular day, many of the questions were about the process of mentoring.

"How do I go about finding a good mentor?"

"How will I know what to do with my mentor?"

"How will my mentor know what to do with me?"

"Is there a particular pattern to the mentoring process?"

This final question prompted me to pick up a marker and walk over to a nearby flip chart. On the flip chart I drew a rough sketch of what we have come to know as the mentoring matrix. I shared what we have observed as a somewhat typical pattern in the development of leaders. It took all of fifteen minutes and was sufficient to answer the question asked.

Later that evening Brenda said to me, "Did you see what happened when you drew that matrix on the flip chart today?"

I replied that I had not really noticed anything.

"The matrix and flow of mentoring you presented resonated with everyone there. They were all diving for a pen and paper. I think you should give more time to thinking about and developing this matrix for us to use with mentors, and our Arrow leaders." With those words, Brenda actually planted the seeds for the book you are reading today. In fact, that flip chart has been taped to the wall in my home office ever since, and it was my son Jon who encouraged me to turn it into a book.

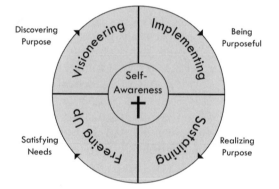

Let me try to re-create that first classroom explanation of the matrix as I stare at this well-used, wrinkled piece of flip chart paper. The center of the matrix, where it states "Self-Awareness" along with the cross, is where all mentoring needs to begin. We start in the middle, move to the bottom left-hand corner, "Freeing Up," and then move clockwise through the three remaining phases of mentoring. Let's look at these phases more specifically.

*Phase One: Awareness*

The first thing I drew was the circle in the center of the page. I wrote the word "self-awareness" but left enough space to include a small cross in the circle. We need to be aware of ourselves, and God.

Self-awareness is at the very core of your development as a leader. You must have an accurate self-awareness, not simply of your abilities, gifts, and skills but also of the shadow side of your life as a leader. Most importantly, leaders must have absolute clarity on who they are as children of God. Self-awareness is about finding and being secure in your identity in Christ.

This is the hub of the mentoring matrix, around which everything else revolves. The spokes of the matrix revolve around this hub. To have an effective mentoring experience, and to develop as a leader, you must start with an extremely clear awareness of who you are and why you do what you do, and a solid theological foundation for your identity in Christ.

## Phase Two: Freeing Up

The second phase of the mentoring process is one of freeing up. Because of our increased awareness of the self, we usually become aware of some things that have been holding us back. It is during this phase that we explore together any areas of life, experience, and history you need to be freed from in order to continue to develop. During our time of discovery together, it may be recommended that you talk with a professional counselor. There is nothing to be ashamed of here. Our desire is to see you free to lead, as God would have you lead. We believe God is calling you to godly leadership. We also recommend being vigilant in prayer—asking the Lord to reveal to you any specific areas where you may be held back in your development by chains of bondage attached to circumstances, unhealed wounds, or spiritual wanderings. Within Arrow, we utilize a couple who are very gifted in guiding leaders through this prayer process.

The freeing-up stage of the mentoring matrix is really all about satisfying needs. It is searching for and understanding your core needs as an individual and as a leader. We try to help leaders understand these needs, and evaluate where they are turning to have these needs met. Many of us try to meet needs ourselves rather than turning to God and allowing him to meet our needs.

## Phase Three: Visioneering

The third phase is entitled "Visioneering"—a word that was introduced to me by Andy Stanley. This is one of the more exciting phases of the mentoring process. In fact, it is so exciting that many people want to skip quickly to this phase. I find that men in particular love to get to the visioneering stage. This is a temptation for both the mentor and the mentee. Let me state this strongly: You cannot skip steps in this process without making the mentoring somewhat shallow. In fact, if you jump to visioneering without having a clear understanding of self, or things holding you back, you may be wasting your time, or even damaging your training if the vision is implemented without a solid foundation.

There's something very energizing about visioneering. I understand why it is exciting, and I personally love mentoring leaders in this phase. Nevertheless, I am not naive to the risks of moving through mentoring too quickly. I have come to see again and again how important it is to ensure that a leader has a very clear understanding of the first two steps in the mentoring process. Within the Arrow program, we walk alongside leaders for a two-year period, and I am happy and willing to spend eighteen months of that time dealing with the first two stages. I find that if we spend the time up front, the following steps will flow rather quickly—the vision becomes much sharper and focused because of a firm foundation.

There are few things more fulfilling for a mentor than to see the eyes of the mentee when they begin to gain clarity and focus on God's vision for the mentee's life. There is a change in the mentee's spirit, countenance, and energy level, and it is often exemplified by a renewed passion.

We want every leader to get to this place, and it is a fun time of mentoring—but we must not short-circuit the process.

### Phase Four: Implementing

The fourth phase of the mentoring matrix is that of implementing. This is the stage where we walk alongside leaders and help them strategically begin to step out in leadership toward the now-focused vision. The mentor is assisting with organizational design and development, with leadership skill and strategic planning. This stage also involves team building and team strategies. It is often important to help younger leaders see the incremental steps required to fulfill a vision. Many young leaders are too eager to get to the finish line without appreciating the importance of stepping out.

### Phase Five: Sustaining

In the fifth stage, "Sustaining," the focus is on assisting the leader to know how to lead and continue to sustain the vision. Often it is at this stage that leaders once again have a difficult time. Once we are past the excitement of visioneering, and the strategic implementation of the vision, it seems as though sustaining is simply not as exciting. The entrepreneurial leader and even those who are less entrepreneurial have a desire to move on. Restlessness sets in.

This restlessness often leads the mentor, and the mentee, back to the core of the mentoring matrix. For you see, after walking through this matrix, leaders learn a great deal more about who they are. Their self-awareness is increased, and as a result, they may find additional things in their person or spirit that need to be freed up.

What I am indicating is that once we have walked through the mentoring matrix, we frequently begin the process again. It is possible for the mentor and leader to walk through the phases of the mentoring matrix several times.

I shared this matrix with a group of leaders in my town, and it sparked quite a discussion. The model, they pointed out, has to be more than a circular journey for us as we develop. One suggested that it would be better illustrated with a three-dimensional model—one that showed us growing closer to God with each cycle through the mentoring phases.

A vertical helix, intersected by the crosshairs of the matrix, may be even better. I like the helix image because of how the circle gets smaller as we proceed through mentoring—and this would symbolically show that we do learn something with each encircling of the matrix cycle.

In my own experiences with mentors over the years, I have gained the insights more quickly when placed within the context and history of my previous experiences.

## Airport Layover

There was a time when several things were converging on me at once, and I knew enough about myself to know that I did not have answers as to direction within me. I thought and prayed about someone I could talk to, and that prayer was answered when a couple, Doug and Gayle Moffat, kept coming to mind. But they lived in Calgary, about a twelve-hour drive or an hour's flight away—how was that going to help me? Then I recalled that I had a flight to Edmonton for a meeting, with a short layover at the Calgary airport. I phoned and arranged to meet Doug and Gayle at the Calgary airport.

Doug was the executive minister for the Baptist Union of Western Canada when I entered pastoral ministry. As a family, they attended the churches where I pastored, and we also had the opportunity to work together for the denomination when I held a new position that Doug actually helped forge. I was charged with developing lay and professional youth workers in 170 churches at that time.

I had come to appreciate Doug as a leader some years before we worked together, and we forged a friendship that has endured for years. Admittedly, at times our friendship was worked out as we "went at each other" over diverging opinions on how something should be handled. One situation, however, absolutely sold me on Doug as a leader I could respect and trust.

Years ago, I went to Doug as the executive minister with news of something I had become aware of. It would have serious consequences for the people involved. I still will not share the details, but suffice it to say, if the situation had not been handled with great wisdom and action, the testimony of Christ would have been tainted. It was so sensitive that if I had been named as the one who "leaked" the information, it could well have been the end of my pursuit of pastoral ministry as a career, due to politics rather than the Spirit.

Doug handled it professionally, wisely, and confidentially. He handled me as a young leader—with respect and protection. In fact, in looking back, I can see several occasions when Doug stood in the gap for me. He contributed greatly to me becoming the man, pastor, and leader that I am today.

That historical note aside, let's get back to the meeting. At the airport, after passing a few pleasantries and showing photos of children, Doug came right out and asked, "So what is on your heart?" As I shared, Doug and Gayle listened and then began to give some insight from their perspective.

Then Doug reached for his pen, and since this was a restaurant where the tablecloths were made of paper, he began to draw an illustration of what he was hearing me say along with a suggested solution.

As Doug began to write on the tablecloth, lights flashed in my head. It was a brilliant solution. He began by talking about who I was, and then described some areas that he felt I needed to be freed up from. Doug also illustrated a vision for what might be next and gave me great wisdom on how to begin implementation.

Do you see what was happening? While we sat at that airport restaurant, Doug had no idea about the thinking I was doing regarding the mentoring process. Yet he had taken me through the phases of the mentoring matrix in about two hours. No question that our relationship and my previous ministry experience allowed us to circle around the main points very quickly; however, I left there with renewed hope and was ready to implement the strategic steps Doug helped me with that day.

Each preceding cycle through the matrix takes the leader to greater and greater depth. The result is a seasoned, self-aware leader with a sharp focus and calling and the strategic expertise to carry out the vision.

## How to Use This Book

This summary of how the mentoring matrix works within the context of developing leaders creates the outline for the chapters that follow. Each chapter is filled with wisdom that will assist Christian leaders at various stages of their leadership and life. The actual phases of mentoring will become clear as we develop each phase more fully, using stories and life-application illustrations from other Christian leaders. As you read about these various stages of mentoring, I ask you to evaluate where you are presently in the mentoring matrix—either as a leader or as a mentor.

*Mentoring Leaders* also contains leadership gold nuggets that are helpful in providing wisdom in discerning your calling, building your character, or enhancing your competencies as a leader. Think of the book as a passive mentor that you can take with you in your briefcase, or have on the desk beside you. Many of the chapters contain material that is helpful for training with your team or congregational leadership.

So here is how I would use this book . . . I'd get out my journal, pour a cup of coffee, and begin reading. Every time I had an "aha" moment, I'd stop to record it in my journal along with a possible application. Sip your way through the book like a hot beverage—allow it to cool naturally and, in that way, soak in.

Give the book as a gift to your mentor, or mentee, and use it as a guide for your mentoring session over the next period of time. Oh yes, and once you have caught it—then go out and teach it. Share it with another. Encourage another developing leader.

PHASE ONE

# Self-Awareness

# 2

# Starting with New Awareness

## THE FOUNDATIONAL BEGINNING
## OF LEADERSHIP DEVELOPMENT

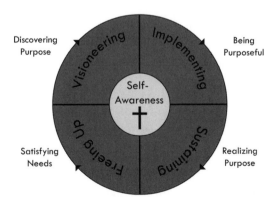

### What Is the Most Important Thing?

Brenda and I are sailors. Over the years, we have cruised the coastal waters of British Columbia aboard *Lazee Gal*—a beautiful, classic wooden power yacht that our friends David and Alison have graciously shared with us. We have been cruising together since before we had children, and during the entire time our families were growing up. Brenda, the boys, and I have developed a deep love and respect for the ocean.

Well, we finally made the decision to purchase our own boat. We spent about a year doing research, with each member of the family undertaking different aspects. Part of the research was to attend the Vancouver boat show—a four-day extravaganza where the football stadium is transformed into a boater's paradise. Brenda and I must have spoken to nearly a hundred boaters at the show, and we made an amazing discovery.

We discovered that although we have enjoyed powerboating for twenty years, we are actually sailors at heart. Now don't get me wrong—the *Lazee Gal* endeared herself to us, and we love the speed, space, and comfort she affords. Nonetheless, we found ourselves drawn to and accepted by the sailors we met at the boat show.

Let me explain the difference we noticed. We discovered that powerboaters were those for whom the destination was of primary importance. Their primary concern was getting to the destination safely, and as quickly as possible. Once there, the concern shifts to having as much fun as possible tubing, waterskiing, etc. For them, this is what makes the cruise worthwhile.

Sailors, we found, had a different priority. For sailors, it seemed that the destination was secondary to the journey itself. The fun was found in the journey, the wind in the sails, the slapping of waves against the side of the boat, and the fact that you could hear it in the silence was part of the attraction. The more pragmatic part was that sailors also used the wind for propulsion—something that was free—and we instantly understood that this would be easier on our personal finances.

Sailing seemed to suit our personalities. While we recognize the importance of the destination—and that has importance ultimately—we thoroughly enjoy the journey. Sailing is the journey.

So we chartered a sailboat as part of the final steps in our research toward purchasing our own boat. I personally wanted to make sure that our family could adjust to the smaller quarters of the sailboat, and handle the additional responsibilities, tasks, and skills involved in sailing. We used the week to study for, train for, and write our certification exams for coastal sailing.

Les Hall is a seasoned sailor. He was also our instructor, and now is our friend. When we were studying for the navigation portion, Les unfolded a chart in front of us. Amidst the clear definition of the islands and mainland was a vast array of shades and symbols showing both hazards and points of interest to any boater for navigation and safety purposes.

I recall feeling overwhelmed at the amount of information the chart contained, not to mention inadequate in being able to lay out the course for a destination. It was at this time that Les asked something that I have not been able to stop thinking about since.

"What is the very most important thing to know regarding navigation?" he asked.

My eyes quickly glanced over the chart. I noticed a compass. I noticed the black markings of hidden rocks and reefs. I saw the current indicators, and signs of rapids. What could it be? Suddenly, I thought this might be a trick question. It may be none of these things. Rather, Les is looking for something more "sophisticated" perhaps.

Brenda spoke out first, and bravely said, "Tides!" (It is precisely this kind of confident attitude that is one of the things I adore about her.)

Les smiled and shook his head no. He then glanced at me. "Knowing where you are going?" I asked, tentatively. I knew immediately from the look on his face that I had not identified the primary nugget of truth he wanted us to attain. We both awaited his response.

*"The most significant thing in navigation—the very most important piece of information—is knowing exactly where you are."*

Of course! If you do not know where you are, none of the pieces of information available to you on the chart are of any use. How could I have missed this obvious truth? The worst thing that could happen to you on a sailing trip would be to lose sense of where you are. This is the core of navigation.

So it is for us as leaders. If we are unaware of where we are, or if we have lost our bearing and wandered off course, any leadership we provide may not assist in leading our followers to the desired destination.

There is a correlation between being aware and your ability to be in touch with your feelings. Leaders appear everywhere on the spectrum of ability to be in touch with their feelings—from not at all, to being very much in touch with their feelings. However, my observation is that the best of the best leaders have a very clear grasp of how they are feeling at any given moment.

Daniel Goleman places a great deal of emphasis on the importance of being able to recognize feelings and sees this as central to his measurement of what he calls emotional intelligence. "Self-awareness—recognizing a feeling as it happens—is the keystone of emotional intelligence . . . the ability to monitor feelings from moment to moment is crucial to psychological insight and self-understanding. An inability to notice our true feelings leaves us at their mercy. People with greater certainty about their feelings are better pilots of their lives, having a surer sense of how they really feel about personal decisions from whom they marry to what job to take."[1]

Goleman goes on to describe in more depth what a self-aware person is like. When you read this, you will agree that we need more leaders with this degree of awareness leading our organizations. "Self-Aware. Aware of their moods as they are having them, these people understandably have some sophistication about their emotional lives. Their clarity about emotions may undergird other personality traits: they are autonomous and sure of their own boundaries, are in good psychological health, and tend to have a positive outlook on life. When they get in a bad mood, they don't ruminate and obsess about it, and are able to get out of it sooner. In short, their mindfulness helps them manage their emotions."[2]

You and I know of too many leaders who lose touch of their feelings and perspective of where they are—and even who they are. Unfortunately, this truth is often not seen clearly until after some kind of fall from leadership.

## What Keeps Leaders from Self-Awareness?

When the behind-the-scenes stories come out after the fall of a leader, we are often left wondering, "What was he thinking?" The leader's behavior or decisions just do not seem to make any sense given what we thought we knew of the leader and his leadership. It seems obvious the leader lost track of his priorities. How can that be?

Actually, it happens all too easily, and especially within Christian organizations and ministries. There are several reasons why leaders lack self-awareness, but let me elaborate on three primary ones: lack of feedback, insecurity, and busyness.

### Lack of Feedback

It seems that the higher one rises up the ladder of leadership "success" (i.e., position), the less feedback one receives. "They don't have any mirrors around them," as Wayman Crosby, president of the Fulcrum Group, says. Too often this is exactly right, and I think I understand how this comes to be.

The battles of being a leader cause us to become isolated. Whether we like to admit it or not, it becomes difficult to trust people. "Only the paranoid survive" is an expression Mitch Whitman used with me jokingly as we were discussing the evaluation of Christian leaders.

Paranoid leaders are those who tend not to trust many people or circumstances. They therefore develop contingency plans for almost everything. Even when paranoid leaders have a trusted friend who provides godly and wise feedback, it is hard for them to hear and act on it, because they always begin to question the motivation of their "friend."

Yes, of course, there are pseudoaccountability structures within every Christian organization. I use the term "pseudo" because they may have the appearance of accountability—without it actually being there. Boards surround leaders; executive committees surround leaders; executive staff, leadership teams, and others attempt to provide feedback. Nevertheless, my experience is that many of these structural attempts at accountability are dysfunctional.

There is also a time and history relationship to accountability where over time boards feel less necessity to hold the founder leader accountable—especially when things are going well. At the same time, the leader may seek less feedback.

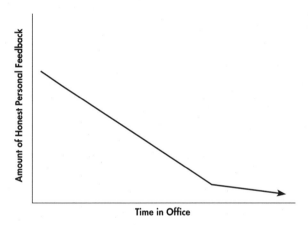

The seminaries and colleges responsible for the equipping and developing of pastoral leaders have not historically been strong in the feedback area themselves. They are caught between their deep desire to provide foundational content and doing anything that might cause a student to withdraw from school—such as providing honest, effective feedback.

I am pleased to note that this practice is changing as more presidents and faculty are taking a stewardship view of their time and energy, wanting to invest in the right people—even if it means that classes are smaller and revenue decreases.

Lack of feedback can also be the result of organizational size. As ministries become larger and more intense in busyness, activity, and importance, the temptation is to begin to believe your own press releases. I am not talking literal press releases here but rather believing your own organizational self-talk that often denies outside feedback or critique.

I believe that all leaders need to have someone in their life who is close enough to them and loves them enough to be able to look them straight in the eye and say "bulls--t" when needed. These are actually the types of close relationships that liberate leaders.

James Taylor, in his song "Shower the People," poetically sings about how being alone cannot hide us from ourselves. He finishes the verse with:

> Once you tell somebody, the way that you feel
>     you can feel it beginning to ease.[3]

It is out of truth telling and the resulting freedom that leaders can shower the people with love and get on with leading. Sadly though, many leaders lack this kind of friendship.

### Soul Friends

I had lunch with Ted Engstrom and Evon Hedley at the University Club located alongside Fuller Seminary. Both men have mentored me over the years, and they are life friends, having enjoyed one another for decades. Enjoying their bantering back and forth with one another, I smiled in appreciation of the feedback I witnessed between them.

They are very close friends! Dr. Ted is having trouble with his sight and asked Evon if he would read the food bill and tally up his credit card slip. What I found very surprising was that Ted allowed Evon to sign. Ted smiled as he looked at Evon and said to me: "We have been friends for so long, he knows my signature."

This is the type of friendship I am talking about. We leaders need someone in our lives who knows our signature, who has our number. Without accurate feedback, we will lose track of exactly where we are.

There has been a flurry of writing in the past ten years about Celtic Christianity, and specifically the concept of the *anamchara* (ahn-im-KAR-uh). *Anamchara* is a Gaelic word that means "soul friend." In the Celtic tradition, a soul friend is a person who provides others with coaching, support, and guidance as they progress along the path toward fulfilling their spiritual and human potential. The word was hijacked from the Druids by the early Christian saints. They took over this spiritual role, providing direction and guidance to anyone who wished to grow spiritually.

Much of what I have read about *anamchara* sounds so warm and cushy. However, think of someone Irish that you know. Generally, the Irish are known for their sharp, crisp, forthright personalities. Yes, they are lighthearted and jovial, but they tell it like it is—albeit in a manner that makes it easy to receive. The Irish are "scrappers" and do not tend to shy away from conflict.

I am from an Irish family, and when I think about a "soul friend," I picture someone who is a very close friend, who will walk along beside me, perhaps with his arm around my shoulder, while at the same time speaking truth into my life and, with a skillful, soccerlike movement, kicking me in the butt when I deserve it. All of this without losing step with me.

### It's Time, Frodo

Tolkien's *Lord of the Rings* allows us to witness this kind of wonderful relationship between Frodo and Sam.

In the last scenes of the movie *Lord of the Rings: Return of the King*, Gandalf is walking toward the last boat to leave Middle Earth when he turns to the hobbits and says, "It is time, Frodo."

Sam looks with shock at Frodo. "What does he mean?" he says.

"We set out to save the Shire, Sam," Frodo replies. "And it has been saved." Frodo's and Sam's eyes then lock as he continues, "But not for me."

"You don't mean that? You can't leave," Sam cries.

"The last pages are for you, Sam," Frodo says, as he hands Sam the leather-bound book *There and Back Again: A Hobbit's Tale* and then takes a moment to embrace each hobbit adventurer, saving an especially long hug for Sam.

Sam bursts into a full-fledged cry as they cling to one another. The violins in the background swell with emotion as Gandalf raises his hand to welcome Frodo when he leaves his friends and enters the ship with the elves.

Frodo and Sam were lifelong friends. During their adventures together, they sharpened one another, shaped their values together, and shared their ventures. Their good-bye told their story without many words.

> Ask your mentee about his closest friends, and ask to meet with both of them together, if possible. Watch how they interact. Is there a level of honesty that will help this leader go the distance? If the setting is conducive, ask very specific questions about their relationship, such as, "How much do you really know about each other? Have you ever shared financial information? Marriage or parenting struggles? What would you describe as your deepest moment as friends?"

## Insecurity

Insecurity breeds misleadership.

Insecurity erodes confidence within leaders and makes it very difficult for them to lead others. Nevertheless, many Christian leaders are insecure. Insecurity is tied to the paranoia I spoke of earlier and is crippling too many leaders.

What causes you to feel insecure? Can you think of the circumstance and setting when you last felt insecure? My experience suggests that there was something about that setting and interaction that triggered the insecurity within you. It may have reminded you of a previous experience. There may have been a personality involved with whom you have had difficulties in the past—or who reminded you of someone you have struggled with.

Insecurity can also rear its ugly head during times of great success. I've met many leaders who actually seem more paranoid when things are going well. Quips of "Well, we never know when things are going to take a turn for the worse" are common, and the mind can begin to imagine all the horrible ways they might do so.

Bobb Biehl, president of Master Planning Group , and one who has invested himself in the mentoring of Brenda and me, believes that confidence is the direct by-product of predictability.[4] There is clarity in this truth that helps us understand why new situations can cause us to feel insecure. Our previous experience helps us to picture how our circumstance might play out. Without experience, our imagination takes over and begins to play games in our mind. Left alone, I seem capable of dreaming up a far more devastating outcome than I usually experience. This is where a mentor can have a significant impact in your life as a leader.

I remember clearly the words spoken to me by Bill Armerding, then Canadian president of the Overseas Council for Theological Education, when he visited me at the Arrow office. Our organization was going through a difficult time financially after the dramatic events of September 11, 2001. I had to lay off half the Arrow staff team. I have fired people before for just cause, but the emotional effect of letting friends and colleagues go because of lack of funds was personally devastating. I inwardly wondered if the ministry or I would survive.

It was Christmastime when Bill dropped by. Just before he left, he prayed with me that I would be able to lead through these times, then he looked me straight in the eyes and said: "You will get through this."

Those words of experience spoke into my life at precisely the right time, when I needed them most.

God really wanted me to get the message. For not long after Bill had left, my phone rang, and it was Paul Sailhamer, then president of the Servant's Trust, who in the midst of a friendly Christmas call acknowledged that he knew Arrow was going through a difficult time. I had been open in communicating with him during our tougher times. Paul echoed Bill's words of not an hour earlier and then added, "Carson, I don't know the president of any ministry that has not had the faith-building experience of going through a financially lean time."

I was getting the message from God, through Bill and Paul: I will get through this. Arrow will get through this, and in fact, we may all be better as a result, for there certainly is a refining and focusing that takes place during the times when you are "on the ropes."

It does not have to be financial hard times—there are many ways that leaders find themselves "against the ropes" and pummeled by the opponent. It may be marriage issues or even a marital breakup; struggles with employees; wrongful dismissal lawsuits; lawsuits claiming ministry negligence; charges of sexual misconduct; moral failure on the part of high-profile staff; or substance or spousal abuse—I'm sure you can add to this your own issues. If you as a leader have not faced these circumstances before, you will feel insecure the first time you do. A mentor can provide tremendous encouragement and see you through tough times based on his previous experience.

Ironically, these feelings of insecurity actually block us from seeking the feedback we so desperately need at these times.

## Busyness

Most leaders function at high rpm. There are so many things to occupy our time any day of the year, any hour of any day, and any minute of any hour. Although I personally do not like it when I am in the midst of it, I recognize that there is a bit of an adrenaline rush that comes from the action associated with leadership.

When I was on the pastoral staff of First Baptist Church Calgary, Dr. Archibald Hart came to spend the better part of a week with us. As part of his visit, Arch had us wear a small "stress dot" on our skin. We were to monitor and keep track of the color of the dot in a variety of situations. It worked on the simple physiological principle that our heart speeds up the flow of blood when we are experiencing stress and the resulting desire to either fight or flee.

I remember hating that little experiment—for I seemed to be under a great deal of stress most of the time. Our first son was keeping us busy at home; I was studying at graduate school full-time; and I was pastoring a growing youth ministry about forty hours a week. (Why should I be stressed, right?) My friend Paul's dot remained constantly blue, indicating calm, cool, and collected, while mine was black, the symbol of death and stress.

What I learned through that time was that we could actually get addicted to the adrenaline rush of our leadership. We get hooked—and so do whatever we can, unconsciously, to feed our need for adrenaline. It actually feels good!

"Most people who die of a heart attack enjoy the process right up to the last minute," Arch says with a smile. "Adrenaline feels so good that we actually become addicted to it. It becomes an energizing force. When most of us wake up in the morning, we don't feel very good until we can get our adrenaline going. So we reach for the coffee with the caffeine that will stimulate us and give us an adrenaline high. If adrenaline arousal is not followed by recovery time, if it is continuous and never lets up, then it is bad."[5]

This manifests itself in leaders today when we cram our schedules with busywork and are always on the go. We leave little room in our lives and schedules for reflection. It is in reflective time that we receive some of the best feedback—for it is in these times that God often gets our attention about his desires for us.

If we are too busy, and have little or no reflection time in our lives, we lack feedback—spiritually, emotionally, psychologically, and intellectually.

## The Cross Is at the Core

> Now if we are children, then we are heirs—heirs of God and co-heirs with Christ, if indeed we share in his sufferings in order that we may also share in his glory.
>
> Romans 8:17

The first time I drew that mentoring matrix on the flip chart, I included a small cross at the very center of the diagram. "The cross is symbolic of our awareness of who we are in Jesus Christ. Do we have a clear understanding of our identity as a child of God?" I asked the leaders.

One would think that a pastor or Christian leader would have a clear understanding of this concept. When we become a follower of Jesus—a Christian—we become joint heirs of his kingdom. We are from that moment on daughters and sons of the King. What do we receive as part of the King's inheritance?

I have just finished acting as the executor of the estate for my mother, and so I am hearing the words from Paul printed at the head of this section with even greater impact. Romans 8:17 uses legal terminology stating that we have a right to a divine heritage (to the estate) because Jesus Christ has a right to that same heritage. We are intertwined with Christ in this—we are heirs as long as we are in relationship with Jesus.

Adding to this, we absolutely have no right to the divine heritage apart from Christ. We can never partake in the fullness of God without being in relationship to Jesus. It is because of Jesus' sacrifice and spilled blood that we are forgiven; because of his righteousness, we are justified; as we are becoming more Christlike in our behavior, it is because Jesus is within us helping us; if we are learning more about God, it is because Christ is our wisdom; if we are kept from harm and able to persevere, it is because Christ Jesus protected us; if we are feeling full and complete, it is because we are complete in him; and if when we die we are glorified before God the Father, it will be because Jesus Christ has been glorified. We are in complete union with Christ, and without Jesus we have absolutely no rights whatsoever.

What is startling in all of this is that Jesus Christ, as eternal God, would leave all of the adornments of the heavenly places—for us!

Brenda received a phone call from a young leader who was about to begin his time with us in the Arrow Leadership Program. He is involved in a broadcast ministry and works very closely with his wife. He was interested in asking Brenda questions about how she and I function together as a couple in ministry. He asked specifically, "What would you say is the most important thing you and Carson have learned about ministering together?"

> Many leaders function without fully comprehending their inheritance. This is the point where many lose awareness of exactly where they are—it's like losing your place on a nautical chart.

Without hesitating, Brenda said the most important thing was having a clear grasp of who you are as a child of God. You and your spouse must understand one another's position in Christ to understand one another relationally.

As Brenda finished relating the story, I asked her what his response was. "Wow!" Brenda smiled as she relayed this one-word response, and I smiled back. For we understand that this really is the case. Christian leaders must have a rock-solid foundation in their faith and relationship to Jesus Christ. Without that, we become like reeds blowing in the wind.

## The Passion

Mel Gibson made cinematic history with his release of *The Passion of the Christ*. His images and portrayal of the last hours of our Lord's life follow what Catholics call the Five Sorrowful Mysteries: the Agony of Jesus in the Garden, the Scourging of Jesus at the Pillar, the Crowning with Thorns, the Carrying of the Cross, and the Crucifixion and Death of Jesus.

As the cross was being raised and the scourged body of Christ hung painfully from the nails, there is a moment when his head falls forward, and amidst shallow gasps for air, he looks at his mother, Mary.

When the base of the cross was dropped into the hole dug for it, the audience in the theater jumped. Not from the "thump" sound as it fell in the hole but because of the surge of referred pain we felt as we imagined the strain placed on the nails by the weight of his body.

Enduring the heckling of the soldiers and the priests, Jesus looked heavenward and said, "Father, forgive them, for they know not what they do." The close-up of his bloodshot eye and the "painful to look at" evidence of his whipping told of the sacrifice Jesus has made on our behalf.

For this generation, the video image of the suffering endured by Jesus has created an outcry of "Why did he allow this?"

Jesus allowed it for you, and for me.

He suffered so that we might truly live. We can be who we are because of him. That is the core, the center, the nucleus, the focal point, the heart of life itself.

What is it about our methodology of developing leaders for Christian ministry that prevents us from spending enough time on this crucial hub? Do we assume that they already have it? Well, most leaders do not. We keep getting elevated in Christian leadership responsibility past the point of accurate feedback—and we are allowed to continue without anyone ever asking us the question, "Where are you in your relationship to Jesus?"

## How at Peace Are You?

I frequently ask Christian leaders to describe how peaceful they are in their lives, on a continuum between one and ten. Peace, you see, is a sign of spiritual maturity. It gives me a quick measure of how they see themselves in relationship to Jesus. While not being very scientific, it has been very helpful in my coaching and mentoring of leaders.

Once leaders have a clear understanding of their place as a child of God, there is a new peace or shalom that embodies their life and their leadership. I have been using a chart I call "Spiritual Development of a Leader" to teach Arrow leaders about their spiritual development.[6] Without my going into all the teaching related to this particular chart, notice the pattern as you move from left to right. Anxiety and drivenness decrease as we mature in our spiritual walk, while at the same time, there is an increase of that inner sense of peace.

When we as leaders lead out of peace rather than frenetic activity, fewer people are hurt and the work of the Lord is multiplied in ways unimaginable.

When leaders are aware, they know who they are as children of God. They find their identity in him and stop the endless seeking of fulfillment by other means. Without awareness on the part of a leader, the collateral damage and lack of progress for the mission can be harmful.

## Spiritual Development of a Leader

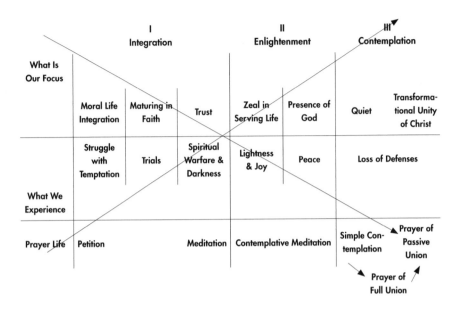

| | I<br>Integration | | | II<br>Enlightenment | | | III<br>Contemplation | |
|---|---|---|---|---|---|---|---|---|
| **What Is<br>Our Focus** | | | | | | | | |
| | Moral Life<br>Integration | Maturing in<br>Faith | Trust | Zeal in<br>Serving Life | Presence of<br>God | Quiet | Transforma-<br>tional Unity<br>of Christ |
| | Struggle<br>with<br>Temptation | Trials | Spiritual<br>Warfare &<br>Darkness | Lightness<br>& Joy | Peace | Loss of Defenses | |
| **What We<br>Experience** | | | | | | | | |
| **Prayer Life** | Petition | | Meditation | Contemplative Meditation | | Simple Con-<br>templation | Prayer of<br>Passive<br>Union |

Prayer of
Full Union

Christian leaders must live and lead with the understanding that we are constantly functioning at two levels. There is the visible leadership level and the invisible spiritual level. But while concentrating on our leadership we may be unaware, and our spiritual foes are not idle. They lurk around us stealthily, ready to take the offensive either by causing us to lean into one or several of the deadly sins, or by the subtler form of leading us into lukewarmness.

## Jim Was Unaware — and Wrong

By the mid-1980s, Jim Bakker had achieved more in his lifetime than most Christian leaders could imagine. Leader of the multimillion-dollar religious empires known as Heritage USA, PTL, and the Inspirational Network, Bakker enjoyed prestige, power, and the adulation of millions.

Jim was a premier proponent of the "prosperity gospel" and was known for preaching an upbeat message of optimism, health, and wealth. But in 1987 Bakker's world caved in when his sexual encounter with Jessica Hahn, a church secretary from

During the season when we leaders are unaware, several points of attack must be fortified against—and each of them tells us we need those in our lives who help keep us aware of where we are at and who we are as children of Jesus. This is a critical role for a mentor to play.

New York, became national news. The loss of his reputation was only the beginning.

Convicted in 1989 of mail and wire fraud for fund-raising efforts at PTL, this Christian leader who was a confidant of presidents was sentenced to forty-five years in a federal prison. There he would lose his freedom, his dignity, and eventually his wife, Tammy Faye. Stripped of power and subjected to the daily humiliations of prison life, Bakker began to face the issues he had always been too busy to confront. As he studied the teachings of Jesus, the former preacher was shaken to his foundations. He realized just how unaware he was of where he had gone in his thinking, his understanding of what the Bible said, and the relevance of his past and its influence on his life.

Released after five years, Bakker wrote *I Was Wrong* and now lives and ministers in rural Montana. In a magazine interview, Bakker gave this advice to younger leaders:

> Get to know Jesus. Seek Him and teach His words. There is no substitute. I was trying to win the world to Christ, but that's not my job. If I have an intimate relationship with Him, then I will be hearing Him and doing my part in winning the world to Christ. We've diluted the gospel with man's ideas. We want a politically forced people to do morally what we think they should do. But if we teach Jesus Christ and the power of the gospel, then people will do right. We won't have to worry about abortion if people are right with God, we won't have to worry about all these things that we keep harping on. We need to fall in love with Jesus Christ. He's the one who never left me in prison. He's all that will last in troubled times.[7]

Bakker is expressing the importance of ensuring that our core is foundationally grounded in Jesus Christ. While many still struggle with some of Jim's past history, it is nevertheless clear that our relationship with Jesus is central to our ability to lead without hurting ourselves, the ministries we serve, and the people who serve with us.

## Seven Personal Fronts of Attack

Jim Bakker became the icon for evangelical leadership failure, but the temptations that blinded him as a leader are just part of the arsenal used by the evil one to bring to a halt the work of the Lord. While trying not to do injustice to this serious subject, allow me to walk you through the dangers and explain the strategies used by the evil one against leaders. There are seven personal fronts of attack. These are: pride, sensuality, spiritual excess, spiritual lust, tiredness and sloth, surrounding with abundance, and lukewarmness. Let's look at each one more purposefully.

## The Inclination to Pride

Leaders of Christian ministries can actually hide the inclination toward pride quite well. The most obvious manifestation appears among those who hold themselves in too high esteem. Others often know what they are doing, but their presumption is so powerful that it is seldom challenged—largely because they have no one close enough to them to confront their posturing.

Another sign of pride is when leaders talk about the things of the spiritual life rather than actually training and mentoring others in how to put into practice these lessons themselves. The shadow side of this leaning is to condemn those who challenge or question their approach to spirituality.

> If you are unable to assess or talk about the seven fronts of attack with your mentee, then do not delay in referring the mentee to someone who can mentor in this area.

Leaders who have slipped to the inclination of pride cannot stand rivalry. Once pride has entered into their lives and leadership, if a rival or challenger appears, they will find ways to condemn and belittle that person until the threat is reduced or removed.

Interestingly, I have observed leaders in this state who seek out and desire intimacy of a spiritual mentor, but when the mentor begins to challenge them, or disapproves of their current ways, they look for another who will be more accommodating.

Mentors need to be cautious of this behavior pattern. If a leader has selected you to be his regular mentor, the leader will want you to affirm his thinking and behavior. When, or if, the leader falls into sin that becomes public, he may seek another mentor whom the leader will say agrees with him or encourages his behavior. Be careful about becoming this second mentor. Ask about previous mentor experiences.

I have had this happen to me on a few occasions—and I wish someone had shared this with me earlier. When a leader begins a relationship with you with a comment about how he has been seeing so-and-so (usually someone you know who has fairly high credibility as a Christian brother or sister) *but* that he really felt led to seek you out as a mentor—it appeals to your ego, and it is easy to get sucked in.

When prideful leaders fall into a serious outward sinful state, they can easily get very disheartened by their own failure and have a difficult time continuing, or facing the music of their action in a proper biblical manner. At this point they become a discouraging model for all the younger leaders watching them. Young leaders think, *If they can't make it—how can we possibly do so?*

A distracting strategy of our spiritual foe is to have prideful leaders season their talk and lifestyle with expressions of their own contributions. They tell the same stories repeatedly about their good works and their success. When you listen to them, you are not sure if they are trying to convince themselves and seeking your approval to boost their sense of security, or if they are so full of themselves that this is all that can flow from their mouths.

The reason is a spiritual one—they have inclined toward pride and forgotten their position. From pride springs envy, which betrays itself by the amount of displeasure they take in learning of the spiritual good others are doing—especially in ministry areas closely related to the ones they are called to.

Behind closed doors, leaders have confessed to me that they feel a sense of pain when they hear another ministry or leader praised. Given an opportunity, they always speak ill of those other Christian leaders whom they view as a challenge or threat to them personally—or the ministries they lead (which are often strongly personalized and identified with a leader in this state).

### Sensuality

There are several other signs of leaders succumbing to the onslaught of the evil one, including several elusive behaviors we can call sensual because leaders receive some personal response that makes them "feel" better. When I wrote to Dr. Mitch Whitman about this, he responded:

> The rigorous demands of ministry may offer fertile ground for compensatory "feel good" behaviors that meet emotional needs. These may include misusing food for comfort, altering mood by alcohol or other drugs, sexual escapism in pornography, or seeking satisfaction through inappropriate relationships.
>
> Most Christian leaders are clear about the moral and ethical constraints of extramarital sexual behavior, but may be naïve about the subtle draw of emotional involvements. In my study of proven Protestant Christian leaders, 27% acknowledged two or more experiences of extramarital emotional connection characterized by a combination of sharing emotional intimacy, sexual energy, and keeping these feelings secret from their spouse and others. In contrast, 8% of the sample admitted to some type of sexual contact on more than one occasion, and these almost never included sexual intercourse.[8]

An "emotional buzz" from the relationship may be experienced positively, but is nonetheless seductive by meeting non-conscious emotional needs without being considered "sexual" in the same way that overt sexual contact is judged negatively. This is often the start of a slide down the slippery slope toward serious relational and ministry betrayals.

Leaders disguise this sensual lust by cloaking it in spiritual overtones and words. One outward appearance is a leader seeking either sentimental or sensual friendship with another person (most frequently of the opposite gender) under the pretext of ministry—either ministering together or the leader ministering to the one from whom the relation is sought. These leaders speak of the relationship as something that is intended to evoke the respect and admiration of others. Often they talk about it as publicly as they can to diffuse their own sense of concern or worry about being caught—or of someone being able to look through them or "read their mail," as one of our Arrow leaders puts it.

### Spiritual Excess

Spiritual excess is usually exemplified in one of two ways: an excessive craving for consolation or the constant need to confess something. Leaders never confess the sin that is at the core of their problem but rather they confess something that is an attempt to draw themselves close to you without revealing the innermost thoughts of their sinful behavior.

Leaders in this state make extra efforts to appear spiritual and do so by sharing something they say they are learning currently.

Leaders, I believe, are wholehearted in desiring the life of devotion they are portraying, but their efforts and longings remain rather barren. If they acknowledge this, then the evil one twists their desire into discouragement and tries to take hold of their soul, which has now become more attached to the attention they get from the consolations and support of others than from God himself.

### Spiritualized Lust

This is craving after spiritual things because of the feelings attached to it. This spiritualized lust is nurtured while doing "good things" like attending prayer meetings and while ministering with someone at church or in the ministry organization. At times of prayer, sensual feelings can be produced. Prayer is an intimate experience and the feeling of intimacy is akin to the feelings of sexual intimacy. Especially vulnerable are those leaders who are tender and affectionate in nature to begin with. Often confused by the feelings, leaders develop a sense of awe about the "feeling" of this new spiritual high and develop a craving for more and more. This may prove to be more of a source of temptation than they can handle.

Teresa of Ávila gave this wise counsel to her brother who had been complaining of this form of temptation:

> I am not surprised at your trouble: but I am surprised to see you so very desirous of serving God, and yet that you find such a light cross so very heavy. You will soon say, "you wish it were lighter, in order to be the better able to serve our Lord." O brother! we know not what we ask. All such desires show a little self-love. Do not wonder at wishing to change your cross, for your age demands this. In spite of this imperfection, do not imagine that every one is as exact as you are in fulfilling their duties. Let us praise God that you have not other faults.[9]

This saint is telling us as leaders today that we can overcome this drivenness toward spirituality. But notice that her brother wrote to her with an awareness of what was going on—he was aware. I have actually come to believe that most leaders have awareness of the indicators that this "false motivation" is behind the feelings they are experiencing although many claim to be completely unaware.

### Tiredness and Sloth

Symptoms of this are weariness in performing even the most elementary of the spiritual disciplines. Reading of God's Word, prayer, devotional meditation, and even public worship are not relished. They are either shortened or omitted altogether.

Not wanting to receive advice or recommendations about their spiritual disciplines, leaders in this state seek out a more amiable sort of spirituality—one that does not interfere with their current lifestyle or sense of ease.

Now tiredness may be a medical condition. If you are troubled by constant fatigue, then make an appointment to see your doctor for a checkup. You may be anemic or your thyroid may be underactive. Your doctor will examine you and order simple blood tests to determine whether either of these easily treatable conditions is responsible. However, your symptoms may be because you are suffering from depression.

### Surrounding with Abundance

Perhaps one of the more surprising of the spiritual strategies employed by our spiritual foe is surrounding Christian leaders with an abundance of resources and opportunities, allowing them to hide from their sometimes less than stellar spiritual life.

This abundance includes spiritual books, readings, and research that consume all of the leader's time and energy and leave nothing for personal interior work. This is a particularly appealing distraction to the more scholarly leaders who have been trained in and are drawn toward academic study rather than introspection of their own soul life.

Another popular abundance is the practice of taking on too many duties and responsibilities—once again leaving no time to get in touch with who they are and what their unique and special calling is. Sadly, this form of abundance is often applauded by the church and ministries because of the amount of "work" that is accomplished—all the while eroding the leader from the inside out.

Another variation on abundance is especially tempting to multigifted leaders. They find themselves surrounded by a multitude of ministry opportunities and end up quitting one thing for another, changing, exchanging, arranging, and rearranging until finally settling on something that is usually expensive financially and in terms of human resource cost (and ironically, often not as potentially far-reaching as what might have been). In addition, during all this time of trying things out, the pressing on of kingdom work is delayed, bringing about a form of temporal victory for the opposing side.

### Roger Kemp on the Opportunities of Technology

Roger Kemp, president of Kemp and Associates, has worked with Christian leaders for over twenty-five years in the local church setting and in Christian broadcasting. When talking to him about abundance as a distraction, he added yet another distraction to my list—technology.

Few things are more seductive than the abundance of opportunities. This, of course, is especially true in our culture where technological advances have afforded a leader to platform his or her message in any manner. That which was unthinkable just a few years ago can now be produced in a laptop. Today, even with limited resources, any leader can generate a dazzling video, record a radio show, transcribe the spoken word into a book, and blast the waking Internet world with email.

And why not? If success is measured by reaching the masses, then why not dabble in every opportunity afforded to see if something will eventually stick?

There's nothing inherently wrong with technology, unless it begins to outpace our heartbeat for ministry. The danger comes when priorities swap positions.

As I have worked alongside leaders for more than twenty-five years, the most effective ones have never lost sight of their core passion. Even the most prominent leaders will tell you, in a simple sentence, the focus of their personal mission. It never includes technology. All of these other new opportunities are by-products that bleed out of their primary focus.

Ministry leads. Technology and opportunity follow.

Several leaders in the Arrow Leadership Program have been overcome by the technology gadget virus—and it is one I have been accused of having myself. There is something very seductive about technology, and gratefully most in ministry are not able to afford the latest and greatest technology. However, we must heed the observation that it is ministry that leads—not technology.

### Dark Night Correction

Each of these distractions is a great hindrance to the spiritual development and progress of both leaders and ministries. Saint John of the Cross says God often introduces leaders in this state to the "dark night of the soul" as a form of correction. Those leaders who do not have a dark night experience often spend the rest of their lives trying to disentangle themselves, using the consuming and ill-effective means we have already discussed of seeking consolation and the dry practice of spiritual disciplines for the purpose of attracting the attention of others more than earnestly seeking God.

### Lukewarmness

Leaders can also surround themselves with an abundance of material possessions and people who genuflect to their every whim and thus shelter themselves from the aforementioned "slippage" strategies. Nevertheless, even if they are able to bypass the discomfort of these, the evil one has saved his best for last. It is not long until the leader falls into the most serious of the spiritual plagues—a state of lukewarmness.

Chuck Swindoll, in his essay "Prophet Sharing," talks about this lukewarm complacency. As you read his words, ask yourself, do I find myself among them somewhere? "Always evaluating where we've been . . . always reacting . . . searching for ways to settle in and find comfort on our sofa-like surroundings . . . yawning . . . slumbering in the sleepy, warm twilight of sundown . . . finding a great deal of security in the mediocrity and predictability of sameness. . . . We are like chatty, laughing tourists taking snapshots of the lowlands through rose-colored filters . . . enjoying today's lull . . . we are yesterday-dwellers . . . avoiding the reality of today."[10]

We know how God detests us being complacent! "Because you are lukewarm, and neither cold nor hot, I will vomit you out of My mouth" (Rev. 3:16 NKJV).

Vomit—that's right. God does not like complacency in the same way that our bodies reject food that is bad.

What is lukewarmness among leaders? It is a place where leaders begin to feel that they have arrived—that they have reached a particular degree of development or stature—and then gradually allow themselves to become complacent in that place. They feel sapped of energy, eventually not wanting to try at all to improve their spiritual life. It is like a slow-working disease eventually taking the life of the host.

Spiritually it is akin to physically suffering from anemia. Our blood is composed of three types of cells (red blood cells, white blood cells, and platelets) that circulate throughout the body. Red blood cells contain hemoglobin, a red, iron-rich protein that carries oxygen from the lungs to all of the body's muscles and organs. Oxygen provides the energy the body needs for all of its normal activities. Anemia occurs when the number of red blood cells (or the hemoglobin in them) falls below normal and the body gets less oxygen and therefore has less energy than it needs to function properly.

Anemia makes it hard to find the energy to enjoy hobbies or other leisure activities, or even to complete basic tasks at home or at work. Particularly for a person with a serious case of the disease, the fatigue, weakness, and other symptoms associated with anemia can compound the challenges of coping with the disease.

Major symptoms of anemia include:

- extreme fatigue
- weakness
- shortness of breath
- confusion or loss of concentration
- dizziness or fainting
- pale skin
- decreased pinkness of the lips and gums
- rapid heartbeat
- feeling cold
- sadness or depression

Because the symptoms of anemia are easily confused with the symptoms of other conditions, it is important to see a doctor for an evaluation if you are experiencing significant fatigue or other signs and symptoms listed above, and especially if you already have a serious disease.

Spiritual anemia in the life of a leader, lukewarmness, reduces the number of "life cells" in a leader, and this gradually weakens the soul, allowing for the door to be open for all sorts of destructive forces that often appear, not one at a time but as many bursting through the door at once.

With the heart and soul poorly guarded, the leader becomes prey to all manner of unwholesome thoughts, suggestions, curiosities, and sensuality. Frequently temptations are only halfheartedly rebuked, and when indulged, the sins quickly multiply and are hardly regretted.

Once leaders are at this stage—while still under God's sovereign ability to be saved from falling—few survive. Their spiritual vitality is so weakened that it is like they are simply preparing for a shameful surrender—they have forgotten that they are a child of the King, and joint heir of the kingdom. It has happened to many, so all readers beware, for none of us is exempt from falling to this onslaught from the evil one. Take heed.

Here are the symptoms of spiritual lukewarmness setting in:

1. Gradual weakening of your ministry energy and spiritual desire.
2. A blinding of your conscience—judgment becomes warped.
3. Gradual weakening of the will—making concessions that were once unheard of.
4. No desire to work hard at repairing—dodging and avoiding restoration attempts.
5. Letting yourself slide in every respect—often this appears with changes in physical appearance.

## Organizational Dangers of Unaware Leaders

You do not have to be a rocket scientist to understand how this type of spiritual attack on the life of the leader is going to have detrimental effects on his ministry. There are too many documented cases of churches that have been set back years by the failing of their pastor. Often the witness of a particular ministry has been damaged and harmed beyond repair by a falling leader. But there is another, less visible danger to ministries by those who lead them, and that is if the leader doesn't know who he is or why he does what he does. It is the failure of the ministry to develop someone to take over after the fallen leader leaves.

Unaware leaders perform with a sense of functional atheism and deny that they are ever going to die, or be sidelined due to poor health or other reasons. Therefore, they have no "Timothy" they are investing in—no one is strategically being developed and trained to serve as the next leader of the ministry.

It is impossible for me to illustrate much of this chapter without casting judgment on other ministries, or disclosing information gathered within the context of leadership consulting—and I will not do that. The Christian leadership world is a small world. Moreover, even attempts at disguising a ministry through the use of a composite will cause you to be distracted trying to figure out who it is. So instead, I will quote a list of spiritual dangers from Paul and Christa Schoeber.

Paul and Christa are intercessors who work on our team at Arrow and have had more experience doing prayer counseling with proven Christian leaders over the past ten years than anyone else I am aware of. As you review the list, you will see many noteworthy "better stay awake" warnings that leaders need to be aware of. The Schoebers list these because they tend to come up repeatedly in their prayer counseling with leaders.

## Spiritual Danger Zones in Leadership

- reliance on own gifts
- fear of humankind (people pleasing)
- perfectionism
- lack of conflict resolution skills or avoidance of conflict
- lack of accountability
- ignoring evil or lack of understanding how evil works
- unawareness of how to guard against sexual misconduct
- empire building
- need for recognition
- need to control
- lack of trust / intimacy with God (solitude, etc.)
- inability to set boundaries (to say no)
- inability to delegate
- lack of discernment

Any one of these is sufficient to bring down or stop a Christian leader; however, we have observed that they often come in groups or clusters. Christian leadership is a significant responsibility, so to those who lead, and those who help them lead—beware. "Be self-controlled and alert. Your enemy the devil prowls around like a roaring lion looking for someone to devour. Resist him, standing firm in the faith, because you know that your brothers throughout the world are undergoing the same kind of sufferings" (1 Peter 5:8–9).

## Gaining His Favor

On many occasions, I have pointed leaders to the passage in the Bible where John the Baptist is baptizing Jesus. The heavens open and there is a spiritual happening with audio where God's voice was heard to proclaim, "This is my Son, whom I love; with him I am well pleased" (Matt. 3:17).

What leaders need to hear is that Jesus had not done anything yet! His ministry career, if you like, was just beginning. So many Christian leaders are caught up in "doing" rather than "being" a son or a daughter.

God loves you as a person even more than he loves what you do as a leader. It brings him pleasure just to think of you, and he longs to lavish you with his attention and his affection. There is absolutely nothing you can do to make him love you less—or more. The relationship you share is based on the character of God, which is unchanging. He loves you with an unconditional love based on his character—not yours. "I have loved you, my people, with an everlasting love. With unfailing love I have drawn you to myself" (Jer. 31:3 NLT).

There is a subtle erosion that begins to take place in many of us leaders, and we begin to question God's intentions for us. We come to misunderstand what God intends of us and begin to compensate by "doing" more. By doing so, we lose track of some of the most important things in life and faith.

We become less convinced that it is all about being a son or daughter of Christ and that the cross is central to our identity as leaders. Our busyness and success in ministry trick us into thinking that it is all about us—when it is all about God.

Try inserting your name within Jeremiah 31:3. "I have loved you, _____, with an everlasting love." (So I would write, "I have loved you, Carson, with an everlasting love.") Write it on your bath-

Review the following table item by item with your mentee and discuss where he is at in his functioning either as an orphan or as a child. It is common that leaders vacillate between the two columns, but as you discuss this you will become aware of areas in the leader's life that need "freeing up," which we will address in the next chapter.

I appreciated meeting with Mark Stibbe of Saint Andrews Church, Chorleywood, in the United Kingdom, and then subsequently reading his book *From Orphans to Heirs*. Mark was adopted as a child, and he brings a unique and poignant perspective to our being adopted through Christ into the kingdom of God. He recognizes that reality and spiritual truth are often separated. Every Christian has a heavenly Father, but that does not mean that everyone has a "father and son/daughter" relationship with their heavenly Father. We can become estranged. When a child of God cuts himself apart from the relationship, we essentially become as orphans as described in Lamentations 5:3: "We have become orphans and waifs, our mothers are like widows" (NKJV).

room mirror using a dry erase marker (for whiteboards). Create a screen saver on your computer. Memorize this and other verses like it until they become part of your innermost being.

Prayer is our declaration of dependence on God. When we pray, we are acknowledging that we need the Lord in our life and it is critical to godly leadership. Many leaders jettison prayer time due to the demands of their position or calling. I think it is completely legitimate to ask any Christian leader how much time he has set aside to pray in a given week.

## Functioning from Your Core as a Child of God

What does a leader look like when functioning with the awareness of being a child of God? The leader is at peace, abiding in the Lord. As leaders come to declare their utter dependence on the Lord, an understanding engulfs them wherein they realize they need only what the Lord can provide, and nothing else. They come to a place of complete trust in Jesus for nourishment, care, nurture, and protection. Often, God does this through their relationships and friends on the journey.

Abiding, staying attached, recognizing who is at the core of who you are and revolving your leadership around this core—that is what mature leaders do. Jesus told his disciples, "You are already clean because of the word I have spoken to you. Remain in me, and I will remain in you. No branch can bear fruit by itself; it must remain in the vine. Neither can you bear fruit unless you remain in me. I am the vine; you are the branches. If a man remains in me and I in him, he will bear much fruit; apart from me you can do nothing" (John 15:3–5).

Notice in the following chart[11] the subtle yet profound difference in perspectives and imagine how this can dramatically alter how one leads and lives.

### Orphan / Child Perspectives

| Orphaned from God | | Child of God |
| --- | --- | --- |
| Bondage | Condition | Liberty |
| Independent / Self-reliant | Dependency | Interdependent / Acknowledges need |
| Guarded and conditional; based upon others' performance as you seek to get your own needs met | Expression of Love | Open, patient, and affectionate as you lay your life and agendas down in order to meet the needs of others |
| Fight for what you can get! | Future | Releases your inheritance! |

| Orphaned from God | | Child of God |
|---|---|---|
| Accusation and exposure in order to make yourself look good by making others look bad | Handling Others' Faults | Love covers as you seek to restore others in a spirit of love and gentleness |
| See God as Master | Image of God | See God as a loving Father |
| Duty and earning God's favor or no motivation at all | Motive behind Christian Disciplines | Pleasure and delight |
| "Must" be holy to have God's favor, thus increasing a sense of shame and guilt | Motive for Purity | "Want to" be holy; do not want anything to hinder intimate relationship with God |
| A need for personal achievement as you seek to impress God and others, or no motivation to serve at all | Motive for Service | Service that is motivated by a deep gratitude for being unconditionally loved and accepted by God |
| Strive for the praise, approval, and acceptance of man | Need for Approval | Totally accepted in God's love and justified by grace |
| Competition, rivalry, and jealousy toward others' success and position | Peer Relationships | Humility and unity as you value others and are able to rejoice in their blessings and success |
| Feel like a servant/slave | Position | Feel like a son/daughter |
| Insecure / Lack peace | Security | Rest and peace |
| Self-rejection from comparing yourself to others | Self-image | Positive and affirmed because you know you have such value to God |
| Conditional and distant | Sense of God's Presence | Close and intimate |
| Seek comfort in counterfeit affections: addictions, compulsions, escapism, busyness, hyper-religious activity | Source of Comfort | Seek times of quietness and solitude to rest in the Father's presence and love |
| Live by the Love of Law | Theology | Live by the Law of Love |
| Difficulty receiving admonition; you must be right so you easily get your feelings hurt and close your spirit to discipline | View of Admonition | See the receiving of admonition as a blessing and need in your life so that your faults and weaknesses are exposed and put to death |
| See authority as a source of pain; distrustful toward them and lack a heart attitude of submission | View of Authority | Respectful, honoring; you see them as ministers of God for good in your life |
| Spiritual ambition; the earnest desire for some spiritual achievement and distinction and the willingness to strive for it; a desire to be seen and counted among the mature. | Vision | To daily experience the Father's unconditional love and acceptance and then be sent as a representative of his love to family and others. |

PHASE TWO

Freeing Up

# 3

# Freeing Up

## THE UNCHAINING OF GOD'S LEADERS

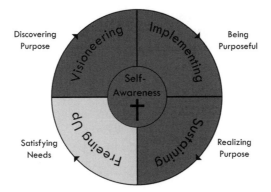

The swashbuckling man suspected of being a pirate was taken from his cell deep in the darkened chambers of the castle. As I watched this video, the picture of this prisoner became a strong image for me. The hero's legs were chained together with shackles. The chains were heavy and capable of being attached to the walls of the cell, but even when released from the confines of the prison, he shuffled along because of the weight of the chains around his ankles.

Although he was obeying the commands of his captors, he could not walk or respond quickly. The shackles were there to prevent his running off or challenging the guards. The disadvantaged prisoner was severely handicapped by the weighted chains around his feet.

Take a mental photo of that scene—for it is symbolic of the duress under which many of God's anointed leaders strive to continue going forward in their leadership. They are chained or shackled by something that our spiritual foe uses to hold leaders captive or keep them moving very slowly—with a shuffle at best.

In working with Christian leaders, there are several categories of freeing up that should be pursued during mentoring. It is common to find that certain areas need attention. In that this aspect of their leadership development takes place after they have become aware of themselves, they are ready and are often able to assist in seeking out areas that need addressing.

## Freeing Up: From Past Experiences

Dale was a leader in one of our Arrow classes, and his assessment materials sparked a great deal of discussion among the members of the assessment team. You see, there was something about Dale that just didn't jibe with his evaluations and test results.

He was an associate pastor at a large downtown church and had significant ministry to the city. He participated in leadership for a Billy Graham crusade and other citywide initiatives. Dale's IQ scores placed him very high among the other members of his class, and there were obvious gifts God had hardwired into him—yet there was still something . . . well . . . off!

I was asked to sit in on the discussion, and specifically whether I would meet with his leadership partner (an on-site mentor assigned to individual leaders in the Arrow program). Without having sat in on the complete discussion of Dale, I knew they were on to something just from my casual observations of him and recollections of meeting him several years earlier in his church's community.

Dale dressed in a different manner and had a very full and somewhat untrained beard that covered his face. He wore a jacket, shirt, and tie at times when other members of his Arrow class were wearing blue jeans and sweatshirts. His tie was a Kermit the Frog tie, and while cute, did not seem appropriate for the setting or the company he was with. What's with that? Appearance alone can cause a "yellow light" response among those watching us as leaders.

Paul Schoeber and I agreed to meet with Dale, and we asked him for some time to review his assessment material with him. Paul and I met in advance and talked through how we might tenderly care for this young leader, and then we prayed, asking God to reveal to us and guide us toward anything that might be holding Dale back as a leader in kingdom work.

Although nothing specific was revealed to us through our prayer time, Paul and I felt ready and somewhat excited about meeting with Dale. Together we have seen many leaders just like Dale freed from the chains that hold them back. While we didn't know what those chains might be or how they got there, we knew God would accomplish his purposes in the right time and in the right way. God is able

> to loose the chains of injustice
>     and untie the cords of the yoke,
> to set the oppressed free.
>
> Isaiah 58:6

Dale was prompt for his meeting with us. He had a nervous smile on his face, which was completely understandable given the intensity of the assessment process he and the other leaders in his class had been through. We entered into some light talk for a couple of minutes and then Paul led us in a brief prayer, thanking God for Dale and his leadership and offering this time to the Lord's leadership and guidance. Then I began the conversation by telling Dale that we were there on behalf of the entire assessment team to give him his assessment materials and talk over with him some of the things we felt were important to help him create his leadership development plan with Arrow for the following eighteen months.

"In looking over your assessment materials, Dale," I said, "there are a few things that just don't seem to line up for us. Let me explain." I described several of his positive gifts and traits that we noticed easily, but then talked about the incongruence of these observations with his appearance, his current ministry position, and the seeming social awkwardness he often portrayed. "Paul and I are here to help you understand yourself and your leadership in a manner that will allow you to be all that God longs for you to be as one of his leaders."

Dale and the rest of his class had been sitting under the teaching of Dr. Martin Sanders that day, as Martin discussed the opportunity to develop and grow past our deprivations and how mentoring was going to be a significant experience in their growth through Arrow. Martin is himself a graduate of the Arrow Leadership Program and a professor at Alliance Theological Seminary in Nyack, New York. He has been training with us at Arrow for years and is a close personal friend. During Martin's teaching time, he asked the class, "How old are you?" He did not mean chronologically but rather the power that something from a person's past has in holding that person back, or chaining that individual to those events in the past so that he stops growing emotionally or psychologically.

Knowing that Dale had just had this teaching session, I asked him about it. "Dale, how old are you?" Chronologically, Dale was in his midthirties, but when I asked the question, his head dropped and he looked toward his lap. He raised his head in a few minutes and with a tear in his eye said, "I am twelve years old."

Paul asked where he saw himself as a twelve-year-old.

Read aloud 1 Peter 2:16 to your mentee: "Live as free men [or women], but do not use your freedom as a cover-up for evil; live as servants of God." Ask the leader what that means to him in his life currently. Is he living free? If he seems free, is it covering up any sort of evil in his life?

Dale shared with us, "I am walking down the hallway of my school and 'the popular girl' of the school, and one whom I really liked, was walking toward me. I was staring at her and she said loudly, 'Who are you looking at, GEEK?' From that moment on, I have been a geek and have been stuck in some ways as a twelve-year-old boy."

Paul then led us in a time of prayer where we renounced the "curse" of those words and prayed that the Holy Spirit would break the chains of any attachment that experience had in Dale's life. We asked Dale to pray the prayers with us, and when we finished, this man's countenance had lightened.

Imagine our delight when we saw Dale arrive for the next residential seminar, smiling, confident, appropriate in both dress and appearance, and longing to grow as a leader. He has since bravely made the decision to leave the pastoral ministry position he held, which his assessment process helped him to see was not the best place for the stewarding of his gifts. Dale was free to pursue his ongoing ministry as a free man. I can see him making an incredible contribution to the kingdom's work in the future.

Each of us has experiences in our past that either enhance or take away from our ability to lead today. Proper reflection and assessment can help a leader be aware of places where chains are still attached. The freedom that comes from being released from the chains is exhilarating. In Dale's instance, it was a circumstance at school. For you or for me it would be something different. But every leader should take the time, with the assistance of a good mentor, to review past experiences and how they have helped or deterred his development as a leader.

## Freeing Up Areas for Women Leaders

Gretchen Englund is an excellent communicator and leadership enabler who works with us at Arrow out of Minneapolis. She serves as a leadership partner (on-site mentor), local mentor, trainer, and coleader. During our work with women leaders within the Arrow Leadership Program, I have appreciated the effort and focus that Gretchen has placed on increasing our sensitivities to the unique challenges faced by women leaders of Christian ministries. On the subject of "freeing up," Gretchen shares:

> Even the most confident-appearing woman can struggle with a sense of low self-esteem. Stemming from one's skewed view of God's acceptance and delight in her, she questions her own worth and doubts who she is. She is a called woman leader who is clearly called of God, but who inwardly struggles with questions of self-doubt, personal shame, and quietly wonders whether God's delight in her is really true.
>
> For some women, an inner experience of God loving her is always elusive. She may understand it, may be able to quote Scripture about it, but her inner experience of God's love and acceptance was shattered somewhere in her past. This shattered place is where a woman leader needs deliverance and restoration through God's careful reshaping. Once her experience of God's love finds a solid inner place, and once her self-esteem is rightly placed in God's esteem of her, she will find freedom around the corner—both in her inner life, and in the working out of God's vision to her.
>
> Finally, women leaders—again because of the many layers of a woman's life—need to address their inner anxiety before they can freely move to the next level. There is a precious reflection of Christ available through an inner "unfading beauty of a gentle and quiet spirit" (1 Peter 3:4). But, women can have an internal tornado, full of questions and unfinished business: Am I okay? Am I really competent? What about being single? Are my kids doing well? Does my husband find delight in me? Am I doing life right? And on and on. . . . A woman will always be called on to multitask her life—she is actually good at that! However, multitasking by the Spirit's leading is quite another thing. If the woman leader is willing to really address that inner tornado which holds questions that scratch at her peace with God, and settle it with God, her ears can be open to hear the quiet voice of God as she leads onward. Inner tornadoes of anxiety may not be obvious to the bystander, but a woman leader who knows herself will allow God's Spirit to discern and calm her anxious heart.

## Freeing Up: From Father and/or Mother

While I'm rather tired of the amount of material written in psychological journals concerning the impact—usually negative—of our mothers and fathers on our lives, there is no question in my mind that, experientially, our relationship, or nonrelationship, with our mother and father dramatically affects our ability to lead.

The divorced and hurting people outnumber what we would consider healthy families in the church right now. The divorce rate in the church is rising. The suicide rate among Christians, due to divorce, is on the rise. The suicide-attempt rate among children ten to twelve years old, due to divorce, is also on the rise. When we are engaged in the development of leaders, we will encounter wounds and scars from experiences with mothers and fathers, or the lack thereof.

There are volumes written about the family dynamics when a father or mother is absent during the formative, growing-up years of the child. This absence can cause an insecurity that lingers for the rest of our lives. Other negative dynamics that emanate from our parents are the aftereffects of overprotection and smothering, alcoholism, physical and sexual abuse, and many more subtle causes.

### Nothing Grows under the Banyan Tree—or Does It?

Arrow works with some of the top emerging leaders in the Christian world, some of whom come from families of significant Christian leaders. It is interesting to note that a leader can be held back by or chained to a mother or father whose ministry has been quite positive, and certainly effective, in kingdom work.

I gave a workshop at a national ministry conference years ago and titled it "Nothing Grows under the Banyan Tree." The Banyan tree is a broad, spreading, dense tropical tree. The leaf canopy is so dense that rain is unable to penetrate—leaving the soil beneath barren of nutrients. I use this image to convey how many young leaders fail to grow under the canopy of existing leaders. They are starved of the essential nutrients required for growth. Such is the case with some of the young leaders we work with.

If the parents are strong and proven leaders in their own right, young leaders often place on themselves expectations to lead in a manner equal to or exceeding that of their parents. It takes great maturity, and restraint, by parental leaders to allow their children to become aware of and at peace with who they are—not who their parents are.

Ron Maines is the new president of Crossroads Communications, which was founded by his father, David Maines. David and Ron had been involved with the ministry for several years prior to Ron's time with us in Arrow. There was a strong expectation that Ron would take over the leadership of the ministry when his father retired. The difficulty and challenge was that Ron is not like David. The gifts and skills David used so easily in this media ministry are not as natural for Ron. If Ron were going to make this move in leadership, he would have to begin shaping the role around who he is rather than what everyone else expected of him. This transition has gone extremely well. Ron's mentor has guided him along the way, and I am able to see how Ron himself is growing into the job.

I actually think about this a great deal concerning our own three boys. They have grown up as PKs (preacher's kids). There are expectations that come with this related to their behavior, their beliefs, and their leadership. Our oldest son, Jason, has faced more expectations than his brothers have due to his ministry involvement and leadership. It is possible that he will need to be freed up from chains inadvertently attached to his legs by Brenda or me. Jason's two younger brothers may also face this as they enter their adult years.

I've asked Jason to comment for himself.

## Father's Shadow

When I was nine years old, I was selected by my Sunday school teacher, Mrs. Oleary, to take the role of the pastor as our class performed our own church service. No one argued or even asked any questions for that matter. In Sunday school it just seemed natural that I play that role. After all, my father was a pastor at the church. When I accepted the role to give the sermon for my class, I did not understand that this was a role that I would be asked to play repeatedly throughout my life.

Over the past few years, I have been in many different ministry roles, from being a youth conference organizer, a camp director, to a youth pastor. In the midst of my ministry one summer, I sat down to talk with a man that I highly respect and love. We talked about ministry and what I was going to do with my future. When I told him about my aspirations of going to law school, I couldn't help but see the disappointment on his face. The obvious dissatisfaction was followed by very honest and good-intentioned wisdom asking me to make sure that I asked God if he wants to use my life for ministry.

I wish that I could say that this was the only time someone asked me to consider playing a ministry role similar to my father. However, little has changed since Sunday school. Time and time again, I am asked to be my father, and by doing so I have been asked to not be who God created me to be. Although I know full well that each person has come to me with only the best intentions, I have had to constantly battle with the world around me in order to bloom into the person that God created me to be. God created me to look like my dad and even more to act like him. However, even though we were created to look and act the same, God created us with totally different spiritual gifting.

The problem was that people don't get to know me well enough to realize how unique and differently God had gifted me in comparison to my
father. I will never say that growing up in my father's shadow has been easy
for me—but I can say that despite its difficulties, it has been the greatest
honor.

As Jason has shared, the influence of our fathers is very real and per-
vasive even without intention. Often the influence is positive; however,
there can be haunting attachments that linger on leaders for years as a
result of the influence of our parents.

### Tell Me about Your Father

None of the witnesses will ever forget the classroom experience we
had with Bobb Biehl as he was training at Arrow holding a one-on-one
consultation in front of the class. He had asked for volunteers to sit at
the front on a stool next to him and allow him to help them with whatever leadership issue they were facing at the time. Everyone else in the
room was to be as quiet as possible, simply listen, and pray during the
individual sessions. The proviso was that the volunteers must allow Bobb
to go absolutely anywhere with his questions—and that is exactly what
he did with a young leader named Nathaniel.

Bobb began by asking him, "If there was one thing I could help you
with today, what is that one thing?" Nathaniel told Bobb that he struggled
with making decisions—that was the essence of his request for help. After
some clarification questions, Bobb surprised us by saying to Nathaniel,
"Tell me about your father."

Immediately the tone in the room and in Nathaniel's voice changed
as he told us of a less than ideal upbringing and relationship with his
father. Bobb was then used of God to break the chains of an unhealthy
relationship with his father that had delayed his development for years
as a leader and as a man.

Bobb asked Nathaniel what his father's first name was, and then told
him to begin referring to his father by his first name—not in person but
rather when referring to him when speaking to others or when thinking
about him. Nathaniel's dad did not deserve to be called "father." Bobb
then shared with Nathaniel how Nathaniel had been trying to seek the
approval of his father for most of his life and desperately needed that approval when in fact his father needed Nathaniel's friendship and respect
more than Nathaniel needed his father's approval.

Bobb illustrated this by demonstrating the difference in height with his
hands. "This is how it feels to you whenever you are around your father,
isn't it?" Nathaniel, through many tears, affirmed this while at the same

time Bobb explained, "In fact, your father feels small when he is around you. Go home and pray for an opportunity to simply be with your father and let him know that there are ways in which you do respect him. Think back to something positive, no matter how small, and begin to nurture a relationship with your father so that you may both be healed."

We received an email several weeks later asking us to pray as Nathaniel was going to visit his father—and later we heard that his new perspective on "Dad" allowed him to begin a new relationship and that it was going well. Since that time, I have watched this leader's ministry leap forward in amazing ways as he moved ahead, unchained from his incessant desire to gain his father's approval. We watched a miracle that day as God used Bobb to bring about healing in Nathaniel's life.

Situations like this have been repeated in our development of emerging leaders. Women abandoned at birth by drug-addicted mothers. Leaders from Muslim families who came to be followers of Jesus and who have been completely rejected by their mothers, fathers, and families. Men and women leaders who have been the victims of physical abuse and who have suffered for years—not so much from the physical bruising as from the emotional scars of rejection, feelings of weakness and vulnerability, and the nagging sense of nonacceptance.

## Freeing Up: From Family of Origin Chains

As part of the course in developing leaders, we individually take the leaders through an exercise of mapping their family tree on a genogram. It is a simple document that works like a flowchart and indicates where, within the family tree, there have been instances of divorce, death, and other spiritual and physical experiences. This helps to begin to bring awareness and give an understanding to family patterns that leaders need to watch.

## What Are Generational Sin Issues?

I had an opportunity to ask Paul and Christa Schoeber about generational sin over lunch, and here is their response.

> Christa: Generational issues are strongholds that in some way or another repeat in generations. It can be "unforgiveness." It can be anger that you can trace in the generations. It can be abuse, immorality—you can trace that, and it is often a stronghold that is there to predispose

the person you are interacting with to this certain kind of sin. Sometimes they are vulnerable to this same thing, but what can happen is, for example, with addiction—there is alcoholism, and a person says, "I will never drink alcohol." That addiction can come out by being a perfectionist or a workaholic. So it can still come out. We have not yet come to any kind of conclusion. We have observed this reality but have no conclusion as to why it keeps on going. Even if they are an earnest Christian who wants to follow the Lord and they really want to be a disciple of Jesus—this kind of thing can really hinder them in their walk.

Paul: The only explanation I can see is from the Scripture in Nehemiah when they built the wall. They got discouraged and stopped building because of the threats from others. Now that is a collective fear, not a single person's fear—it has affected the whole community. Scripture says that they looked at the rubble, so they allowed the fear to focus on the wrong thing. When you do this, and churches can do this collectively, when we focus on the wrong thing, and not on God, we focus on something else. There can be a generational pattern there. When we confess to Jesus Christ that we, and our fathers, have sinned against him, that power is broken. We do not know how it works, but we know that it does work. When it is confessed, that power is no longer the strong influence on that person's life. It is really quite a mystery, but it works.

Christa: It does work!

Paul: Also with the fear of confrontation or conflict or conflict resolution—there are certain people, and groups of people, that simply do not deal with conflict.

Christa: Many people do not even acknowledge that conflict is there.

Paul: They pretend it is not there, and that can lead to enormous anger and even lead to violence. When you see that, then you have to start looking for the root cause. I often point out to leaders that there is a freedom that they will never get until they deal with this. Freedom is a choice word for that. Sometimes I point out to them how Saint Augustine wrote about this, "Where fear is, God is not." That gives a shock to some people to make them realize the position they are in. When they realize that God isn't in that part of their lives, then they have a desire, most of the time, to rectify that.

Christa: Most of them are aware that it has a negative effect on their lives. Getting to the stage where they recognize it and the desire to overcome it is also a huge factor. It is rare that people don't want to address it and be free of it.

Paul: We must mention vows. Often people have made vows earlier in life and a vow that needs to be dealt with and confessed because at a certain point, a vow becomes sin, and that prevents us also from making good choices. That is a separate issue, but it ties in with this.

## Freeing Up: From Spiritual Chains

It amazes me how Christian leaders who are functioning at a significant level of ministry leadership still have unfinished business in their background spiritually. My assumption has always been that most Christians know that spiritual dabbling or bondage from their past must be confessed and renounced to produce freedom. I now know that this is a broad assumption to make.

One of the strategies that Screwtape and Wormwood use today is to infiltrate Christian ministries with leaders who function like "sleeper" cells. Their spiritual dabbling in the past has left a door with a key—just waiting to be opened.

Let me explain how this works in the spiritual realm. Imagine a young leader who has made choices in his past in the area of the occult, New Age, voodoo, witchcraft, or Eastern or native mysticism. He then commits his life to the Lord and seems to break free from the bondage this had in his life, but he does this without any prayerful and intentional breaking of the spiritual attachment.

Our spiritual foe quickly goes into dormant mode in this area so as to draw as little attention to this as possible. The leader develops and grows in his circle of influence and ministry leadership position. Once that leader has risen to a place of responsibility, the evil one begins to awaken the attachment from the past.

> Take the time to go through this inventory as a mentor and seek help as required to pray through any generational or personal involvements.

The leader recognizes that something is just not right—but it is still very subtle. How it tends to show itself is in the nonachievement of results in the ministry and little or no spiritual growth in his life.

Another major area of attack from the sleeper cell is through the family and marriage. Just when the leader's ministry is about to make some significant breakthrough for the sake of the kingdom of God, the sleeper cell is activated and all hell breaks loose within the family or marriage.

There are several charts or series of questions that can help to flush out the more obvious types of spiritual attachments. Neil Anderson's "Non-Christian Spiritual Experience Inventory" is one such reference tool.[1] It provides a list of possible spiritual involvement areas, and it can be used in a mentoring or prayer-counseling situation. It helps you get to know more about the spiritual history of the leader. Leaders can also be asked to indicate any involvements they know of within their family lineage.

### Non-Christian Spiritual Experience Inventory
(Please place a checkmark beside any where you, your family,
your father, mother, grandparents, great-grandparents may have been involved.)

- [ ] Astral-projection
- [ ] Ouija board / Automatic writing
- [ ] Table or body lifting
- [ ] Dungeons and Dragons
- [ ] Speaking in trance
- [ ] Magic eight ball
- [ ] Telepathy
- [ ] Using spells or curses
- [ ] Séance
- [ ] Materialization
- [ ] Clairvoyance
- [ ] Spirit guides
- [ ] Fortune telling / Tarot cards
- [ ] Palm reading
- [ ] Astrology/horoscopes
- [ ] Rod and pendulum (dowsing)
- [ ] Self-hypnosis
- [ ] Mental manipulations or mind swapping
- [ ] Black and white magic
- [ ] New Age medicine
- [ ] Blood pacts or self-mutilation
- [ ] Fetishism (crystals, charms, etc.)
- [ ] Incubi and succubi (sexual spirits)
- [ ] Other

- [ ] Christian Science
- [ ] Unity
- [ ] The Way International
- [ ] Unification Church
- [ ] Mormonism
- [ ] Church of the Living Word
- [ ] Jehovah's Witnesses
- [ ] Children of God (Love)
- [ ] Swedenborgianism
- [ ] Unitarianism
- [ ] Masons
- [ ] New Age
- [ ] The Forum (EST)
- [ ] Spirit worship
- [ ] Other

- [ ] Buddhism
- [ ] Hare Krishna
- [ ] Bahaism
- [ ] Rosicrucianism
- [ ] Science of the Mind
- [ ] Science of Creative Intelligence
- [ ] Transcendental Meditation
- [ ] Hinduism
- [ ] Yoga
- [ ] Eckankar
- [ ] Roy Masters
- [ ] Silva Mind Control
- [ ] Father Divine
- [ ] Theosophical Society
- [ ] Islam
- [ ] Black Muslim (Movement)
- [ ] Religion of Martial Arts
- [ ] Other

## Vows and Leaders

Most leaders worth their salt will have gone over this list and taken steps to renounce or deal with anything regarding possible Masonic involvement or occult involvement in their past, including generational involvement. However, we are astounded by how many leaders we mentor who have made vows that tie them to the past spiritually. Leviticus 5:4 says that if we make vows, even good ones, we are to confess these to the Lord—we are guilty and need to seek forgiveness—once we become aware of them. "Or if they make a rash vow of any kind, whether its purpose is for good or bad, they will be considered guilty even when they were not fully aware of what they were doing at the time" (NLT).

What is that all about? Well, think of these examples. A leader who grew up in a home with a smothering mother who instilled fear in him as a child by her constant overprotectionism makes a vow, saying, "I am never going to be like my mother!" As a young adult, then, this person seeks out relationships with "wild women" who are risk takers and quite irresponsible. Now in his leadership, he often aligns himself with people who are much the same way, and as a result he has never progressed to the level of leadership one might expect given his capabilities and calling.

In another instance a young woman, hurt because of the divorce sparked by her father walking out on the marriage, says, "I am never going to trust a man again in my life." To this day she remains single and has never been able to enter into a meaningful relationship with someone of the opposite gender. Since she ministers within an environment that is predominantly male, she has developed a reputation of being an "angry woman" and is often overlooked for leadership opportunities because of this. It is her attitude, not her gender, that holds her back from being all that she could be as a Christian leader.

So why does this vow thing not kick in until we become aware of it? Well, I am not precisely sure, but I think God allows us as children to make vows at times as a form of protection. I know of too many leaders who have had experiences in their past—from physical or sexual abuse to chronic neglect—from which their only means of surviving was to make a vow: "I'll never be like this or that . . ." The vow sees them through the trauma and so is permitted.

However, when I say, "I will never . . . ," it is like cutting God out of that area of my life—and he longs to be Lord over all aspects of our lives. Therefore, when we become aware of having made a vow in one area or another, we need to let God back into that part of our life. We do this by confessing that we made the vow and in prayer turning that back over to God's control.

## I'm Vow Man

The Schoebers and I met with a young leader who is one of the most gifted communicators of the gospel that we have met in a long time. Christopher had experienced many setbacks in moving ahead as a Christian leader and was longing to deal with and push through any barriers still in his way. We asked him whether he had made any vows and shared with him Leviticus 5:4.

Christopher thought about it carefully and then said he could not think of any vows he might have made in his past. This is not uncommon, for we find that, spiritually, our foe does not want leaders remembering such things. When this occurs, we ask young leaders to make it a matter of prayer and ask the Lord to bring to mind any vows they might have made.

Three days later he called me and told me he was "vow man," like it was some kind of supervillain. I didn't understand at first, but he clarified by stating that the Lord had brought to mind over a dozen vows that he had made, and that he had begun to confess them and had invited Jesus to exercise his lordship over these parts of his life as well. And so the sleeper cells were discovered and dealt with.

In this, as in many encounters with the enemy, we must always be aware that once the light has been turned on to an area in a leader's life, the enemy will try to hide some aspects from being discovered. Often the leader will give up the least damaging vows first, and those that hold the leader back the most are not given up without a bit of a fight. I say bit of a fight because the evil one has already lost the war—these encounters are like minor skirmishes among some remaining soldiers.

## The War Is Over—and Jesus Won!

I remember my father telling me a story about the Second World War in the South Pacific. The Pacific War ended on September 2, 1945. However, when Japan signed the surrender agreement aboard the USS *Missouri*, there were still hundreds of Japanese soldiers dug into shelters among the many islands of the South Pacific. Long since cut off from their command headquarters, they had not heard that the war was over.

In September 1974, an amazing twenty-nine years after the signing of the peace treaty, an Indonesian Air Force pilot noticed a man in a clearing on the island of Morotai. Rumors of Japanese soldiers holding out had persisted for years, and Japanese officials had tried many things to coax loyal troops out from the mountainous interior, including the playing of their wartime national anthem by loudspeaker.

The man seen from the air was Private Nakamura Teruo, who had spent more than twenty years in complete isolation. Nakamura did not know the war was over and was convinced he would be killed if he were found. It took until December 1974 to surround him, at which time he turned over a very well-maintained rifle and five rounds of ammunition. He was still ready to kill for the cause twenty-nine years after Japan's surrender. He was a threat to anyone who happened to stumble into his holdout territory.

Spiritually for Christian leaders, the war is over and Christ is the victor, but we are prudent to realize that we can still get hurt in minor battles. Vows are very similar to this holdout soldier. We are able to call out these hidden vows from the life of a leader and renounce them with the support of others alongside praying that the Lord would reveal all that needs to be known in order to see the leader released from these spiritual chains that are hindering his growth as a leader. Again and again, the Lord faithfully reveals all that needs to be known at the time in order to proceed.

## Freedom from Addiction to Power and Control

The fifth area leaders need to be freed from is the appeal of and addiction to power and control that come from their leadership position.

Anyone who has been around ministry leadership for any length of time has witnessed and probably experienced a variety of responses to power. Consider the following example.

Doug, a very intelligent and gifted young leader, has been greatly used of God throughout his life. His leadership abilities were first noticed as a young person. However, his leadership came into full blossom during his time in seminary. Following the advice of his mentor, Doug began working as an associate pastor in a significant church. His denomination recognized the effectiveness of his ministry and frequently asked him to be involved in conferences, and in the training of other pastors. Seeing the need for further education, he began work on a doctorate in ministry. While still completing his degree, he was offered an administrative position within the denomination. Over a five-year period after seminary graduation, Doug had demonstrated competence and was well liked.

As he climbed the leadership ladder and began to take on national responsibility, power began to stimulate him. He loved this new position, but he began to change. Those closest to him noticed it first. He preferred to be called "Dr. Doug" and liked to show off the new technology that came with the position. He seemed to default toward decisions that made him look good rather than helping the organization perform well. Doug was largely elevated to this leadership role through his vast network of friends, constituents, and colleagues; however, he began to communicate differently toward them—and often it was in emails or letters, seldom face-to-face or by phone.

This young leader probably enlisted support from other ministers and leaders on his way up the ladder. Such interaction helped them feel included and increased the organization's effectiveness. Therefore, when the communication disconnection begins, the seeds of leadership downfall have already been sown. As problems or breakdowns occur, the toxic effects may even increase. The leader is pushed away from interacting with staff.

Doug's ability to function professionally and his effectiveness began to decline. Sensing the growing tension and seeming unable to identify his own deprivations and turn things around, he began to withdraw. Before being asked, Doug resigned his leadership position, and after a short stint in another church, where the same patterns repeated, he withdrew to a job with a company that seemed to encourage his desire for and love affair with power.

## What Is It about Power That Is So Seductive?

In their book *Blinded by Might*, Ed Dobson and Cal Thomas comment on why leaders get hooked on power.

> Power is the ultimate aphrodisiac. People may have wealth, position, fame, but unless they have power, many of them believe their lives are incomplete. Power cannot only seduce, but also affect judgment. It can be more addictive than any drug, because it deceives the one who "takes" it. Power can be used to rationalize the most outrageous behavior because the power abuser sincerely believes his ends are justified and so any means of achieving them are legitimate.
>
> When a preacher or any other person who claims to speak for God, and who already holds sway over sometimes large numbers of people, is seduced by power, he can become destructive, not only to himself and to those he is charged to lead, but to the cause and objectives of the One he is supposed to be serving.[2]

While their focus was on political power in *Blinded by Might*, Dobson and Thomas's observations about the influence of power should be heeded by Christian leaders. There are several sources of power we encounter in our leadership. Money, especially lots of it, creates power in the hands of the beholder. Position naturally creates authority that can be used positively or negatively. Age in some cultures, where one is never to question one's elders, is another source of power. No matter where our leadership leads us, we will always have an encounter with power.

## Power in the Boardroom

You may have noticed in an in-flight magazine a tear-out advertisement for a seminar on negotiating skills. In these seminars, business leaders are taught that the very best negotiators understand what creates power and how they may gain the upper hand through this knowledge. They are taught that for each party in a negotiation, there are eight sources of power. These are need, options, time, relationships, investment, credibility, knowledge, and skills. This is remembered through the acronym NO TRICKS.

We can place this approach into one of the settings where power is wielded and expressed often in the leadership of a ministry organization like a church—at the board meeting or elders meeting. Many Christian leaders—especially those whose training has been confined to seminary or pastoral training—are outmaneuvered by skillful and not always spiritual negotiations by those who are simply better at this than they are. Here is how the NO TRICKS negotiating approach can be used against leaders.

*N* stands for need. When a board member assesses the need for a given idea or program to move forward, the essential question is who has the greater need for it: the community you are trying to reach out to, or the church or organization for internal or pride reasons. The more intense the community's need, the more power you will need to get the board behind your leadership.

*O* equals options. Skillful negotiators can stall progress by seeking options and not wanting to move forward without a selection of choices. Often the other options they put forward consist of the ideas or opportunities that "may be" waiting in the wings—ignoring the real opportunity before you. The more options you have, and the fewer acceptable options you have, the greater the negotiating power of people being used to freeze ministry.

*T* stands for time, which refers to any impending events that place a deadline on either the board or you as the leader. If the board is under time pressure, the leader usually has negotiating strength—although I have seldom seen the board of a Christian organization able to respond quickly to opportunities.

For example, at an urban church where I served as minister of evangelism and community outreach, I heard that the building across the street was being converted from an office building to apartments. We had an opportunity to purchase a unit and encourage a family from the congregation to move into the building as missionaries to this new minitown, literally across the street.

I approached the leadership of the church, and we even went over to view one of the display suites that had been set up. The vision was shared and was exciting. We shared the vision with a few more, and momentum was building. Then we discussed what process we would need to undertake to move forward on this. It required going to a committee of the board to create a financial model that made sense and that was attainable and sustainable. That meant calling a meeting. This would be followed by a presentation to the governing board of the church—another meeting. The governing board met monthly, and if their endorsement was received, we would present it to the congregation as a whole and buy the condominium. I was excited!

Two days later, the vision and dream vanished.

I was driving to the church office that morning fueled by this exciting and visionary ministry opportunity. I was already beginning to picture potential candidates being developed as urban missionaries. As I was on final approach from my commute and nearing the church parking lot for another safe landing in my parking spot, the dream was shattered.

I rounded the corner and looked up at the soon-to-be high-rise condominium next door to God's house. I envisioned the 300-plus people who would be living there—with our church missionaries right in the midst of them. Then my eyes lowered to the FOR SALE sign, where I saw a brand-new SOLD OUT banner hung across it in a triumphant manner.

Time was not on our side. Opportunity was lost.

*R* is for relationship power. How strong is your relationship with your leadership? If you have many high-quality relationships with your board and congregation, you have relationship power. But some board members may not allow you to develop these relationships. Obviously, in such a situation you will have a hard time developing relationship power.

The *I* in NO TRICKS stands for investment. How much time and energy have you already invested in the idea or process? The more effort someone invests, the more committed he will be to seeing it fulfilled. If you put twenty hours into preparing a proposal, you'll have a hard time walking away from the idea. Investment gives you power through the investment—especially when you have thought through the issues at a level that those with "day jobs" have not.

*C* stands for credibility. You must have personal leadership credibility for big visions or ideas. This comes from a witnessed faithfulness over time, a track record of wisdom and character. We also gain power when others with credibility come alongside our vision and are willing to add their names to it.

In the early years of Arrow, prior to any historic record of accomplishment of leadership development, there is no question that Leighton Ford was the credibility carrier. His international reputation and leadership of the Lausanne Committee, as well as his leadership with the Billy Graham Association, opened the door for Arrow Leadership International Ministries to come into being.

Shortly after taking over the presidency of Arrow, I visited with one of the initial donors who helped start Arrow. He shared with me that he did not even know what he was funding in the beginning. "It was just something that Leighton was involved with," he told me. It was Leighton's credibility that drew in his financial support.

How comfortable does your leader feel in a boardroom setting? Many Christian leaders can benefit from seeing other boards in operation. This is one of the values of volunteering for other ministries. Are there other ways you can help coach your mentee in the area of boardroom leadership?

*K* stands for knowledge. Knowledge is power. You have knowledge power when you thoroughly understand the issues, problems, and needs of the community and can foresee how the ministry or services you are envisioning will help the community meet those needs.

*S* stands for skill. Who is the most skillful organizational leader? In mentoring leaders, I have heard many stories where leaders who possessed many of the "powers" we have just discussed in their leadership lacked the organizational leadership skill to "pull it off." They were outsmarted in the boardroom. Today, as Christian leaders we must constantly improve our skills, just to keep up.

PHASE THREE

# Visioneering

# Visioneering

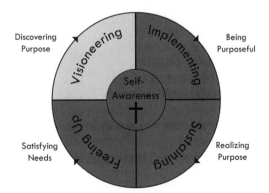

## Vision: A Problem for Gifted Leaders

Without vision . . . the people perish.

Most books, courses, and seminars on leadership deal with the subject of vision. There is no question that it is a valuable and essential part of the leader's life and ministry. Whenever you study a successful ministry effort, you will find a leader who was able to provide a guiding coalition for people, centered on an image of the future that was well communicated and appealed to those under his care. I'm speaking about something that goes deeper than five-year strategic plans or brainstorming sessions. God's vision is a burning desire that fuels hope.

Much that is written about vision gives the dangerous impression that we can somehow have a much more important role in the developing of vision than we ought. Followers of Jesus who are called to lead are not self-made people on some personally concocted journey. Vision is God's taking you from one place to another for his purposes—not our own. Vision is more about being "taken."

Vision intended for a group of people or an organization or ministry almost always begins with one person. It becomes personal to the extent that we refer to it in possessive terms such as "my vision" or "my calling," yet the intent is usually to minister to or impact many others. Sometimes our first attempt at expressing vision creates a blurry image that is not clearly seen—nor understood—by others, including the leader. But wise leaders learn to gather around them trusted mentors who, under God's guidance, help to sharpen the vision.

## Vision Percolator

I find that most young leaders have an experience with vision that is similar to a coffee percolator. On our sailboat, we make coffee using a stove-top percolator. You pour water into it, then add coffee grounds, then place the lid on tightly and set it on the stove. As the propane flame heats the water, it is forced up the center tube where it bubbles into a glass knob on the lid. The pot begins to take on a life of its own as it gurgles and sputters until the water takes on the color and aroma of the coffee grounds.

In a similar way, vision begins to percolate up within the life of the leader. God is the one who provides the energy—and yes, sometimes it is in the form of heat! We can be stimulated by our situations to such an extent that our lives become open to dreams, and it is out of dreams that vision emerges. Without a vision, any ministry effort can quickly dissolve into a schedule of repetitive and often unfulfilling projects that take the church or organization in the wrong direction or cause it to miss a window of opportunity by doing nothing at all. Without a clear, compelling vision, all of your effort, and that of your team, will not add up in a very meaningful, purposeful way.

An embarrassingly high percentage of churches have either plateaued or declined in attendance and ministry impact. Within these churches, you usually find plenty of plans and programs—but no vision. The vision that is needed is one that clarifies the direction they should be going, and out of that eventually will emerge the strategic steps that will get them there.

Young leaders are at the same time both excited and fearful of vision. They know the power of vision, yet question their ability to be visionary. It is almost as though our current leadership culture has created an image of the visionary leader that they feel they will never live up to. That may be true, but it's really not about them. Vision is not about you and me. It is about God. God is the originator of vision.

## Baring My Heart to Barry

In one of my brown leather journals, I wrote notes in 1992 about the vision and passion that was beginning to percolate up within me regarding the development of emerging leaders. It was so heavy upon me that I did not know what to do with it. I shared it with Brenda, but it almost seemed too overwhelming for us to deal with alone. So I mustered the courage to speak with Barry Hawes, the primary mentor in my life.

Barry is an amazing Christian executive, a philanthropist, and an insightful mentor. We had been friends for several years, and he has known me since I was a youth pastor. Yet it was with a great sense of tenderness that I began to share my vision with him. I was baring my heart.

It reminded me of a time when I went with my father to Saint Joseph's Oratory in Montreal, Canada. On a rise of earth known as Mount Royal stands a religious edifice of staggering proportions. It is 361 feet high, taller than either Saint Patrick's Cathedral in New York or the Cathedral of Notre Dame in Paris. I remember climbing to a small room at the back of the oratory where the mortal remains of Blessed Brother André lie in a black marble sepulchre. There on a pillar was displayed the now shriveled heart of Brother André. Seeing this heart exposed made me think that if it had nerves that allowed it to feel, even the slightest breath of wind on it would cause pain.

It is like that with sharing vision. When we expose our vision heart, it is always with extreme tenderness. We try to shelter it always from a breath of breeze that might cause us to withdraw in pain.

Barry listened carefully as I explained that the Lord was inspiring me with a new vision for my life and ministry. As I sensed his openness to hearing what was on my heart, I began to unfold the vision. Little did he know that I had written out four pages of ideas to share with him. It was like he was trying to drink from a fire hydrant, as I burst forth with passion and excitement, tinged with fear.

My experience with Barry as my mentor has been extremely positive. I realize that many younger leaders have trouble finding a mentor with whom they connect. However, it is well worth the effort to continue searching for a mentor who is not just a good fit—but a God fit. As a mentor, please prayerfully evaluate if you are the right person to be alongside the leader at this time. Allow the leader to move on if you think it is best for him. Remember, mentoring is not about you—it is about the young leader and his development by the Lord. Yes, you may experience some personal blessings as a result of mentoring—but it's not about you!

As I started into page 3, he smiled and continued to listen, asking a few questions of clarification. When I had finished, I asked him what he thought of it.

Barry's response at this point was critical to me as a mentor, and ended up becoming the bedrock on which I would begin praying and pursuing the vision further. He told me that the vision was a great vision, and certainly something I was not only being called to but was uniquely gifted to fulfill. He did not dive into specific strategies at this point, even though my four pages included many suggestions as to how I might engage the vision in my life. Rather he shared with me the various ways in which God had been preparing me for such a mission. At the end of our session together, Barry sent me away encouraged, feeling believed in, and supported. He promised to pray with me about this and led us in prayer, asking the Lord to lead and guide me on—bringing increasing clarity to the vision.

So why is vision a problem for many younger leaders? There are three primary reasons:

1. Younger leaders are often multigifted and capable of doing almost anything—therefore dreams and visions do not have the natural filter of capability or capacity that other people would use as a foundation in decision making.
2. Younger leaders are often far too busy to notice God or allow him to percolate his vision to the surface. They do not take enough time in life for solitude and reflection.
3. Young leaders have tried to proceed to the visioneering phase of their leadership development without having dealt with self-awareness and subsequently seeking freedom from those things internally and externally that hold them back. We spoke earlier of these chains.

## What Is the Vision Process Like for Women?

Gretchen Englund has made some excellent observations about the "vision quest" and its specific nuances for women leaders. In an email dialogue we had she writes:

A man and a woman encounter the same basic walls to climb as each discerns God's vision—questions of confidence, discerning God's voice, how God affirms the vision, and what steps one should take. Unlike men, however, a woman is seldom urged to take risks in God's economy, to move out, and to bring others with her. Add to this discernment process a woman's natural reflection regarding her singleness, marriage, and/or children—and she is now in a complex situation. She often wears many "hats." Because embracing God's vision involves a degree of added risk, she will need to not only discern God's vision and call, but also look to God for a new, bolstered confidence in Him. If she is living by conviction in the known priorities of her life, when the vision becomes clearer, she will be able to accept the call to move ahead. Without settling God's revealed call in the foundational areas of her life, the vision can be eclipsed. However, a settled conviction about known priorities and her own identity in Christ allows God's Spirit to assist her in warding off self-doubt and hesitation to "move out."

Is it actually more difficult to discern vision as a woman? I contend that it is more complex, but not more difficult. A man, for example, will never need to ask himself, "What does it mean to be a man in ministry?" But a woman must ask and wrestle with the question, "What does it mean to be a woman in ministry?" In the first place, the question of women in Christian leadership needs to be addressed. There are competing voices within current Christian culture about women's roles in leadership; therefore, the emerging woman leader must answer whether she has freedom to serve God in every capacity, or if there are limitations. That question adds a profound, additional dimension to the visioning process. Every woman I have mentored has come to this crossroad, and each must negotiate it. The woman who settles this question will find she is able to move ahead with courage, resting solely on God's call to her and his Word, and not on the competing voices.

When she begins to get clarity discerning God's life vision, she must then take responsibility to steward the vision. Again, men are easily taught to take responsibility, move ahead, and trust God for the best, while women are not always challenged in this way. But God's vision requires bold obedience that stems from knowing one's identity and position in Christ. If a woman questions who she is as a woman following Christ, she will likely also question her ability, or responsibility, to carry out the vision.

Even Esther exhibits self-protection in her first response to Mordecai, saying she had not been summoned to see King Xerxes in thirty days and would be killed if she entered the court unasked (Esther 4:1–17). She apparently had not fully reflected on the position God had placed her in. When God uses Mordecai to challenge Esther that her call to save the Jewish people may be "for such a time as this," she then realizes the call and her "royal position," and that it is God who raised her into the position. She stops hesitating, calls the Jews to a three-day fast, and proceeds to carry out the vision—placing her life in God's hands. Women discerning God's vision may need to be guided to see not only that God gives vision but also that he gives the responsibility to steward that vision.

Finally, even if a woman understands her womanhood and vision, even if she sees that God is calling her, she can still remain stuck. The complexities of womanhood require women to be persons of many layers and cross-fibers. The joy is that women and men, together in ministry, express a great richness of God's image. The problem a woman often faces, however, is remaining stuck in unresolved personal issues that halt even the most outwardly confident woman. It is very difficult—nearly impossible—for a woman to segregate her unresolved issues from the rest of her life, and it is certainly an issue of integrity if she does. Once a woman submits to the painful process of inner change, her full receipt of God's vision will become clearer, and her freedom allows God to expand his kingdom through her.

## A Patient Visionary: The Story of Barnabas Family Ministries

When we walk with leaders through the Arrow Leadership Program over a two-year period, part of our desire is to help them sharpen their vision. We do this not by a single module where we teach on vision but by weaving a thread of sharpening vision throughout the devotions, trainers, sharing times, and case studies. One example of this is a devotional we use by Rob Bentall.

Rob is the executive director of Barnabas Family Ministries. Barnabas is an incredible facility on Keats Island—about an hour by boat from Vancouver. We try to take every Arrow class to Barnabas at least once during their time with us. It is one of my favorite locations from which to do leadership development. It provides a sense of isolation and surrounds us with an incredible view of the mountains and the ocean and the forest. When the Arrow leaders get their first glimpse of the facility and location in daylight—they are often speechless.[1]

Barnabas is a first-class facility that is tended by true servant leaders. The lodging, the meals, and the staff are incredible! The young leaders often joke, saying, "Please don't tell my spouse how nice this place is." Brenda and I have known Rob and Kathy for many years, and the Barnabas these young leaders experience today is the result of a vision that took decades to mature. After the students have had sufficient time to be wowed, we ask Rob to share a devotional about the visionary story of Barnabas. We do this because young leaders often struggle with how long it takes to prayerfully and continually proceed forward with a vision.

Here is how Rob Bentall tells his story:

In 1972, I had just finished my undergraduate degree and had thought I would go into the family business. However, I was sensing that God was calling me into ministry. So I began to pray over a number of months and, because I'm a very practical person—I like designing and building things—I asked God for a very specific and precise vision.

In October of 1972, I was running a discipleship camp at the other end of the island—at the Baptist camp there. On the second night of that retreat, in the evening session, I had a strong sense that God spoke to me and that God answered my prayer and gave me a vision. The vision was for family and adult ministry and on a very specific piece of property. I shared it with two fellows who were helping me out on that weekend. The three of us walked down to the property. There was no one around at the time. It was owned by a retired high school principal from Vancouver. We sat in the upper field and prayed, "Lord, if this vision is of you, protect it, preserve it, and bring it about in your time."

The next summer I came back with my father and met the gentleman. He had been my father's high school principal and my father had a good relationship with him. We met him on the front porch of the old farmhouse across the field. He was not a believer, so I very carefully shared the dream with him. Well, his response was anger and he kicked us off the property. That was 1973. The door closed, but the vision was very much still there. So I proceeded to go to seminary and then into ministry. I was first an associate pastor and then later got involved in a ministry called Young Life in Canada. The years ticked on, the elderly gentleman passed away, left all the property to a young nephew from Nova Scotia, Richard. Richard moved out here as a single person and made this his home. He met a local gal, married, had three children, and it looked like the vision would never come about.

One side note: when I was at seminary I remember sharing the vision with some of my professors and basically being gently reprimanded that God doesn't work that way. I struggled with that. I really believe that God gave me that vision, and yet the counsel of those around me was saying no. So I carried on, believing that God had done this, but rather than just waiting and doing nothing, I pursued other ministries as God would open the door and lead. This prepared me.

So the years went on. In 1986, we had been in Young Life for seven years and my wife and I were sensing that our time was done. So we asked a group, whom we respected, of six or so people to pray with us over a number of months. That culminated with us getting together for a weekend with that group. And as we met together for that weekend, we just felt God saying, "Move ahead. Take some steps. See if I will open some doors." We continued to talk with that group, and right away we realized there would need to be some kind of endorsement or affiliation if we were to get started. I mean, who were Kathy and I that we would start this family ministry?

We talked amongst the group, wondering who would that be. One person in the group said Dr. Dobson would be perfect, and my response was to laugh. "Well, yeah, sure, that would be great, but who am I that Dr. Dobson would want to do that?" Another person said, "Well, wait a minute, he's coming to Vancouver in two weeks' time and he's going to meet with our prayer breakfast group. There are twelve of us. Why don't you and Kathy come and share with him?"

Well, two weeks later, we attended the group, which grew from twelve to ninety. But as God would work it out, four of us sat at a table, Jim and Shirley [Dobson], Kathy and I, and we got to share the vision over that breakfast with him. I won't go into the long story, but over the next month, it was amazing how God opened the door. What ended up happening was that Focus said, "Yes! You won't know this Rob, but you just met a criteria that we had prayerfully laid out but not shared it with anyone. We have wanted to encourage and support others who are called to family ministry but left it that we would not approach anyone. They had to be led to us, just as you have."

A few years ago, I was sharing the same story with Arrow, and one of the presenters came up to me after and said, "I was on the Focus board when we made that decision." It was so exciting for him to see what God had done with their decision many years ago.

So, we started moving ahead; God had opened that door. Then all of a sudden Richard, the owner of the property, became homesick and wanted to go back to Nova Scotia. Dialogue began to happen. A foundation stepped up and said, "We'll underwrite the cost of the property and the buildings in order for this to happen." And so it was clear, we felt, God was calling us to move ahead.

Thus we began. We started in 1987 by doing conferences up at Whistler, the ski area just north of Vancouver, by renting hotel space. We would do marriage enrichment, family, and parenting conferences during their low months between the end of summer and the start of ski season. At the same time we began to develop the property here. The first two years were very exciting. After waiting for so long, door after door just kind of flung open. Then all of a sudden, the wall came down.

The funding that had been pledged to us—evaporated overnight. All of a sudden, we were left with a very small support base that was completely inadequate, even just to make ends meet. And God began to do a deep work in me, to teach me what it means to trust and depend on him for everything, every step of the way.

I grew up in a fairly wealthy family, and now I didn't know where the groceries were coming from the next day. For me, that was a big lesson, but it was an important one that God needed to work on in my life.

Others started to see that we were out on a limb. They began to catch the vision and come on board. I could share story after story of God's amazing provision. From putting a road in with all volunteer help in the middle of winter that should never have happened, to the pier out at the front of the property. In fact, there's a neat thing that just happened a few years ago. Expo '86 in Vancouver was a big world's fair, and at the end they auctioned off everything that they had built and didn't need. The government had paid half a million dollars for those blue bridge sections that are out front there, and we put a low bid offer in for $15,000 thinking that we could use them as a pier on our property. The fellow that gave us the counsel and helped us put it all together was in the marine industry and very knowledgeable, and we managed to get them for $15,000. But they were too big and very expensive to move; they weighed twenty-three tons apiece. You don't just put them in the back of your boat and bring them here. So this fellow let them sit on his property for five years. It's a complicated story, but this fellow and part of the foundation that pulled the plug on us were connected relationally. So he and I had a broken relationship.

The time came to move the bridge pieces and God started to raise up people. An engineer who had just retired donated his time to design it, another fellow had contacts to get a tugboat donated, and another person donated the biggest barge on the coast. Yet another friend of the ministry had the largest crane in Vancouver to lift them onto the barge, so it all came together in an amazing way. So God did it in his way and in his timing.

Thus the years have continued. We chose the name Barnabas because Barnabas in the New Testament was known as son of encouragement. We felt our mission statement was to be encouragers of families and to strengthen the family. So all summer long we provide family conferences. Then the rest of the year we mostly do marriage enrichment and preparing for marriage weekends. We also do some specialty weekends, like our adult mother-daughter retreat.

So we continue to move ahead, trusting God to lead and direct, trying to be obedient every step of the way. Vision is in God's timetable, not in ours. It may not be that you have to wait seventeen years before God will open the door—it might be years or it might be two months. It wouldn't have been right for us to start building in 1973. The needs just weren't the same, the culture wasn't the same, and Kathy and I sure weren't ready. But in 1987 the time was right and even more so today. So I encourage you to hang in there for the long haul because God knows what he's doing. He's the wise one, and not us.

Rob's story is an inspiration to the younger leaders attending our Arrow residential seminars. Why is that? It is because they are actually sitting in the fulfillment of the vision as they listen to him speak. They are witnessing a gentle, faithful leader who did not stray from the vision God gave to him in spite of great obstacles. He becomes like a mentor encouraging them to first of all seek God's vision, and then pursue it with their whole life, not giving up but being patiently obedient.

Today, Barnabas Family Ministries is a world-class Christian conference center in one of the most beautiful places you can imagine. The work that God does there, through the ministry of marriage enrichment, preparation for marriage, and family camps, has transformed so many families and continues to this day. It would not have been possible but for the patient visionary God has in Rob Bentall.

The Barnabas team has a new vision for another building that will greatly enhance their capacity for ministry and move them toward sustainability as a ministry. And just as Rob shared about the securing of the property, Rob and Kathy are waiting on the Lord to provide the resources necessary to build without debt. We are praying with them, and I am confident that the Lord will provide.

## Following a Path Set by Others?

Some leaders have expressed to me a sense of despair after hearing Rob share because they came to realize that they have never sought the Lord's vision for their life but rather have been following the path set by others.

Lorna Dueck is the executive producer of the current affairs program *Listen Up TV*. A popular television host and public speaker, Lorna is a regular commentary writer on faith and public life in Canada's largest national newspaper, the *Globe and Mail*. *Listen Up TV* exists to use news and current affairs as a bridge to help people discover Christ.

Each week Lorna examines current affairs for their spiritual meaning for our lives. She hosts studio interviews and field reports as Canadians share stories of how their view of faith influences the world. Crises, politics, pop culture, home and international news—the program listens to the world and looks for the spiritual side to the story. It is an amazing program and ministry.[2]

*Listen Up* was birthed when Lorna realized it was time to set out on her own. I remember the look in her eyes as this realization was percolating to the top of her vision world. For eight years Lorna had been cohosting Canada's most watched daily Christian television program, *100 Huntley Street*. That career created and launched *Listen Up TV*, first within *100 Huntley Street*, and now as an independent program.

Lorna would be among the first to confess that stepping out of a path that someone else had you on, to start moving in your own direction, is very scary. It requires a special determination to "say good-bye" to all those things that are common to you, with no idea what may lie ahead.

## Passion, Vision, Mission

Someone once told me that vision is the beginning of leadership. Our leadership really begins when the vision emerges within us. Certainly, vision is a principal key to our understanding of leadership.

As the Lord was creating within me a clarified vision of developing emerging leaders, it gave me a clear direction to embark upon, and I knew it would take the rest of my life to invest in. I knew that no matter where I worked, I would seek to fulfill the ministry that I believed wholeheartedly God had placed me on this earth to undertake.

Although I had been in several leadership positions and roles prior to this time, now everything seemed different. I realized that without a clear, compelling vision, I was acting out a part—pretending and trying to conjure up what I thought I should be and be about. Now, I was taking steps toward real leadership.

In reading several leadership books on vision and mission, I find that there are somewhat confusing definitions for the words that are bandied about. Let me state a simple definition of the terms as I have experienced them in working with leaders.

### Passion

Passion is where it all begins. I often speak to younger leaders and refer to passion as "the burn" within them. I think about the story in Luke 24 of Jesus on the Emmaus road, where after his resurrection he came alongside the disciples and walked with them without revealing who he was. When they broke bread together and finally realized that Jesus was with them, he moved on—but the "burn" stayed with them.

They asked each other, "Were not our hearts burning within us while he talked with us on the road and opened the Scriptures to us?" (Luke 24:32).

That is the burn that passion brings. You see it often in leaders who are completely committed to their cause. Who would daresay that Tony Campolo does not have a burning desire for justice and a passionate love for the underprivileged and those who do not yet know Jesus? For twenty years I have heard him speak, and I always sense the burning passion within him.

Chuck Swindoll has a burn for preaching the Word of God. I was with Insight for Living (IFL) when Chuck stepped down as the senior pastor at the Fullerton Evangelical Free Church in California. For about a month he seemed okay with taking a break from the pulpit, but I remember Roger Kemp, then vice president of broadcasting for IFL, saying to me, "Carson, if we don't find a pulpit for Chuck to preach in soon, he is going to explode!" We laughed at the thought, but knew there was a lot of truth in that statement. God was continuing to instill in Chuck messages from his Word that had to be preached. It is what God hardwired Chuck to do.

Much to our delight, Chuck got the opportunity to preach at a church up the coast from Los Angeles where his son-in-law was the pastor. It was a small church, a tiny church that some might think unworthy of a preacher/figure like Swindoll—but it was a pulpit. Making arrangements to preclude a big fuss over his coming, he just showed up in the pulpit one Sunday—and the internal pressure in Chuck was released for a short period.

Chuck became president of Dallas Theological Seminary, and in that role had several opportunities to preach to students and faculty there, but it still was not enough to release the buildup of the burn within him—his passion for preaching the Word of God through the gifts God had given him. That is his passion and it burns within him! Chuck reminds me of the psalmist who could not contain himself from speaking out:

> My heart grew hot within me,
>     and as I meditated, the fire burned;
> then I spoke with my tongue.
>
> Psalm 39:3

Mothers have told me of the experience of carrying a child and the heat generated by this new life growing within them. This is another great metaphor of the burn I am speaking about. There is new life—a passion—growing and developing within them, and it will continue to create this sense of heat, like an internal heater, until it is birthed and takes on a life of its own.

### Vision

Vision is a clear picture that a leader sees of the future for the people and organization he leads. It emerges from "the burn" God places within. When God gives a vision, and a leader picks it up and begins to run with it, the people break away from any restraints or resistance in order to pursue it with all their ability and gifts. This is the actual meaning behind Proverbs 29:18. People will shed constraints—all those things that seem like barriers—to fulfill the vision.

It is often said that Canadians define themselves as a people more by who we are not than who we are. Vision is somewhat the same, for it is more easily recognized by the effects of its absence. When there is no visionary leadership, you will see confusion, disarray, disobedience, and lack of progress on any number of fronts.

I'd go so far as to say that without a clear vision you have not really begun your role as a leader. You may have been a managerial leader, but it is vision that sets leaders apart. Now vision involves more than just the leader, for the vision must have followers. Perhaps the major responsibility of every leader is to effectively communicate the vision and clarify it for the followers. The leader lives with the vision day and night. It is a cherished possession that is guarded and protected. The leader spends time thinking, dreaming, and praying about the vision, and then conveying it to others so that it might be accomplished.

Staying focused on the vision generates action. It inspires an expectation of accomplishing great things and fuels the striving for excellence.

## Mission

So the burn (passion) percolates up a vision and then the mission is birthed—the commitment to act on that vision. The mission is undertaken by a series of programs or goals that fulfill the vision in meaningful, measurable ways.

Many leaders fail right at this point. They have recognized the burn, have clarity of vision, but are too quick to abandon the vision when nothing seems to be happening.

Missional leaders are those who have the ability to design and develop a program out of the vision they have received, whereby other people can be engaged in assisting the fulfillment of the vision and overcoming the obstacles that will undoubtedly form in front of the vision.

In the spiritual realm, this is one of the places where leaders face resistance, for it is a place of action. A vision given by God is of little threat to our spiritual foe if never acted on or communicated. Therefore, when a leader begins to formulate the mission, all hell can break loose, often starting with those closest to you failing to align with it. Then it can branch out into financial fears and external rules and regulations, which prevent the mission from proceeding. Screwtape and Wormwood will use whatever means possible to stop progress right at this point.

Sometimes vision and mission are blocked through a weakness within the leader that has been lying dormant or in a stealth form prior to the vision.

## Your Affectionate Uncle Screwtape

Hear these words of C. S. Lewis as he writes of the senior demon Screwtape counseling Wormwood on distracting his "patient"—the Christian man he is assigned to stop in his relationship to Christ:

> A few weeks ago, you had to tempt him to unreality and inattention in his prayers: but now you will find him opening his arms to you and almost begging you to distract his purpose and benumb his heart. He will want his prayers to be unreal, for he will dread nothing so much as effective contact with the Enemy. His aim will be to let sleeping worms lie. As this condition becomes more fully established, you will be gradually freed from the tiresome business of providing Pleasures as temptations. As the uneasiness and his reluctance to face it cut him off more and more from all real happiness, and as habit renders the pleasures of vanity and excitement and flippancy at once less pleasant and harder to forgo (for that is what habit fortunately does to a pleasure) you will find that anything or nothing is sufficient to attract his wandering attention. You no longer need a good book, which he really likes, to keep him from his prayers or his work or his sleep; a column of advertisements in yesterday's paper will do. You can make him waste his time not only in conversation he enjoys with people whom he likes, but in conversations with those he cares nothing about, on subjects that bore him. You can make him do nothing at all for long periods. You can keep him up late at night, not roistering, but staring at a dead fire in a cold room. All the healthy and outgoing activities which we want him to avoid can be inhibited and nothing given in return, so that at last he may say, as one of my own patients said on his arrival down here, "I now see that I spent most of my life in doing neither what I ought nor what I liked."[3]

## Vision: Getting the Theology Right

What does the Bible teach us about vision? As you glance through the leadership books on the shelves of your local bookstore, you will find illustrations and examples of vision that are taken from every kind of historical leader you can imagine—but what does God teach about vision?

Who originates vision? God? Human beings? Or both?

Titles like *Personal Power* and *Finding the Vision Within* come across as though vision were something that we conjure up from within ourselves. Is that what the Bible says? No, Scripture tells us vision is a product of God working in us. He creates the vision and we receive it. It becomes a rallying point, a future goal for us and for those around us.

## Biblical Vision Stories

When we review vision activity in the Bible, we find that:

1. God initiates.
2. God speaks.
3. God connects.
4. God invites.

God uses vision in the lives of leaders to manifest his will, to move us and motivate us.

People's experiences in the Bible exemplify this in a wonderful variety that speaks to both the individuality of the people and also the breadth and expanse of God's intentions. God uses vision for a range of purposes.

### Vision of Purpose

Abraham had a vision that just said get moving! And with that simple vision, Abraham continued to believe that God would lead him wherever he needed to go.

### Vision of Empowerment and Freedom

Moses had a vision of empowerment and freedom. He endured constant leadership headaches, but the vision was strong enough to keep his focus on the promises of God despite the circumstances.

### Vision of Victory

Joshua had a vision of victory. As a result of God's vision, Joshua led his people across the barrier of the Jordan River, knowing they would overcome any challenges. No challenge would be too great since God preceded them and Joshua believed in the power and might of the Creator.

*Vision of Change*

Deborah was a great judge and leader of her people who had a vision of change. She overcame the discrimination toward women in that day and stood firm on her faith in God. Deborah's vision called on her to trust that God would equip her for the task, overcoming all of society's preconceived notions about her ability as a woman. She was living out what would later be written in Romans 8:31: "If God is for us, who can be against us?"

*Vision of Destiny*

Caleb stood with his warrior friend Joshua, both in their eighties, before the hills of the Promised Land. Giants had once inhabited these hills, yet Caleb did not fear, and said: "Now then, just as the LORD promised, he has kept me alive for forty-five years since the time he said this to Moses, while Israel moved about in the desert. So here I am today, eighty-five years old! I am still as strong today as the day Moses sent me out; I'm just as vigorous to go out to battle now as I was then. Now give me this hill country that the LORD promised me that day. You yourself heard then that the Anakites were there and their cities were large and fortified, but, the LORD helping me, I will drive them out just as he said" (Josh. 14:10–12).

Even at an advanced age, Caleb was not afraid of one more push into that hill country because Caleb had a vision of destiny and wasn't afraid to reach out and claim it.

Leaders I work with today still encounter God's vision in similar ways to these biblical examples, yet they are often confused about what to do. God is seeking our obedience. I believe that leaders become stuck because they are still trying to understand the vision and calling in its entirety before moving forward.

## Attempting to Define Vision

The word "vision" is like the word "mentoring" in that it is currently popular and is used by a wide variety of people with many different meanings. In a Christian context, there seems to be blurriness about vision. The word can mean any of the following:

- a focus or direction
- the biblical stewardship of spiritual gifts and life experiences

- a specific "calling"
- a specific task given from God by special revelation
- a "passion" or "dream"

In communicating vision, it is important to beware of the human potential movement, which sells many books by helping others discover their dreams and achieve desired results.

If we asked Christian leaders at different points in history, "What is your vision?" we would likely receive a range of answers:

"A restored and safe people." Nehemiah

"A promised land." Moses

"Evangelized Gentiles." Paul

"A converted China." Hudson Taylor

"A youth-targeted church." Dr. Dave Overholt

"Transformed families." Dr. James Dobson

"The campus and the world won to Christ." Dr. Bill Bright

Based on these usages of vision and the particular focus of individual leaders, we can draw out components of vision that help us in defining it.

## Future Focused

Bill Hybels defines vision as "a picture of the future that produces passion."[4] There are some challenges with this definition in a ministry context. For example, Hitler's vision of Germany's future produced much passion—but was destructive.

## Faith Potential

J. Oswald Sanders defined vision as "faith," with a future focus and a focus on potential.[5]

## Compelling

Leighton Ford defined vision as "the ability to see in a way that compels others to pay attention."[6]

*About God's Purposes*

Based on Dr. J. Robert Clinton's definition of a leader as "a person with a God-given capacity and a God-given responsibility to influence a specific group of God's people toward His purposes for the group,"[7] vision must implicitly involve identifying God's intended purposes for the future.

With the concept of vision including a compelling picture of the future based on God's desired purposes, the logical next questions are: "Do we receive vision or is vision developed?" and "How?"

To answer the question of how it is formed or developed, I find it helpful to break vision into three distinct expressions—corporate, special, and process vision.

## Corporate Vision

Through Scripture, God has revealed significant general principles that provide the foundation and direction for much of life for all believers. For instance, the two great commandments from Matthew 22:37–39 provide both general and specific direction to living life. "Jesus replied, 'Love the Lord your God with all your heart and with all your soul and with all your mind.' This is the first and greatest commandment. And the second is like it: 'Love your neighbor as yourself.'"

In addition, God's desire is that all people come to a saving relationship with him. "The Lord is not slow in keeping his promise, as some understand slowness. He is patient with you, not wanting anyone to perish, but everyone to come to repentance" (2 Peter 3:9).

The life of Jesus also provides us with an example of a truly complete and healthy life. Specifically, there are four primary interdependent components of Jesus's life—intimacy, character, community, and ministry.

*Intimacy.* Jesus repeatedly demonstrated his need for and dependence on a deep and vibrant personal love relationship with his Father. Christ followers are to have the same kind of intimacy.

*Character.* Jesus was tempted in every way, but by God's strength Jesus chose and lived a life of complete obedience. Christ followers are to live obediently.

*Community.* Jesus chose to live, love, serve, and suffer in the context of community. Jesus enjoyed community through individual relationships as well as groups. The church was established as the ongoing community of Christ. Christ followers are to live accordingly.

*Ministry.* As a servant leader, Jesus boldly challenged, loved, and led others in their quest toward a relationship with God. He called disciples to count the cost and radically follow him. He invested his life in training and developing others who would continue the mission in their own unique ways. He finished well and left the world a different place. Christ followers are to do the same.

Church history offers many examples where one or more of these four key components were magnified or ignored with significant consequences.

We also often elevate ministry to a level of primary importance. In other words, we often think about "vision" exclusively in the context of the ministry component. We are tempted to seek what God wants us to do rather than what he wants us to be. As Dr. Os Guinness says, "First and foremost we are called to Someone (God) not to something . . . or to somewhere."[8] Also, "We are not called first to special work but to God."[9]

Within the ministry component, the corporate vision God gives is based on spiritual gifts given by his grace and by his power for the purpose of serving the body of Christ and God's eternal purposes (not our own).

As per the priesthood of all believers, followers of Christ are to steward these gifts for the maximum benefit to the body of Christ and God's eternal purposes. Biblical stewardship would include the creative and focused care and growth of the gift: "Each one should use whatever gift he has received to serve others, faithfully administering God's grace in its various forms" (1 Peter 4:10).

## Conclusions regarding Corporate Vision

Through these general principles on corporate vision, God has given *all Christ followers* more vision about who we are to be and how we are to live than most of us can implement.

We must be careful not to pursue vision through ministry at the expense of the three other components of a healthy life.

It may be easy to confuse "God has given me a vision for _____" with the simple, good stewardship of our spiritual gift. In other words, a vision statement may be more a statement that flows out of good stewardship and the Holy Spirit working together than a direct and specific revelation from God.

Corporate vision is given to all Christ followers (leaders and nonleaders) and may not require the mobilization of others.

## Special Vision

Beyond the comprehensive general principles of corporate vision, God reveals more specific personal vision *to a few select people* through special revelation.

### Common Characteristics of Special or Personal Vision

Those who receive special vision do little or no specific "vision seeking." God's initiative and grace is paramount, and there is no "work" that will bring it on—or turn it off. It is not a light switch that we can flick. For example, Saul/Paul wasn't on the "right team" at the time he was called. David and Moses were minding their business tending sheep when they were called out and given a vision.

Vision may be conveyed through swift and sudden and clear communication. God isn't shy about getting people's attention when he wants to communicate his vision: angels, burning bushes, dreams, etc.

The task given by God is often seemingly impossible without supernatural intervention—see Abraham, Moses, etc.

The recipient isn't necessarily passionate or happy about receiving the task. (For example, Jeremiah was unhappy about being a prophet—speaking cutting truth to a disobedient people is not a job that many line up for.)

The task God gives may not provide "successful results" from the world's viewpoint. (Would Jeremiah sell any books in his day on the "success" of his ministry?)

The vision requires life-changing obedience that may or may not see results in the recipient's lifetime (consider Abraham's Promised Land or even some great missionaries' investments).

Specific vision may be given to people with or without the gift of leadership. However, if the vision requires the mobilization of people, then the gift of leadership will be present or given.

### Conclusions regarding Special Vision

The special revelation complements rather than contradicts corporate revelation.

Also, special revelation brings a greater burden and sterner judgment.[10] God generally communicates it through "road to Damascus" type experiences where he supernaturally intervenes in an individual's life to communicate a specific vision or responsibility.

## Process Vision

After hearing a report on the state of his people and the walls of Jerusalem, Nehemiah "sat down and wept. For some days [he] mourned and fasted and prayed before the God of heaven" (Neh. 1:4). The outcome of this was Nehemiah's step of faith to ask the king for permission and assistance in rebuilding the wall. Then, as the story goes, Nehemiah surveyed the situation, cast the vision, organized the workers, prayed often, stood against opposition, encouraged the workers, and then celebrated the miraculous completion of the wall.

Nehemiah's vision for the restoration and safety of his people did not arise exclusively from general principles/corporate vision or special revelation. Instead, it was a process where he was overcome by a need, and prayed and waited before the Lord; his position/experiences as a member of the king's court were factored in as well; and he was led to an obedient and visionary response.

John Maxwell says, "One of the most valuable benefits of vision is that it acts like a magnet—attracting, challenging and uniting people."[11] He states:

- Vision starts within.
- Vision draws on your history.
- Vision meets others' needs.
- Vision helps you gather resources.

Nehemiah's "vision" meets Maxwell's points 2 through 4, but point 1 gets close to the human potential movement. Nehemiah's vision came through his anguish and prayers but was framed by God and the words of Matthew 6:33: "But seek first his kingdom and his righteousness, and all these things will be given to you as well."

Leighton Ford quotes Terry Fullam, saying, "Vision is a product of God working in us. He creates the vision and we receive it; it becomes a rallying point, a goal toward which we move as his people. . . . Vision arises out of our burden to know the will of God."[12]

### Conclusions regarding Process Vision

For many leaders, vision seems to develop through a "Nehemiah-style" process of discovery. Bobby Clinton outlines a detailed process-based theory of leadership and vision based on developmental stages in his book *The Making of a Leader*. This can be very helpful to young leaders.

To accomplish his purposes, God will utilize leaders to mobilize people.

Leaders (those gifted in leadership) will seek out God's desired purposes and mobilize others to accomplish his purposes.

Steve Brown, my colleague and director of programming at Arrow Leadership, is the one who has given a great deal of thought to these categories of vision for us. He has put these thoughts into a helpful chart so we can review these three facets of vision side by side. I thank Steve for his thorough and thoughtful reflections on vision from God's perspective.

### Vision Comparison Chart

|  | Corporate Vision | Special Vision | Process Vision |
|---|---|---|---|
| Initiative of Vision | Individual to Apply | God | Combined |
| Timing of Vision | Now, Anytime | God | Individual/God |
| Based on Good Stewardship of Recipient's Gifts | Yes | Not Necessarily | Partially to Yes |
| Recipient's Response | Obedience/Faith | Obedience/Faith | Obedience/Faith |
| Focused on God's Purposes | Yes | Yes | Yes |
| Task Size | Individual to . . . | God-sized | God-sized |
| Mobilize Others | Not Necessarily | Yes | Yes |
| Gift of Leadership Required | Maybe | Yes or No | Yes |
| Experience of Leadership Required | Not Necessarily | Not Necessarily | Not Necessarily |

James Lawrence, author of *Growing Leaders* and director of the Arrow Leadership Programme in the United Kingdom, expresses aspects of implementing vision as being three-dimensional:

Vision of God: Seeing God for who he really is.

Personal Vision: A God-given perception of what he wants for our lives.

Organizational Vision: A clear mental image of a kingdom-honoring preferable future given by God to his chosen servants, based upon an accurate understanding of God, self, and circumstances.

Christian leaders are people of vision. Mentors can help leaders understand and clarify God's vision for their life and act as a check to draw them back into the Scriptures and ensure that it is confirmed by the written Word.

# Practical Vision Helps

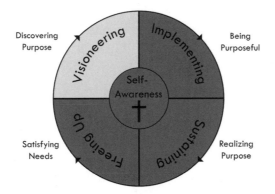

Leaders are both intrigued and haunted by talk about vision.

Taking time to think about the future and dreaming about what is over the horizon where they serve can be exciting! It gives an energy that wells up with that "now we can really do something" surge. However, for some leaders visionary talk is disturbing, for not all leaders are visionaries. George Barna categorizes church leaders into four types: directing, strategic, team-building, and operational. However, in *The Power of Vision* George says it is a myth to believe that some leaders are visionary and some aren't.[1] True leaders have vision and seek God's vision. How you mobilize the vision may vary considerably from category to category.

Some visionary leaders struggle with this topic, not because they lack vision but because they lack the discernment or wisdom to know which visions to pursue and which to leave alone.

Brenda and I were meeting with Bobb Biehl, who, as I mentioned has taken us under his wing and mentored us into presidential life and leadership. Brenda was asking what we were to do with the vision and ideas that we had for which we seemingly had no capacity at the moment. Bobb shared wisdom with us by encouraging us to write them down, journal them, and then pray—asking God if this was a vision for this time or for another.[2]

I found that just writing them into my journal seemed to release the pressure I often felt from vision. It also provided an extended time line in which to view the ideas. Often younger leaders want to see instant results or feel that because they have an idea or catch a glimpse of a new vision, God wants them to actuate it immediately.

During several years of journaling my visions, I have seen again and again how God desires to get us ready prior to the vision being enacted.

For gifted leaders, the size or scope of the vision is not a sufficient criterion to help them decide if it should be pursued or not—these leaders may have the capacity to accomplish any vision placed before them. So how do we decide which visions God desires us to pursue?

## Duck Hunting

When I was a child growing up on the Midwest prairie, there was an annual event that was part of our family rhythm. It surrounded the southward journey of migratory game birds from the north. In a family of three boys, it was our project to help fill our freezer with enough fowl to serve many suppers during the cold winter.

The hunting was done with a 12-gauge shotgun. I understand that many reading this volume may have never held a shotgun, so let me describe how one aims in order to hit a target. At one end of the barrel, closest to your shoulder, is a V-shaped metal gun sight. At the other end is a small bead threaded to the barrel. With the shoulder butt pressed against your body, you lower your face to look through the V and try to place the small bead in line with your intended target.

Now keep this image in mind as I transition over to leaders and vision. To discern vision there has to be an alignment between the gifts and ability of the leader, the specific calling, and the potential opportunity or vision. The V sight represents the gifts, talents, and capability of the leader; the bead represents a specific calling; and the target represents the vision.

If either the V or the bead is missing from the gun, then every vision looks like the target. Every opportunity looks like it should be pursued. It is crazy-making for leaders caught in this space, and it emphasizes the importance of understanding who you are as a leader—your gifts and abilities, as well as the unique and specific calling God has placed on your life. For multigifted leaders it is very important to seek this alignment in pursuing vision, and mentors have a very important role in providing the guidance to understand gifting and calling in order to release leaders to pursue God's vision for their life.

David Phillips, president of Phillips Management Company, is an executive coach, an athlete who was a World Cup freestyle skier, and a Guinness world record holder for endurance waterskiing. Over two decades Dave has worked with people processing as many life issues as you or I could possibly imagine. In the midst of all this experience, there seems to be a recurring theme underlying all the symptoms presented by business and ministry leaders.

Dave says it seems that every honest soul keeps calling out for the answers to three essential questions:[3]

1. What is my purpose for living (why am I here)?
2. What will my mission be in this life (what am I best designed to do)?
3. What will be the vision for my life (where am I going in my life)?

"It is equally important that these questions be answered in the context of one another. Often I see a vision statement or a mission statement written that is confusing to the author and readers which ends up being functionally irrelevant because it doesn't answer these critical questions of the soul," Dave thoughtfully adds.

## Clarifying Focus

On the spiritual side of the vision quest is the confusion caused by the evil one around the pursuit of vision. In the spiritual realm the demons are instructed to disrupt a Christian leader's pursuit of or engagement with God's vision plan. It is therefore a spiritual battle to follow God's vision from the onset, but one of the evil foe's most strategic moves is to confuse the leader from the onset as to the validity of God's vision.

When I was in my early thirties, I spent an afternoon with Michael and Rosemary Green discussing how we can know for certain when it is God speaking to us or giving us vision. Michael was a great encourager to Leighton Ford at the start of the Arrow Leadership Program and continues to spur us on in the development of God's leaders. Michael and I had also done some evangelistic ministry together, and I was just beginning to develop a relationship with Rosemary. We always enjoy time together, seeing God at work, and also there is usually a lot of laughter, as was the case this day.

I was describing to Rosemary some interaction with God that I had been experiencing that she helped me see as the spiritual gifts of "wisdom" and "word of knowledge." Michael was listening and laughing at my story. Rosemary was amused too, but in a slightly more constrained way. When I asked Michael what was so funny, he responded, "Carson, there are charismatics that would do anything to receive the gifts that you as a Baptist pastor have received without even seeking them." For some reason, Michael found this particularly funny, so Rosemary asked him to settle down and leave us for a moment.

"But how do I know if it is God speaking to me, or the devil trying to speak into my mind and life in a way that will ultimately distract me from the things of God?" I asked.

"That's easy," replied Rosemary. "Come with me." She rose and led me across their living room to the front window. "Hand me your spectacles," she said, reaching out her hand to receive my eyeglasses. "Now tell me what you see."

I could see pretty well without my glasses, so I began to describe the sidewalk, my automobile parked in front of their house, and the trees across the street and the fence behind them.

Rosemary then handed me my glasses and asked me to put them on again. "What do you see now?" she asked.

"I see everything that I just described to you—except it is much clearer."

"Look at the trees. How are they clearer?" Rosemary smiled as she asked.

"Well, I cannot only see that there are trees there, but I can also see the leaves—and not just the leaves but the distinct edge of the leaves."

With the gentle tone of a mentor/teacher, Rosemary said, "That is exactly what it is like when God is giving you a vision—it is crystal clear. It is God's responsibility to make it crystal clear to you, and if there is any cloudiness or blurriness, pray and ask God that if this vision is divine, for him to make it crystal clear. Then search the Scriptures and ensure that the vision is in no way contrary to his written Word." That simple word of counsel has guided me for almost two decades since and has prevented me from running ahead with something that ends up being a huge distraction.

I like the story told of Paul in Acts 16: "During the night Paul had a vision of a man of Macedonia standing and begging him, 'Come over to Macedonia and help us.' After Paul had seen the vision, we got ready at once to leave for Macedonia, concluding that God had called us to preach the gospel to them" (vv. 9–10).

The last verse tells us that dialogue took place between Paul and the other disciples regarding the vision God had revealed to them. Together, they concluded that God had called them to take the gospel far beyond the borders of their thinking prior to this. Leaders do need sounding boards to bounce things off of, and a good mentor (or two) is a good source for discerning God's vision for our lives.

Back when I was praying and searching for God's vision for my life, it was my mentor, Barry Hawes, whom I trusted more than any other to help me work it out. He prayed with me every time we met, and in and through those times together, God forged a vision imprint that still guides me today—"To bring about biblical life-change in unchurched men and women internationally by encouraging leaders through example, mentoring, and teaching the Word of God in a contemporary manner."

In a Johns Hopkins medical letter addressing eyesight and vision, I read that some degree of blurred vision is common among adults of all ages; however, the most frequent causes after age fifty are either refractive errors or disorders of the eye such as cataracts, macular degeneration, and diabetic retinopathy.

Refractive errors are an imperfection in the way the eye bends light. The spiritual equivalent among Christian leaders seeking God's vision is a faulty theology—not being Christ-centered in their thinking but rather incorporating too many of the world's ways in defining the vision for their life. These refractive errors can almost always be corrected with prescription lenses, and for the spiritual leader I would suggest the corrective lens of the Bible to restore godly vision.

Six leaders sat together in the living room of Larry Brune, founder of One Way Ministries in Ottawa.[4] We talked that evening about what causes blurred vision in the lives of Christian leaders. They created a useful and notable list of causes of blurred vision—most of which require surgical removal or healing in the lives of leaders to clear the vision "lens" in their lives. These included:

1. Busyness—being consumed in a rat-race-style leadership that gives little or no time to even think.
2. Comforts—things become just a little too easy and you no longer want to move outside this comfort zone.
3. Too many options—we get confused by the array of opportunities before us.
4. Insecurity—if we don't really know who we are, how can we know what we are suited to do or where we should go?
5. Your past—issues not dealt with will hold you back, and this is often expressed as fear of failure. This may include generational sin or family of origin issues.
6. Laziness—not pursuing vision merely because of the deadly sin of sloth.
7. Good things using up all our capacity and keeping us from pursuing the great things of God.
8. Lack of prayer and fasting that is needed on the vision quest.
9. Logistics and outside factors cause pressure, and as leaders we sometimes just want to take the easy way out.
10. We try adopting someone else's vision, and it simply does not work because it is not the vision for the time or place where you or your followers are.
11. Perhaps there is no expectation of having vision in the ministry where you serve, and therefore you never even begin to seek God's vision.
12. Secret sin residing in the life of leaders often dulls their senses and blocks their ability to enjoy clear reception without the "static" caused by sin.

Disorders of the eye causing blurred vision require different treatments and often can be minimized through lifestyle changes. Spiritual blurred vision can also be treated by addressing issues in life and leadership through prayer. Often it requires "spiritual surgery," where others pray for and over you, asking God to sever any spiritual ties that are holding you back from pursuing all that God desires for you and his people under your leadership. Any one thing from the above list could prevent leaders from clearly seeing what God desires of them. However, these symptoms often come in multiples, actually blocking vision in the life of a leader—like a cataract over the lens of the eye—and must be removed, and that is done by prayer and changing lifestyle by the leader to be obedient to God's call.

## Getting Vision

George Barna devotes a chapter of *Building Effective Lay Leadership Teams*[5] to the importance of vision for a team. To summarize, George emphasizes that discerning the vision is one of the primary tasks of a leader or a team. After years of studying the topic, he has come to see that the process of clarifying vision is actually quite simple. George noticed four steps:

1. Get to know yourself inside out.
2. Know your ministry environment and circumstances.
3. Know God through prayer, worship, and reflecting on his Word and principles.
4. Test it. Get feedback from a few people you can trust.

## Inside-Out Illustration

Karen Souffrant is an Arrow alumna from New York City. As she developed through the Arrow process, God began to work within her, allowing a new vision to emerge. Listen to Karen describe processing vision in her own life, and note how she journeyed through Barna's clarifying process.

One day as I was traveling on New Jersey's main parkway (the Garden State Parkway), my mind was suddenly flooded with vivid thoughts and ideas about starting an organization for women leaders. At that time, I was not sure what that meant or how it would unfold. Yet, the thoughts were so compelling that I pulled my car over on the shoulder of the road, grabbed a piece of paper, and began to record my thoughts. The name InsideOut occurred to me, and I wrote it down. I had never had an experience like this and have not since. I was not completely sure what that all meant at the particular time. However, I later typed up these ideas and placed them in a binder on my bookshelf, believing that they would become useful sometime in the immediate future. I had recently graduated from seminary and was anticipating my first job assignment, so I suspected that my ideas would be directly linked to my new role.

I was hired to work for a very large church in the New York metropolitan area upon graduation. When I assumed my new positions, I learned that there were no predecessors in the positions and that I was responsible for creating and implementing these ministries. The task ahead of me was both exhilarating and frightening at the same time. I took the plunge with minimal experience and training and was able to successfully develop and execute both ministries. I remember in trying to establish the ministries, I thought several times about ascribing the name InsideOut (the name I wrote down that day on the Garden State Parkway), primarily to the Young Adults' Ministry. However, I felt unsettled and so I held off, convinced that the vision was not for this appointed time and place. While I functioned in my capacity as director of the two ministries, I kept the vision of InsideOut in the back of my mind, waiting on God for clarity and direction.

During this time, I was enrolled in the Arrow Leadership Program. It was just the kind of program that I needed at this stage of my development. The lessons I learned about myself and leadership are priceless. Arrow provided for me a safe place to confront my fears and to venture into the world of possibilities for my life and ministry. God used my Arrow experience to help shape my character and sharpen my vision. I really began to learn what it means "to be led more by Jesus, lead more like Jesus, and to lead more to Jesus." While going through the Arrow Leadership Program, I found myself standing at the crossroads—I had some critical decisions to make regarding my future. The vision I received on the parkway about InsideOut was brought back to my remembrance. I had a clear sense that the appointed time for the vision had come and it was now the season to take it off the shelf. It was during one of my Arrow sessions—"Keeping Your Life in Crystal Clear Focus"—that I really began to assess the matters of my heart—wrestling with questions like, Why do I do what I do? I was also required to list ten critical steps in turning my dreams into reality. The exercises in this session invoked a stirring in me that propelled me toward pursuing the vision that God had placed in my heart. The process of developing the vision was a daunting one, but I kept one word in mind: "FOCUS."

Subsequently, I revisited the vision I had written down previously. By this time, ideas and concepts had become clearer as a result of my own personal leadership journey. I spent a lot of time in prayer seeking God for wisdom and direction as it related to turning this dream into reality. I spoke with trusted advisers and friends about what God had placed in my heart and sought their input, insights, and prayers. The responses were generally very encouraging and positive. Knowing that others were in my corner helped tremendously. Known for being an initiator and developer, I delved right into the process and established InsideOut International. It quickly became apparent to me why InsideOut could not have been established when I first received the vision.

First, my character had to match up to where God was taking me and what he was about to accomplish through the organization. The very name InsideOut represents leadership that is based upon character and authenticity. I had begun to experience early in my career that a lot of people were capable of rallying the crowd, but up close and personal, their character did not match their public reputation. Secondly, graduating from seminary did not provide me with the depth and breadth of experience that I needed to spearhead this kind of undertaking. I was quickly stripped of my naïveté as an aspiring leader and thrust into the real world of hard knocks, where I had to learn the tough lessons of leadership. It was like a jungle most of the time, and I felt more like I was on the reality TV show *Survivor*. Although very challenging, this kind of experience prepared me and gave me the credibility to establish an organization like InsideOut. Theories are great, but my experiences gave me the kind of connection I would need to relate to the people I was attempting to reach.

InsideOut was birthed out of my own quest for personal and professional development as an emerging woman leader. As I began sharing my frustration and concerns with ordinary women like me about the lack of support and resources for emerging women leaders, I soon discovered that my struggle was not an isolated case. It was through these shared experiences that InsideOut was able to move from its dream phase to become a reality. Many people have inquired about the process of seeing the vision being actualized. My response is always the same. Once I was convinced that the vision was from God, I chose to make myself available and I responded in obedience. In addition, I admitted my fears and embraced the risks involved in moving forward. I am often reminded of a quote by Eleanor Roosevelt—"You gain strength, experience and confidence by every experience where you really stop to look fear in the face. You must do the thing you cannot do." I knew that I had to do the thing I cannot do, but I was assured that God could and can do it through me.

My first step was to pray about the vision. I wanted to make sure that I was receiving this vision from God and that the timing for executing the vision was the appropriate time. Next, I wrote the vision down in order to make it as clear as possible. Then, I learned how to communicate the vision concisely and effectively to others. I would generally ask for feedback to see if the vision was being communicated clearly.

I enlisted others to join me in the process. As I shared the vision with different women, I learned that they also had similar sentiments. I surrounded myself with a team who had like passion for the work that I was embarking upon. At times the task ahead seemed overwhelming and too vast to attain. However, I constantly assured myself that there was no vision too large for God to accomplish. The challenge was going to be for me to relinquish control and to allow God to be my compass.

My team and I met together regularly to discuss the progress of Inside-Out. We set specific goals that we wanted to achieve at specific times. We held each other accountable for delivering on the specific tasks assigned to each team member. The greatest joy was to watch each person embrace and take ownership of the vision of InsideOut.

On Saturday, October 2, 2004, InsideOut was officially launched. The event was a success. The responses from attendees were both encouraging and rewarding. The work has just begun, and we look toward the future with great anticipation.[6]

Karen formed InsideOut International as a nonprofit organization to respond to the burgeoning needs of emerging women leaders for personal and professional leadership development. Women are progressively assuming leadership roles in every sector of society in unprecedented numbers. Yet, there is a significant lack of resources and programs available to address and meet their developmental needs.

Karen now uses the word "develop" as an acronym that helps her present the vision to others:

**D** iscover—Our aim is to work alongside emerging women leaders by helping them to discover their calling, gifts, and purpose.

**E** quip—Our aim is to equip emerging women leaders with the practical skills necessary for their personal and professional development, through a process of intentional and professionally designed training programs, workshops, seminars, and conferences.

**V** alue—Our aim is to assist emerging women leaders in identifying and embracing their unique value as women in leadership, so they are better able to lead with greater authenticity and congruency.

**E** mpower—Our aim is to connect emerging women leaders with a network of safe people who will encourage, affirm, and empower them in their ability to lead with character, confidence, and competence.

**L** ead—Our aim is to produce world-class leaders for the twenty-first century and beyond through a unique combination of leadership training programs, mentoring, and personalized coaching.

**O** ptimize—Our aim is to provide opportunities and forums for emerging women leaders to interface and network with their peers and other experienced women in diverse areas of leadership to achieve optimum growth and development.

**P** repare—Our aim is to prepare emerging women leaders to maximize their fullest potential through the integration of their personal, spiritual, and professional lives.

The organization was birthed out of Karen's quest for personal and professional development as an emerging woman leader herself. As founder, Karen began sharing with other women her frustration about the lack of support; it became apparent that her internal struggle was not exclusive to her. Being a woman who has been mentored and intentionally developed by some very highly respected people, both men and women, Karen says she enjoys and appreciates the benefits Arrow's kind of personalized development has afforded her. Yet, she realizes that this opportunity (that of being a part of a leadership development process like Arrow) is not accessible to many women, especially minority leaders.

Karen's eyes saw clearly, and God gave her crystal clear clarity as to what he was calling her to do—and now she is giving her life to this vision with the help of a great team of women she has gathered around her, and the support of her husband.

## Vision Is Birthed in Solitude

Yes, of course, there are occasional times that God chooses to inspire vision when leaders are with others, but it is usually delineated within the sanctuary of solitude.

John Haggai, founder of the Haggai Institute, met with my two life friends David Bentall and Bob Kuhn and me while he was visiting Vancouver with Randy Manery. It was actually that meeting with John and the gift of his book *Lead On* that started me on my own vision quest. In particular, his chapter on solitude and its relationship to vision struck me as a new insight I had missed during my life up to that point as an evangelical.

Specifically, I was motivated by these words: "You're more likely to discern a vision in the cloistered halls of solitude than in the screaming jostle of the metropolitan concrete jungle. Perhaps in a cathedral of trees, under the silence of the stars, or by the moaning sea, you'll be most likely to see the true light and hear 'the still, small voice.'"[7]

I was an urban pastor at the time I read those words. I loved the metropolitan concrete jungle (and still do); however, I did realize that I had no solitude in my life and I longed for it.

Have you ever noticed how some of our best ideas tend to come to us while we are in the shower? This happens to me all the time. Why is that? I think it is because it is one of the few places in our lives where we are alone.

We live in an action-packed, noisy environment, and yet we are expected to lead with clear, visionary thinking. Our clearest thinking occurs in silence . . . solitude provides us the opportunity to be quiet.

Restlessness is the sin of the enthusiastic leader. We long to move forward for the sake of the kingdom, and we are impatient that we move so slowly. We also feel the reality of evil deeply and realize that the number of evildoers is very large, and we can't help fretting about what we should be doing for the kingdom's sake. Our very zeal for ministry makes us overanxious and overactive. So, in our churches and organizations we tend to multiply machinery. We add organization to organization, program to program; our voices get hoarse from speaking too much; our bodies and our souls get weary with too much doing.

In the front of one of my Bibles I have written something that Barry Hawes shared with me early in our mentoring relationship. Barry's words are recorded on a yellow sticky note still stuck to the front flap: "Ministry for God can often be the greatest enemy of devotion to God." He was encouraging me as a pastor to discipline myself in the area of regular devotional times and the reading of the Bible for nourishment. However, ministry for God and the busyness we find ourselves in can also be a great barrier to experiencing solitude. Bob Lupton of Atlanta's FCS Urban Ministries put it well: "The chaff of the bright idea is blown away by tomorrow's busyness. The kernel of vision drops down into the ground of the human spirit and begins to take on a life of its own, pushing its way up through the conscious attention of a person until it demands action."

We confuse solitude with "getting away," but Jesus says, "Come with *me* by yourselves to a quiet place" (Mark 6:31, emphasis added). He wants leaders to be quiet there with him—to stop talking and to listen.

## Can't Hear the Forest for the Trees

While I was a participant in the Arrow Leadership Program in 1993, we gathered in the seminar room, preparing ourselves for another day of interaction with Leighton Ford. Little did we know what kind of interaction was going to be part of our day.

Leighton entered the room and explained that we were going to participate in a special exercise, and we all crowded into vans and were driven to a nearby lake. Leighton then asked us to take the next two hours and find a place where we could be completely alone. We were not to sleep but rather to seek solitude, listen, pray, and journal. We departed the vans in silence, and I climbed up into the forest with my journal and Bible.

It seemed like a rather silly way to spend the morning when I had traveled a long distance to learn about Christian leadership and evangelism. These thoughts spun through my head as I walked up higher and higher on the hill seeking a dry and hopefully soft place to sit and endure the next two hours.

I do love the forest, and when I first sat down I thought this little time in God's creation would be a welcome change. That lasted only about five minutes.

The mind traffic began, and my thoughts began to scatter between some new ideas for the church and meetings I needed to have next week. Then I jumped over to thinking about Brenda and our relationship, to wondering how our boys were doing and what I should buy them as a little treat from this trip to Charlotte.

Wait! What was that noise?

Oh, it was just the sound of a car.

I wonder what kind of tree that is—we don't have those trees where we live.

How much longer do I have to be here?

Six minutes had passed.

I'll start reading the Bible. What should I read? But wait, I already read my Bible this morning (as I flipped it open to any page and then glanced at the middle of the page). Nothing! Nothing is happening. How much longer?

Seven-minute mark—I think I should just lie down and pray. Yes, that's it. I can pray for other people—there is always lots to pray about. "Now I lay me down to sleep," I mused—oh, but I am not supposed to sleep.

Wait a minute . . . I am an ENFP on the Myers-Briggs. Surely ENFPs are not built for solitude. I want to be with people. I wonder where my other Arrow leaders are? Are they feeling like I am? Bet I could find another ENFP who is dying to break out of this solitude just like I am.

Stop it! Stop the mind traffic and pray.

So I began praying, and talked to God for the rest of the hour . . . but wait, I was asked to listen, and I have been doing all the talking. So I stopped and for the next twenty minutes sat perfectly still. My mind traffic now stilled, I just listened.

I began to hear some things around me that were new. I had not realized that if I was very still, I could hear some traffic on the highway. I heard the wind blowing through the top of the trees above me. Then with a snap, crackle—pause—I listened to something on the forest floor very close to me. It was a small bird picking up seeds among the leaves on the ground at the base of the trees. I'm certain it had been there for quite a while—I was simply too busy to notice.

Thinking this is something worth recording, I picked up my journal and pen—and that is when the thoughts, ideas, and prayers flowed from my pen.

It had taken one hour and forty minutes for me to come to a place of solitude where I could listen to God.

When we all gathered back by the vans for our return trip, Leighton asked if any of us wanted to share about our time. Many of these capable and successful leaders had struggled with the exercise at first—but almost without exception we had heard from God in ways that were unique and specific to us and our ministries. For some, it was so personal that they were unable to share and instead found themselves crying due to the incredible sense of affirmation and love they felt, while others experienced the conviction of the Holy Spirit concerning some areas of "work needed" in their lives.

## We're Not Big on Quiet

As Leighton listened and cared for those needing a touch at that moment, he reminded us that God was always waiting for us to listen to him. I realized as I stood by that lake that most North American leaders spend far too much time talking to God and far too little time listening. Even our church services reflect this and are often quite noisy. Most evangelical churches are not big on "quiet" or solitude, but for leaders to lead, this must be a component of our personal lives. Our Arrow confession begins with stating our need as leaders to be "led more by Jesus," and the only way that is going to happen is by listening to him as he speaks through the Word and by the Spirit.

Being still amidst the restlessness, noise, words, and relentless activity— that is what leaders need to do. We must choose to develop the discipline of silence. I do not believe there is a better way that a leader can move toward a deeper relationship with God than through protracted times of stillness. "Be still, and know that I am God" (Ps. 46:10).

I love how Eugene Peterson says this: "Step out of the traffic! Take a long loving look at your High God."[8]

Chuck Swindoll says, "Noise and words and frenzied, hectic schedules dull our senses, closing our ears to His still, small voice and making us numb to His touch."[9]

At least once or twice a year David, Bob, and I retreat to various locations where we commit ourselves to periods of listening. One such place is Westminster Abbey. It is a silent place, and the monastery by its very location and design nurtures a respectful quietness. Another place of silence for me is in the cockpit of our sailboat, where the sounds of the ocean and wind create an audio backdrop that functions like "white noise." White noise is produced by combining sounds of many different frequencies together. It is used to mask other sounds around you. It is similar to being in a hotel room where the air conditioner prevents you from hearing the sounds in the hallway or outside your window.

Some years ago my friend Mitch introduced me to Bose Quiet Comfort headphones for traveling. You may have seen something like them—they look like extremely comfortable earphones where the wires lead to a small black box the size of a matchbox. The black box has a switch that when activated creates a silent-to-the-ear white noise that blocks out almost all the ambient noise. In an airplane it mutes the constant droning of the engines, the circulation of the air, and even the voices of those talking around you. When I wear them on long flights, either listening to music through them or with them simply turned on, I find that I arrive in a less-stressed state than I used to.

Sometimes as I have been writing this manuscript, I have put on my headphones in my home office to block out the distractions of noise around me.

What type of "noise" do you have around you? What is preventing times of solitude and listening? Here are some of the things we have learned in working with Christian leaders.

1. Many leaders feel too busy to take time away to listen. They have mind traffic that both distracts and exhausts them. Good opportunities continually present themselves or people continually cry out for their attention—keeping them from spending time in quiet.
2. Many leaders are actually ambivalent about solitude.
3. Many leaders are afraid of being alone. It is helpful to explore what is behind this fear with a mentor.

Solitude and silence balance out the noisy, public, hectic lives most of us live. It is an excellent way of regaining internal balance and of mending the confusion caused by a harried and distracted existence—and yet it is within this fertile soil of quiet that vision begins to grow.

As you begin to scrutinize why you are not spending more time alone listening to God, ask yourself, "Doesn't it make sense to invest a relatively small amount of time in solitude in order to make the rest of my leadership more effective?"

## Vision Quest

I remember when my friend Bob was thirty-nine years old. It was a very reflective time for Bob, and a time when we as friends were talking a great deal about vision and what we were to be about in our lives. As a lawyer working in a significant law firm downtown, Bob had begun an internal shift from success to significance. He was on a journey and reflecting on dreams that were still unmet. Listen as he shares from his heart.

## "Death of a Dream, Birth of a Vision," by Robert Kuhn

I'm thirty-nine.

For the most part, the dreams of my youth have come true. Or in some cases I have realized they are unlikely to.

But it's time to ask myself some serious questions. Perhaps they are the same questions asked by others who have apparently reached the age of midlife confusion. (I prefer "confusion" over "crisis." "Crisis" leaves the impression of an event rather than a state of mind.) Like Larry, the successful young lawyer who had just made partner in his law firm, who, as we rode up the elevator together, said, "I wonder if I'm doomed to ride this elevator to the same job for the next thirty years?" It seemed like a strange question to ask when the road ahead looked so full of promise.

Perhaps it is the same question asked by Michael W. Smith in his song "Place in This World." He is crying out to know the reason for his existence and asks: "Is there a vision, that I can call my own?"

Or from the halcyon days of the seventies, the question posed by Diana Ross when she said, "Do you know where you're goin' to? Do you like the things that life is showin' you?"

Or the same question posed by Billy Crystal in the movie *City Slickers*, when sitting around the campfire with his midlife cronies, he says, "Is this the best that it gets?"

Or perhaps it is the same searching which Arthur Miller wrote about in *Death of a Salesman*, where Willy Loman's sons concluded after their father's suicide that "He had the wrong dreams." I fear that Willy's dreams may be the same as mine.

Whatever the question is, it seems time to answer it. It seems that now, more than ever, it is time to choose, to make a decision as to what I will live for. What is my aim in this life? What do I want to accomplish in order to know my days have been worthwhile? What am I really living for? What is my life purpose? What is my definition of success and a life well spent? There seem to be many ways to ask the question, but the answer must define, in some way, my future. I want an answer that will give context and meaning, overcome my current sense of aimlessness, and liberate the passion I want to experience in a positive, constructive way.

This all sounds like the complaints of a man who has lived too long as a rudderless ship, but I really have nothing to complain about. As the psalmist said, "The boundary lines have fallen for me in pleasant places; surely I have a delightful inheritance." I have a wonderfully supportive and understanding wife; three miraculous children (nine, six, and three, and all adopted, healthy, and gifted in unique ways); a career in law which has been rewarding, challenging, and more successful by most definitions than I would have dreamed possible. I have had roles to play in church, nonprofit, and community opportunities which have enriched my life. I have a group of friends with whom I can relate deeply and from whom I gain precious wisdom, accountability, and love.

I am healthy and reasonably fit, even being able to compete as a middle-of-the-pack triathlete for the past two years. Truly, I have been blessed far beyond deserving or expectation. But lately, as I reach the middle of my life where the future and the past seem to hang in a delicate and frightening balance, I have felt a deep longing for something more. As if a part of me was dying, a part I hate to lose, something that reminds me of the carefreeness (my parents might say irresponsibility) of my youth and its limitless dreams. I feel the need for a new beginning.

Perhaps it was my parents who instilled in me this search for meaning, this vision quest, as some native Indians call it. I was their hope, the carrier of their dreams. My father completed grade eight and my mother grade nine in a world in which university education opened the door to opportunity. As long as I can remember I was told that my education would give me everything I would want, everything they did not have. It was the ticket to success.

So now I am "successful." Why is it I still have the vision quest? Why is it I sometimes feel angry that life is skipping by like a flat stone thrown across the surface of time, touching every so often but slowing, inevitably slowing to sink and skip no more?

I seem no longer able to recite my teenage motto, "I can do anything if I just put my mind to it. I can have it all if I really want." Cocooning has become a comfortable way to merely survive without my dreams.

Lately, I seem to be constantly reminded of the great needs in our world, our country, our city, even the overwhelming demands within my own limited personal environment. I see how much needs to be done to turn things around, make things right. I am confronted with the compelling need to make a difference in my world, even just in my own small sphere of influence. But I feel helpless, small, and insignificant—an angry, but very controlled, rebel without a cause.

The cry is for leadership, for people with vision, a sense of mission. But I fear these are my childhood fantasies of superhero deeds of courage and conviction speaking, not the reasoned considerations of a man slip-sliding into his forties. After all, what can I do? I am no Gandhi, no John F. Kennedy, and no Albert Einstein. They all knew their calling. They had a passion for what they felt compelled to do with their lives. They were special. They knew or at least had a passionate conviction about what I am struggling to find: What unique pursuit will give my life worthwhileness?

So if the dreams of my youth are dying, and I need to reestablish direction, how do I do that? I am far too skeptical to believe I can reinvent my anarchistic adolescence. I have seen the personal and relational havoc wreaked by those who want to start over in their lives. I have concluded I cannot really start over; I can only move on. But how? Where is my purpose? Where does my vision come from? What is the source to which I must go to find that passion and my personal vision for the second half of life?

The gurus of humanism would have me reach down deep inside and "create a vision of greatness." As highly respected management writer Peter Block says: "A vision exists within each of us, even if we have not made it explicit or put it into words. Our reluctance to articulate our vision is a measure of our despair and a reluctance to take responsibility for our own lives, our own unit, and our own organization. A vision statement is an expression of hope, and if we have no hope, it is hard to create a vision."

He goes on to define the qualities of "great vision":

1. It comes from the heart. A vision is in some ways unreasonable. The heart knows no reason. When our vision asks too much of us, we should begin to trust it.
2. We, alone, can make this statement. The statement needs to be recognizable as ours. It needs to be personal, and those who know us should be able to recognize who it came from.
3. It is radical and compelling. A vision dramatizes our wishes. This makes it radical and demanding. Radical in the best sense of service rather than rejection. Our willingness to take a unique stand is what empowers us.

But this all sounds like the philosophy of a reckless explorer steering to some destination using a compass with true north defined not by the pole but by visceral instinct (or indigestion) he experiences. Where does God fit into all this? Is it possible to have a vision defined by each of us without it being somehow grounded in truth or absolutes? Vision without such a foundation seems like nothing more than guesswork, the artistry of a blind man, a nightmarish life of grab bag uncertainty, humanistic wishful thinking.

I choose to believe that God loves me. That he sent Christ his Son to die on a cross for me so that I might not only live in eternity with him when I die but also so that I might live today with purpose and meaning. He is deserving of my worship, service, and love, for without his love for me I would truly be destitute, left to rely on my own puny efforts and ideals to make sense out of the few years of my life. Without him there would be no truly significant answer to the question, "Why?" I know of no one else who can establish true north for the compass I must steer my life by.

And believing as I do, I have no difficulty agreeing with Stacy and Paula Rinehart in their book *Living in Light of Eternity*, when they say: "God offers us a purpose-filled, integrated life. He is more than willing to help us discern what shape that life should take for each of us individually."

But a conundrum emerges. If the vision is mine, how can it be God's? But if the vision comes from God, where is it and how is it mine? Is it hidden like some needle in the cosmic haystack? Or is it reserved for only an anointed few?

Surely the God of the Bible is interested in each of us uniquely, including the details of our lives. He is interested in our visions.

While I will never rank with the great Bible heroes, I found it instructive to examine people such as Moses and Paul and their visions. I discovered some helpful things from my study which gave me some guideposts in my search for a vision.

1. Both Moses and Paul had or were provided with the basic character, qualities, and training to carry out their missions, despite Moses's protestations and Paul's thorn in the flesh.

2. Both were men who had their own misguided sense of calling which they were acting on. In the case of Moses, he saw himself as the hero of his people long before he was confronted with the burning bush. Paul was obviously driven by his religious passion in his mission to exterminate the "heretical" early Christians.

3. Both had experiences that indelibly marked them and validated God's role in their ministry: Moses with the burning bush and Paul on the road to Damascus.

4. Both experienced lengthy periods of "wandering in the desert" without a precise understanding of their calling. Moses watched his father-in-law's sheep in the Midian plains, and Paul spent some time in the Transjordan desert cooling his heels. John Haggai, in his book *Lead On*, says our visions often remain unformed or half developed because we spend so little time alone with God.

It appeared from my reading in the secular wisdom, measured by the truth contained in biblical accounts of God's involvement in the processing of a person's vision, that certain tentative conclusions could be drawn:

1. Having a vision means choosing for some good things and against other good things. I cannot do it all. I must forgo some of my dreams in order to lighten my load for the climb to the summit.

2. I need not look in some distant place for my vision. God has given me unique experiences, qualities, circumstances, and character, which provide a setting in which my vision can be defined and played out.

3. While I may need to step beyond my current frame of reference in order to act upon my vision, it is likely a change of focus I need. In other words, before I run off and change what I am looking at, I should consider a change in glasses.

4. My vision must be defined in partnership with God and therefore requires time for contemplation and meditation with him. It is not imposed upon me nor framed in his absence if it is to have personal and ultimate significance. I like the term "imagineering" as an expression of the merger of two apparently inconsistent concepts. It is like many other elements of God's plan. It involves the apparent paradox of a sovereign God and a man with complete freedom of choice.

5. Vision is often formulated in the context and with the help of others. There is accountability for my vision, which could otherwise so easily become a fetish for personal gratification. This process of accountability has been especially helpful in refining my sense of calling and giving it concrete direction.

6. While vision gives living direction, it is not necessarily measurable in the temporal context. Success must be defined by the journey, not by the destination or one's distance from it.

7. The greatest enemy of vision is the fear of failure. But I may see things in a way few others do, and therefore I should expect that my steps

toward that unseen horizon may be criticized. The direction I must walk should be defined by faith, not my eyes and my ears. Vision in this sense isn't vision at all; it's faith.

8. The vision quest involved the following questions:
   a. How has God equipped me? What are my talents, personality, experiences, circumstances?
   b. What ideals stir and motivate me? When I get beyond my skepticism, what do I feel strongly about?
   c. What do my time expenditures tell me about my current priorities?
   d. Having spent time seeking God's direction, what do I believe he would have me commit myself to?
   e. Am I really prepared to commit myself to the vision? It may require more dedication than I have given to anything.

Considering the alternatives, who wouldn't want a life with meaning and purpose molded in partnership with our Creator and the Creator of this world we inhabit? But I recognize that the mere desire for a focused and meaningful vision is not enough. It requires effort to both define my vision and then to carry it out. It requires time with God, not just to discover what he would have me do but also how in dependence on him I am to carry out the vision.

From the vision come plans and goals which, as one lecturer said, are dreams, or using the preferred term, visions, with deadlines. I have found in my own search that both the vision and the plans and goals which flow from that vision are best refined and understood when written. There seems to be something about seeing my thoughts and prayers in black-and-white that gives them reality. I understand and can see them as true or false.

I wish it were an easier process, this vision quest. No wonder so many avoid asking those hard questions like, "What's life all about, anyway?" But the alternative of living life in the shadow of unmet expectations or glare of empty dreams achieved is too frightening.

As the Rineharts said: "If someday we sit in the rocking chair of our old age and look back on life with regret, with a sense of having wandered aimlessly over a faceless terrain, it will be because we never stopped long enough to assess our direction or because we chose to give ourselves to empty dreams."

I'm thirty-nine. But even as I feel these last days of summer slip into autumn, I have begun to sense a new beginning; a new sense of vision for the uncertainty ahead; a new confidence and excitement in the direction of my path.

In Bob's open letter, he is candidly expressing the process that I hear many leaders go through. As you read his letter, what does it cause you to think about? Here are some questions that help leaders reflect on their quest for vision.

## Vision Reflections

What is my aim? What do I want to be remembered for?

Why do I still have that vision quest?

Do I "sometimes feel angry that life is skipping by like a flat stone thrown across the surface of time"?

Do I wonder "what I can do"?

Where does my vision come from?

How would I define the qualities of great vision?

What do you learn about vision from Moses, Paul, and the others in the Bible?

What are your reactions to Bob's conclusions? Which ones do you affirm? What would you add? What would you change?

What "dream deadlines," plans, and goals will flow from your vision?

# Implementing

# Implementing the Vision

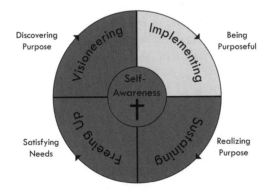

Right around the same time my friend Bob was writing about his journey, I also found myself on a quest. It found expression in my teaching about the importance of vision in an adult Sunday school class held in the five-star Sutton Hotel down the street from First Baptist Vancouver. This spurred me to begin praying about God's vision for my life, daily, and I did so over a nine-month period. It took nine months for God's vision to be birthed within me—the same gestation period God orchestrated for my physical birth. Nine months of relentless pursuit of God, daily seeking his vision for my life: not what others wanted me to do; not what I am capable of doing; not what I even necessarily liked doing. I wanted to know what God had designed me for. Why was I on this earth and what was my mission? Was I doing it now? Was it yet to be revealed?

I remembered Leighton Ford quoting Calvin Miller during an Arrow residential seminar as saying, "God does not shout his best vision through hassled Christian living. It's in the quiet that he gives the most delivering visions of life." I knew that if I earnestly sought God's vision, he would give me the clarity I desired. So at least once a day, sometimes two or three times, I would be at his doorstep, knocking once again to let him know I was still waiting—and then I would listen. For nine months I listened . . . and nothing happened, until one day while driving home from the church office.

It happened as I crossed over the Arthur Laing Bridge. I remember being a little frustrated at God that day, for I was getting tired of listening—but suddenly, all was well. As I reached the third lamppost from the start of the bridge, a vision statement came to me so strongly that I had to pull the car over as soon as I was off the bridge. As I scrambled for a piece of paper and a pen, the vision came clearly and I scribbled on a napkin from a fast-food restaurant that was in the glove box. I wrote: "To bring about biblical life change in unchurched men and women by encouraging leaders internationally through example, mentoring, and teaching the Word of God in a credible contemporary manner."

As I shared this statement with Leighton, he encouraged me to add the word "internationally" following "leaders"—for he had insight that was beyond my ability to comprehend at the time. To this day, the statement is etched on my life, guiding and directing my days.

In the days that followed, I returned to the church with a new set of eyes. Sifting what I was able to do in my ministry through the grid of this mission statement, I began to change my focus to the encouragement and development of leaders within the congregation. I found my time training leaders, within the various outreach ministries, to be very fulfilling.

This vision statement also began to affect my prayers, prompting me to focus them on asking God for opportunities to do more in the area of developing leaders. Ultimately, this led to my resignation from the pastoral position I held, as I waited for the platform God would provide to enable a greater fulfillment of this calling. It was the ministry of Insight for Living that provided my next growth and training season in the development of godly leaders.

At Insight for Living, while giving leadership to the Canadian broadcast ministry and to the team at the Canadian office, I was also able to begin ministering to pastors by speaking at pastors' conferences; organizing some pastor and spouse gatherings with Chuck and Cynthia Swindoll;

and engaging in hundreds of one-on-one conversations with Christian leaders.

The purpose behind all these endeavors was to encourage Christian leaders in the work of the Lord and to spur them on in the ministry of the gospel. One of the mission statements of the Canadian ministry at that time was to "provide support to pastors, churches, and listeners." In a booklet "The Calling of a Country" it was made more specific:

> We believe the local church is the most significant rallying point for Christians on this earth today.
>
> As part of "our calling of a country," we desire to support the mission of the local church. We envision equipping churches, Christian colleges, and seminaries with practical and doctrinally sound materials. We foresee creating a Christian resource center at our office to make Christian materials more available to listeners and members of the local church.
>
> A committed effort to support and encourage pastors has been an ongoing effort for IFLM. Currently, we are organizing a network of communication with pastors. Special bulletin inserts, pastors' newsletters, and conferences are being planned in order to provide helpful information and encouragement.
>
> God is calling us to come alongside pastors, lay leaders, and listeners with encouragement, equipping materials, and prayerful support.

You can see the alignment of the mission of the ministry and my personal vision and calling. This season of ministry in my life was extremely fulfilling. I grew a great deal and learned from a broad spectrum of Christian leaders what was needed in their lives to encourage them in their ministry. Many of us are engaged in ministry out of our desire to see people come into a saving relationship with Jesus Christ. However, the busyness of church ministry and the demands of congregations can subtly cause the flame of that passion to go out. As we engage Christian leaders in their development, anything we can do to reignite the "pilot light" of evangelism will reap benefits for the kingdom.

My daily regimen includes a commitment to pray about bringing biblical life change in unchurched men and women through encouraging leaders internationally by example, mentoring, and teaching the Word of God in a credible contemporary manner. Praying this regularly has helped order my weeks and months and years.

A few years later, without my seeking it, the Lord challenged me with another opportunity to expand on this vision. Brenda and I were approached by Leighton Ford, and later by Dr. Ralph Newton (chairman of the board for Leighton Ford Ministries), asking if I would consider a call to become the president of what is now known as Arrow Leadership International Ministries. The mission of Arrow was and is to identify, develop, and network emerging leaders worldwide who will be led more by Jesus, lead more like Jesus, and lead more to Jesus. Since I knew the ministry well, as a graduate of the Arrow Leadership Program, Brenda and I knew this was in perfect alignment with my personal vision and calling from God. It took almost two years from those initial conversations for that call to become reality, and I was able to draw to a conclusion my five years with Insight for Living. Together, Brenda and I then gave ourselves fully to the ministry of developing God's leaders through Arrow Leadership.

Now, is it possible that I may one day continue to fulfill this purpose through another organization or in another form? Absolutely! It is possible—and that is a test a leader can use to affirm a life calling.

## Vision Principles

As we mentor leaders in the area of vision, there are two fundamental principles we must reiterate to leaders:

*God is the instiller of vision.* There are too many conferences we attend and books on the shelves of our libraries and bookstores that reduce vision to some kind of personal exercise and discipline. We can help leaders by pointing them back to the vision stories found in the Bible and asking them to study how God went about instilling vision and what his purposes were in doing so.

*God is also sovereign.* He can change plans and even change vision, especially if leaders are not ready and need to grow before they can embrace the fullness of his vision for their life.

## Discerning God's Vision

So how do leaders discern if they are pursuing God's vision for their lives or following a personal drivenness fueled by their own deprivation or need? It is helpful to consider the following questions to help discern the calling or vision.

Is the vision consistent with Scripture? While this may seem like an elementary question, it is not as easily answered as one may think. The subtleties of some visions may require a great deal of searching the Scriptures—not simply to validate the vision but to seek the living words of God affirming the call.

As a mentor, I also find it helpful in discerning vision with a leader to ask myself, "Does the leader demonstrate the core competencies necessary to give leadership toward this vision?" By core competencies I refer not only to skill but also to the necessity of character, righteousness, love, wisdom, and grace.

In that God is always about preparing his leaders for service, is there a history or a thread of preparation that would make the leader uniquely qualified to carry out the task? Again, this is not always obvious. The biblical example of David shows how complicated this could be. David's preparation for leadership began as a shepherd in the fields, tending to sheep. Part of Jonah's preparation for God's evangelistic vision in Nineveh took place in a great fish. I often ask leaders facing significant difficulties whether they are running from a calling God placed on their lives previously.

In the Western world, in particular, is the leader simply responding to the latest best seller? While at a meeting in Los Angeles, discussing leadership among American pastors with the leaders of the Evangelical Christian Credit Union, I blurted out that the trend was that of M.B.BS.— Management by Best Seller. (What did you think BS was?) As we laughed about it, we acknowledged the wave of new "vision" that washes across the continent after the release of each new book about a particular church. Suddenly, many Christian leaders try to rewrite their vision to align with the best seller rather than earnestly seeking the Lord for his specific vision for their place in their time.

It is essential to pray about God's vision. I encourage leaders to utilize solitude and to understand that it usually takes time. Yes, there are examples when God uses vision to motivate people into action quickly because of a particular window of opportunity. However, life vision, and that is primarily what I'm referencing here, requires time.

I vividly remember a conversation with my friend David when I was several years into my ministry with Arrow. He commented, "It really seems to me that you have found your lifework." He was recognizing the alignment of my calling and the mission of Arrow, and seeing that this was something I could give my life for. I said I had found my life calling, but that I could pursue that calling while working in a variety of settings. My desire is to see the leadership of Arrow turned over to a younger leader well before I retire. This means that I will have another opportunity to pursue my calling and vision in another setting. I cannot imagine a better fit than Arrow. However, my sovereign God may deploy me to another field of service that is not currently on the horizon.

Some leaders actually need practical help in knowing how to pray about vision. Left alone, their minds get spinning with new ideas often generated from deep-seated, internal needs. It can take a while for the leader to quiet down, "tune in," and get used to being in the Lord's presence and to hear his voice. Invite mentors and other intercessors to pray for leaders throughout these times, asking God to show himself clearly over the coming weeks in what he is calling the leader or the ministry to do for him. The leader may also ask others to pray, such as a small group, or perhaps an entire congregation, that God will make his calling clear to the leader.

## Vision Prayer

To assist leaders with the discipline of praying regularly for God's vision, I have found it helpful to provide a short prayer that they can utter as they begin a time of solitude and listening. The prayers of others can become an inspiration to help leaders ask for God's vision for their life.

Heavenly Father, you are the one
who created me and put me on earth for a purpose.
Jesus, you died for me
and called me to complete your work.
Holy Spirit, you are the one that empowers me
to carry out the work for which I was created and called.
In your presence and in your name
I now begin to seek your vision.
May all my thoughts and inspirations
have their origin in you
and be directed to your glory.

## Journaling

When a leader is seeking God's vision for life, journaling is a very helpful tool. Not all leaders are into the practice of journaling, and my experience is that most mentors seldom journal.

Exodus 24:4 tells us that Moses "wrote down everything the LORD had said." In Deuteronomy 31:19, we find Moses once again writing down the words and perhaps the music to a song that he then taught to the Israelites. Whether as a song or words on parchment, Moses was creating a written record of his interactions with the Lord.

In Daniel 7:1 we read of this young leader who had dreams and visions passing through his mind as he lay in bed. Many leaders have thoughts, dreams, and visions at night just prior to falling asleep. It is a "time between times" when we seem to be open to listening and hearing from God. At the same time, leaders can be filled with what I call "mind traffic" or the leftover remnants of a busy, stressful, or stimulating day. If we can quiet the static of mind traffic and listen carefully for the Lord to speak to us, new visions and ideas often call out. Daniel took the time to write down the substance of these dreams and visions. This gave him a written record in the morning. Many leaders have inspiring visions during these times but quickly forget them as they are blown away like chaff in the busyness of the next day.

Leaders often shy away from journaling because they have legalistic ideas about the frequency required and the content to be recorded. When we begin working with Arrow leaders, we gift each of them with a new journal. Inside the front cover we include several questions to help them make good use of this discipline while God is developing them in their leadership.

Questions to guide you in your journaling:

What am I trusting God for today?

What are the joys in my key relationships right now? What are the stresses?

Why are these people important to me?

In what ways am I experiencing inner peace? How am I lacking?

What are my three most significant prayer requests?

Am I entertaining any fears at this moment? What are they?

Do I feel discontent in some way? Describe it.

What has made me laugh recently?

Have I read something convicting or stimulating recently?

Is there someone I need to forgive? What's holding me back?

Am I really accountable? To whom? For what?

Am I putting in too many hours away from those I love most?

How am I cultivating a wholesome sense of humor?

What can I learn from this test I'm enduring?

Have I affirmed someone lately? Has someone affirmed me? How did it feel?

Am I in full control of the way I spend my leisure moments? If not, what's out of control?

Are my priorities the best ones?

Overall, how has my attitude been this past week?

Is there anything I need to release to God so I might worry less?

Is there anyone I am consistently encouraging with no thought of return?

Am I spending time with the right friends? How do I know?

What is unique about this period of my life? Is anything out of the ordinary happening?

What decisions am I facing right now for which I need divine guidance?

What am I learning from Scripture passages I've been studying, or sermons I've been listening to?

## Casting, Sharing, Communicating the Vision

All the great Christian leaders I have met in the past two decades have one thing in common: the ability to communicate vision so clearly, with such feeling, that people—many people—are moved to follow.

Any book on leadership that you pick off the bookstore shelf will in some way address the topic of vision. Leaders today often experience outside pressure to produce or come forward with a new vision. However, producing the new vision is often easier than communicating it in such a way that others are moved to follow. Creating and communicating vision is an absolute requirement for leaders wanting to achieve their goals and future dreams for their ministry or organization.

Using comprehensive data from 900 senior executives in 100 American corporations, as well as in-depth interviews with 150 top managers in fifteen successful companies, including General Electric, Citicorp, IBM, Hewlett-Packard, and Coca-Cola, John Kotter singles out the practices that develop superior leadership. According to Kotter, leadership "is the process of creating a vision for others and having the power to translate it into a reality and sustain it."[1]

Communicating the vision is the first step in strategic planning, and yet many ministry leaders do not take enough time, nor involve enough people, to effectively communicate the vision. A vision that is grasped by one's entire congregation or all the constituents of one's ministry can help everyone set goals to advance the ministry of the organization. A vision can also motivate and empower staff team members. Visioneering skills are used by great leaders to draw people toward themselves and their ideas through the communication of a vision. Without a strong vision, strategic plans cannot be properly set down, since there is no guiding principle or compelling ideal to plan around.

A vision is an aspiration or a description of a desirable future that exists within the leader's soul that can inspire people, bring meaning to their work, mobilize them to action, and help them decide what to do and what not to do in the course of their work.

## Effective Vision Resonates

My son Jeremy is a guitar instructor, and although he has now left me in the dust with his amazing ability, I did introduce him to the instrument. I shared with him how to tune his guitar by the use of harmonics. Harmonics is the reverberation of a guitar string causing another string to vibrate—even though you have not physically touched it—due to the matching sound wave.

Here is how it works. I have a digital watch that produces an alarm tune that begins with an E note. Listening to the alarm's E, we could tune the top string. It is the sixth and largest string on the guitar, therefore it will not go out of tune as easily as the others. Once the sixth string is in tune, we sound the harmonic at the fifth fret of this string, and it should be the same as the harmonic at the seventh fret of the A string. Likewise, to tune the D string we match the harmonic at the fifth fret of the A string to the one at the seventh fret of the D string. Harmonics, when properly struck, will ring for a fairly long time, usually allowing us to tune the string before it stops resonating.

An effective vision resonates in people much the same way. As you communicate the vision, your "sound" waves cause them to vibrate in harmonics to your calling. The vision motivates people by arousing desire for great things and appealing to their aspiration to make a difference in the world.

Back in 1994 Peter Senge said a vision is "an idealized picture of the future organization and it expresses the organization's reason for existence."[2] Vision grabs people and brings them into the fold. When a leader's vision is effective and strong, staff team members and stakeholders absorb the vision, get caught up in what they are doing, and commit themselves to the goals and the values of the leader, or the leader's vision.

If vision is so important, how can we mentor leaders to communicate effectively their vision?

I believe the process starts with making sure the leader understands and is grounded in the core values of the ministry. There has been so much talk about vision in the past years that almost every ministry or church I visit has a vision and mission statement posted on the walls of their offices. Yet I frequently do not see it empowering what is taking place among the staff or congregation. Delineating core values is an often lengthy but extremely worthwhile endeavor. It is a step that many leaders can assume they have already covered. When setting out to understand the core values of the company, the business leader embarks on a journey of discovery rather than a mission of invention or creation. The first step is to identify the core values that already exist in the organization.

I was asked to make a presentation about Arrow's core values for the Evangelical Christian Credit Union, our strategic partner in Los Angeles, who expressly wanted to know how their core values aligned with Arrow's. As we prepared for the presentation, I asked our entire staff team at Arrow what they thought the core values were for the ministry. What emerged were a series of excellent core values that had never been stated formally but were in fact a key part of how we have functioned since 1992. This is what emerged:

**Arrow Values . . .**

### Jesus Is Our Model

- We desire the leaders who experience Arrow to be led more by Jesus, lead more like Jesus, and lead more to Jesus.
- Our motivation for the development of Christian leaders is to ultimately see more people come to faith in Jesus Christ.

### Biblical Leadership

- Biblical leadership is God-originated. God raises up leaders, we do not. Therefore, we search for leaders with potential, not potential leaders.
- We value empowered Christian leaders and encourage development to their fullest potential.

### Kingdom Seeking

- Leadership and evangelism development are transferable concepts that should be "given away," resulting in kingdom growth, not the growth of personal empires.
- Arrow is not ministry-, gender-, or culture-specific.

### Character

- Biblical leadership is character focused. The key to the effectiveness of leaders is their spiritual character formation more than their skills.
- We value and recognize that integrity is essential for the credibility of our ministry—we must "walk the talk."

### Excellence

- Excellence honors God and inspires people. We value being and giving our best in all our efforts.[3]
- There is no excuse for mediocrity. Leaders have little time for average ideas, average experiences, or even average ministries.
- At Arrow we believe that every residential seminar should be better than the last one.

*Assessment Process*

- God uses a highly personalized leadership development process that takes time.
- Leadership development should be individualized and based on accurate assessment.

*Mentoring*

- Christian mentoring is a dynamic, intentional relationship of trust in which one person enables another to maximize the grace of God in his life and service.
- God uses older mentors to develop leaders.
- God uses peers to develop leaders.

*Experiential Learning*

- God develops leaders in community.
- God develops men and women leaders in the midst of their leadership.
- We combine experiential learning with scholarship in all our programs to produce educated leaders who are awake to new possibilities.

*Praxis*

- We invest in training, research, and evangelism as an essential foundation for preparing Christian leaders for their generation.
- Arrow wants learning to be immediately beneficial for leaders' ministries. Their organizations should experience tangible benefit over time as a result of their development with us.

*Communication*

- We value open, creative communication throughout all levels of the organization, programs, and partnerships.
- Communication is the glue that keeps networks together—therefore we will invest in excellent communication through time, technique, and technology.

*Balanced Life*

- We value the importance of personal and professional balance—physical, intellectual, spiritual, and family.

*Building on Strengths*

- We build on our existing strengths, which include:
  - A proven history of developing transformational leaders
  - Leadership assessment expertise

- Mentoring development and facilitation
- A network of proven Christian leaders, trainers, and partners
- A kingdom focus and pursuit of productive partnerships with other outstanding Christian ministries and foundations
- Entrepreneurial responsiveness

The defining and articulation of values are difficult tasks for leaders to undertake if the intention is to reach a level of depth and uniqueness that will endure beyond the many changes the organization will face in the future. As a mentor it would be a tremendous gift to arrange a short retreat to assist a leader in beginning or refining existing values. It requires more listening than talking. Ask leaders to tell you about their ministry organization or church. This will reveal existing values, so as you listen write bullet points on a flip chart for further discussion.

These values undergird our organization, and as we increase capacity in the development of leaders by adding new programs and staff, these core values will remain.

Core values are those ideals that are intrinsic to the organization. Core values define the ministry and what it stands for. Core values should endure the test of time. They are essential and foundational to an organization. So as we introduce new vision for growth in our development of leaders through Arrow, we must constantly hold up new developments alongside our values to ensure alignment.

## Core Purpose

Once we identified the core values of the ministry, it was time to define and understand our core purpose. The core purpose is the organization's reason for being, and it reflects idealistic motivations for doing the ministry's work. For Arrow I use the phrase "To experience the joy of identifying, networking, and deeply investing in God's anointed leaders worldwide for the benefit of the kingdom of God."

This core purpose is the answer to why we work at Arrow. Whereas we might achieve a goal or complete a strategy, we cannot fulfill a purpose.

Once the core values and purpose are clear, then vision tends to flow more easily both to leaders and to their congregations, because communication from the leader to others will usually be clearer because of the core value process.

## Sharing Vision

Communicating vision is achieved when it goes both deep and wide. Vision needs to be driven deep into the organization and staff, and to the far reaches of the organization. But how do leaders practically share vision? Here are some of the important ingredients to helping leaders share vision.

Give specific examples of "mission accomplished" factors. In other words, tell people what it will look like when you have achieved the vision.

Don't go cheap! So often leaders begin to count pennies when it comes to sharing vision, and yet sharing vision is perhaps the single most important thing you could do for the ministry. Effective communication requires resources and effort. Get input from a professional communicator; there may be one right in your congregation or ministry who could help. Develop a plan, and then allocate the resources to ensure that it happens. Go all-out—your actions speak louder than words. Posters on the wall and a vague statement on a quickly thrown together website aren't enough to create a consistent vision for your staff, community, and congregation.

Use a wide variety of communication vehicles and styles. Also, integrate the vision into as many communication channels as possible—personal presentations, written communications, emails, ministry newsletters, meetings, advertising, marketing campaigns, and by placing plaques and engravings stating the vision in hallways, offices, and lobbies. Determine who your audience is and then target the type of communication that is going to connect them to your vision.

Seek input as you share the vision. Hold brown-bag luncheons and try sharing the vision while seeking some feedback. Find out what is connecting and what needs more work. Vision does not communicate well when it comes from a completely informed perspective. When leaders have been working with something for a long time and understand it themselves, as is often the case when leaders have been immersed in planning, we can think we are communicating even though it remains confusing to the recipient. Beware also of time pressure or pressure by the board, as this can cause difficulties at the receiving end of the communication process.

Evaluate the communications channels you are already using such as newsletters and announcements, and augment them with new expressions to capture those on the fringes.

Constantly use connection illustrations. These are opportunities to highlight actions or accomplishments consistent with your vision. Connect your vision rhetoric with actual examples of your people doing it.

Model the vision yourself as the leader. If you want your people to engage a new vision, roll up your sleeves at specific points and work alongside them. You are a powerful communicator through action. Truly great business leaders act in accordance with their vision and serve as living examples of the ministry they wish to model.

Make the vision part of your staff meetings and organization's conversations. Discuss the vision regularly. Ask, "How are we doing?" to ensure that every staff member can make it a reality. The ministry leader must insist that all staff model behaviors that are consistent with the organization's vision. It is through such action that all members of the ministry will believe in and live a meaningful expression of the vision.

Share it at every opportunity. Repetition breeds awareness, acceptance, and understanding of your vision. Use every opportunity to share the vision with people both inside and outside the organization.

Visitors to your ministry organization should understand its vision not by reading it posted on a wall or printed on paper but by seeing the ethos of the place, based solely on the conversations they hear and the behaviors they observe. Effectively communicating vision is more than placing a vision statement on the wall in the lobby. Effectively communicating the vision means the ministry lives the vision it promotes; the ministry means what it says and practices what it preaches.

## Come into the Kitchen

One of the finest examples of vision casting that I have seen is at Northpoint Community Church in Atlanta, Georgia, where Andy Stanley has a vision of 100,000 people being connected to small groups. He uses a DVD to share how the church has been designed to function like a home. "We invite guests to the foyer, develop friendships in the living room, and grow as a family around the kitchen table."

These three environments are a great expression of Peter Wagner's teaching about the "Three C" model: celebration/congregation/cell. The foyer component is the weekly worship service for adults and is an entry point—the big event. From the foyer, Northpoint seeks to move people into the living room—medium-sized groups usually focused on specific need areas.

From the living room, people are directed toward the kitchen. These are small groups. This is the place where lasting friendships are made.

I have visited Andy's church several times and am impressed with how the congregation knows this language and has caught the vision of multiplication and deepening

To come alongside a leader during the vision casting is such an encouragement that it often makes the difference between success and a fiasco. After the initial euphoria of creating a vision, many leaders become somewhat paralyzed with "how do we get there from here." Strategic steps are necessary for implementing vision, and mentors can be of great assistance to leaders at this stage.

Leaders also face another challenge at this point, in that if they are communicating the vision well, others will ask, "What can I do to help bring this to fruition?" As a mentor, you can help them think through how to get people involved with their vision.

of relationships. They understand that success at Northpoint is defined by how effectively their ministries move people from large environments into small groups.

Ministry leaders can harvest the benefits of a strong vision by defining the core values of their ministry, defining their purpose, describing what they see for the ministry in the future, and then clearly articulating, communicating, and living the vision at every opportunity.

# Stepping Out Vision

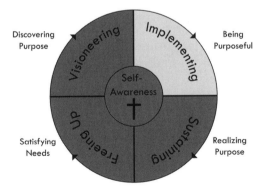

I have become a great believer in incremental steps and have seen the value of helping leaders, or congregations, follow a vision by breaking it into smaller sections or steps. This enables you to celebrate successes along the way and to measure progress more effectively.

We need to begin helping leaders by asking a series of questions to see how ready they are to establish some steps toward the vision. Here is a sample checklist:

1. Does the organization currently have a comprehensive ministry plan or some form of long-range strategic plan?
2. Do you belong to a denomination or larger coalition that also has a strategic plan your leadership fits into?
3. Do your team members have individual plans that help them with their focus for the year?
4. Do you meet regularly with your individual team members to review their progress toward their part of the overall plan?
5. Do you meet with your team regularly to review overall progress toward the plan?
6. When a specific step is created, do you make sure it doesn't fall between the cracks of day-to-day busyness?
7. Are you in the practice of building your relationships with your staff around the steps that have been mutually identified? For example, do you bring the vision back into performance reviews, staff meetings, or congregational meetings?
8. How do you feel about releasing control for steps and passing along responsibility to others?
9. Are the steps for the plan set by all of your key staff and stakeholders rather than just by you?
10. Do you praise your staff team freely when they accomplish their steps?

If leaders answer these questions positively, they probably require little help in this area of their leadership. However, that has not been my experience with most ministry leaders.

After stating the vision, each leader should ask of each of his staff team, "What do I expect this person to do?" Each member of the team should be able to answer the question, "What does the ministry expect of me?"

If a leader and his team members can answer these questions completely and with considerable detail, they are part of a ministry that will have few interpersonal and operational difficulties.

The establishment of steps toward a vision works best when they are part of a larger strategic plan. For the majority of churches and smaller organizations, the plan should set out some objectives for the first few years. Having these in place will set the foundation for short-term goals. In very small churches or organizations, the leader should sit down with a mentor and perhaps some key individuals and write down where he sees the ministry going. Try to describe the ministry as you see it today, and how it should be evolving as you pursue the vision.

## Different Styles of Steps

There are two aspects to establishing steps:

1. Organizational steps and objectives for the ministry or your staff team are usually established in group meetings.
2. Individual steps are established between the leader and the team member.

Some ministries go overboard by establishing numerous goals and steps that become unwieldy to manage. I have reviewed pages and pages of details, printed on reams of paper, that Christian leaders have spent hours producing. We usually find only about 20 percent of this work is worthy to use as individual steps. Usually included in their lists are series of items that are routine to the day-to-day running of the ministry. They are already covered as part of clearly understood duties related to the role.

> When helping leaders establish steps, you may find ongoing resistance. Don't be afraid of pursuing why they are not willing to undertake a given step. It may be that their leadership style is one of not breaking down life and tasks in this manner.

Steps should be concisely stated. If they go beyond one piece of paper, I would recommend cutting them down to size.

Try to be as specific as possible when establishing steps. A vague statement such as "Our church is going to increase giving to missions" does little to move people. There is nothing about the statement that specifies action. It is important to communicate in specifics, such as, "We will increase our giving to missions by 10 percent within the next six months."

Many ministries are resistant to setting measurable goals. Often the leader feels that the work is far too spiritual to be encapsulated in a specific measurable step. There could be lingering issues in the freeing-up phase of the mentoring matrix that need to be addressed. Whatever the reason, leaders must be able to lead others with some sort of measurement or clear way to recognize that the steps have been reached.

Every time we establish a step, it should be accompanied with some action bullet points. How are we going to get there from here? Make sure these steps are realistic. For example, it should be possible to achieve the step within the time frame that you specify. To use my example of increasing giving to missions—is a 10 percent increase unachievable within six months? If extenuating circumstances make it impossible, then it would actually be destructive to establish this as a step, since it is largely out of reach.

When we are creating steps toward vision, the value the step has to the ministry and the people assigned to carry it out should be obvious. It needs to be important to them. This is another test to see whether goals being set are simply for routine matters.

## What If I'm Not a Goal Setter?

Bobb Biehl says some people are simply not goal setters. They are actually problem solvers. If you are not a good goal setter, try restating all goal-setting language in problem-solving language. Here is an example.

1. State the problem as best you can.
2. State what you would like to accomplish.
3. State the end result. What will it look like once you have solved the problem?
4. Set down some possible actions you can take to solve the problem, and include some measurements you would use to tell when the problem has been solved.
5. Now take these problem-solving possibilities and refine them into a clear, detailed action plan.

It is amazing to watch how people who are averse to goal setting can quickly engage in the process once it is restated as problem solving.

## Out-of-Control Leaders

Effective ministry leaders actually like being out of control. No, I'm not talking about a leader who is constantly wigging out. Nor am I referring to a leader who is a control-freak micromanager. I am talking about being comfortable not being in control of every detail of every step. It is only as we become able to release others to do the work that our ministries have capability for growth and achievement.

## *West Wing* Friday

In the Arrow office we have a special event that takes place weekly. It is called "*West Wing* Friday," and we each bring a bag lunch into the boardroom—which we have renamed the "situation room." There we watch an episode of this popular television series about the White House (on DVD). We have fun giving Arrow staff members nicknames after the characters on the show, but we also discuss and think a great deal about leadership due to the themes presented and the interaction of the White House staff in this drama.

My nickname around the office is POTAM, which stands for "President of the Arrow Ministries," and is a play on the American president's POTUS. The team also humors me by saying, "Thank you, Mr. President," whenever I dismiss a meeting, mocking the formal nature of White House meetings. Following a private meeting with Jeremy (nicknamed Toby) Tjosvold, who works in the area of communication and assessment in the Arrow office, I found myself smiling long after he left the room. We had been talking about a particular communications piece and several problems related to our getting it out in a timely manner. Jeremy suggested a couple steps that would lead to resolution, and I heartily agreed.

As Jeremy left my office, he turned and said, "It shall be done! Thank you, Mr. President." I heard nothing more about the project for a couple days, but the silence was rather pleasing to me as a leader. I knew Jeremy would take care of the assignment, and I felt very relaxed. Jeremy is competent and well organized. I knew I would be pleased with the results.

> When leaders take the time to establish a clear process of the steps toward the vision, it gives everyone something to reference and work toward. It also provides leaders with markers to see if the organization or ministry is accomplishing the stated desires. It also gets an entire staff team energized and working toward their strengths.

How can we help leaders to feel comfortable with being out of control?

The key to any leader being able to trust others is found within. Does the leader actually trust himself? This question should be addressed during the first two phases of the mentoring matrix when we are looking at the inner life of the leader. Each leader must identify circumstances and situations that cause him not to trust others. It is usually a disappointment from the past or an unhealed wound—both of which can be healed through the Holy Spirit's work in our life.

Another area of trust that must be scrutinized is the competency level of the people we work with. My relaxation with Jeremy was spurred on by my collective experience of his competency in previous tasks.

Leaders who are good at being "out of control" are usually positive people. They also set high standards and expect the team to achieve them. They do believe that the task will get done properly, and that the staff team will work hard to see that the vision is achieved. Noncontrolling leaders are also comfortable allowing people to do the job their way—believing the end result will still be achieved.

If an "out of control" leader wants to live a more relaxed life, there are three leadership actions that can be taken to help achieve this.

At the beginning of each year, the leader should sit down with each member of the team individually and together work out a plan for the year. All the individual goals should feed into the ministry's master plan. Push for real clarity and check to make sure that the team member understands clearly. Often this is a matter of language. How the leader speaks to the goal may be interpreted differently by the team member. In the end, both the leader and the team member should have a written plan for their achievements in the coming year.

Throughout the year the leader should meet with each person to discuss the latter's progress. I find it helpful to ask the person to show evidence of what he is doing. This is better than a simple verbal report, which can easily be romanticized by those who want to maintain harmony. When looking at clear evidence, it is very easy to praise the team member if things are going well. It also provides an opportunity to discuss things that are not going as well. Together you might explore new ideas or approaches and possibly reflect on whether the goal itself needs to be reset because it was either too high or the circumstances have changed. Everyone benefits when a leader allows for midcourse corrections.

Gather your entire team together two or three times a year to discuss goals. It is during these times that a fresh exchange of ideas can take place and others on the team can focus on some of the more demanding projects you are undertaking.

When you walk into a ministry office, you should be able to sense if it is a smooth-functioning, people-sensitive, and productive place. Such a place is marked by healthy activity. There is fluidity to how the staff interacts. You don't sense friction and nothing gets logjammed for very long. In addition, the people who work in a healthy ministry have a high level of appreciation and excitement.

## A Team Visioneering Retreat

Often a retreat setting is a great place to focus on stepping out a vision. There is something about being out of the office that allows brains to engage in creative and stimulating thinking. So what does a leader do at one of these retreats? Well, here is one suggestion for how to break up the retreat time.

- Write down all the major problems facing your ministry or organization and pick out one that requires attention. It doesn't have to be the most important one—just one that you feel capable of handling.
- Have your team come up with a statement of the problem in one sentence. This will help to define what the central issue is.
- Have each team member write down a desired solution in one sentence.
- Have individuals work on the previous sentence so that the desired solution is specific and measurable.
- Brainstorm together and list all the various activities that could be done to help achieve the solution. Do not analyze them at this point, but rather, try to get out as many ideas as possible.
- Review this list as a team and seek consensus on the activities that will realistically accomplish the desired outcome. Everyone involved should be able to support the activities listed. Test this before moving on to the next step by asking members individually if they are supportive.
- Assign a specific project leader for each of the action items you identify. Have each project leader write out a proposal for accomplishing the desired outcome and bring it back to the team for their endorsement.
- Beside each action item place a start date, a completion date, and who will be responsible.
- Together, discuss who should be the overall coordinator for the plan. Have this person be responsible for managing the progress.
- Decide together as a team what the measuring devices should be. What are the markers? How will we celebrate the milestones? And how will we ultimately verify the results?
- Discuss when progress reports should be due and who will make them. At the same time, create meet-

Engage, don't tell. Many mentors can get extremely excited about the strategic phase of their mentoring relationship. This is especially true, it seems, with men. So let me raise a caution to those of you mentoring leaders. Be very careful that sure emphasis in this phase is on engaging the leader in the process of creating steps rather than telling him what to do. This is critical to his continued development as a leader. Our ultimate goal is not only to teach leaders how to step out visions they will receive in the future but also to equip them so that as they work with their teams they will be able to transfer the concepts and skills to their colleagues.

ing dates and times for the team, so that together you can monitor the results of your progress.

- Have a recording secretary write out the complete plan in as few words as possible. Try to keep it all on one page, and give each member of your team a copy.

Learning to lay out the steps toward a vision is a transferable skill that a visionary leader will be able to apply on numerous occasions and in a variety of situations.

## Teams and Time

The execution of vision requires our ability to work with people and to manage our time. There are so many excellent resources available on these subjects that I will not rehash the topic in depth but rather will point leaders to some excellent sources of information on the nuts and bolts of both building an effective team and learning to manage time effectively.

I do, however, want to help leaders understand that working with teams is critical to effective ministry today, and if you are unable to steward your time as a leader, the days will fly by with little accomplished for the kingdom.

## Please, No More Lone Ranger

For those of us old enough to remember, even the Lone Ranger did not ride alone.

Today Christian leaders have to function with a mind-set of team. Working with others in a collaborative relationship is central for any leader, but the next step is to work with a team. That is when we can really accomplish the vision.

On May 25, 1961, President John F. Kennedy made a special address before the U.S. Congress on the importance of space exploration. His famous vision began, "First, I believe that this nation should commit itself to achieving the goal, before this decade is out, of landing a man on the Moon and returning him safely to the Earth."[1]

When Kennedy established this objective, he inspired and led. He did not sit down and design the spaceship that would carry the astronauts. He did not weld it together, fire up the engines, or create a process to allow foods to be consumed in a weightless environment. To accomplish all of this, it took thousands of people functioning as a team.

Most ministries or missions, whether large or small, require teamwork. It is incumbent on today's leaders to not only be able to inspire toward a vision but also to draw together the team to make it happen. A delicate balance is required: leaders must use all the skills they possess to inspire and lead a team, but they must never lose sight of the fact that they themselves are a member of the team, subject to its rules and dynamics, responsible for its shortfalls as well as its successes.

## Do You Really Work on a Team?

When working with younger leaders in the Arrow Leadership Program, we find that the new generation of leaders seems to come hardwired toward working in teams—which is generally not the case for my baby boomer colleagues. However, their definition of teams can be distorted because of the misuse of the term in many of the environments where they have worked or ministered. Many of their experiences have actually been in what we call work groups rather than teams. There are two things that distinguish a team from a group:

1. A team will always have common goals that everyone clearly accepts, and will understand that if they are to accomplish them, they must work together.
2. A team will invest a substantial amount of time in learning how to work together.

The definition we use for a team in our training is:

> A ministry team is a group of interdependent people
> committed to a common purpose
> who choose to cooperate in order
> to achieve exceptional results for the glory of God.

Pat MacMillan, founder and CEO of Team Resources, Inc., has taught the module on team building in the Arrow Leadership Program. I have often referred to the notes I took during this module over a dozen years ago. Pat asked us to answer a series of questions for our ministry organizations. Our answers were then graphed on a chart divided into several distinct sections that helped define where the team baseline was, and more importantly for me, what a high-performance team looked like. Here are his five categories:

*The Working Group*: This is a group for which there is no significant incremental performance need or opportunity that would require it to become a team. The members interact primarily to share information, best practices, or perspectives, and to make decisions to help individuals perform within their areas of responsibility.

*Pseudoteam*: This is a group for which there may be a significant incremental performance need or opportunity, but it has not focused on collective performance and is not really trying to achieve it. It has no interest in shaping a common purpose or set of performance goals, even though it may call itself a team. Pseudoteams are the weakest of all groups in terms of performance impact.

*Potential Team*: This is a group for which there is a significant incremental performance need, and which is trying to improve its performance impact. Typically, however, it requires more clarity about purpose, goals, or work products and more discipline in hammering out a common working approach. It has not yet established collective accountability.

*Real Team*: This is a small number of people with complementary skills who are equally committed to a common purpose, goals, and working approach for which they hold themselves mutually accountable.

*High-Performance Team*: This is a group that meets all the conditions of real teams and has members who are also deeply committed to each other's personal growth and success. That commitment usually transcends the team. The high-performance team significantly outperforms all other like teams and outperforms all reasonable expectations given to its membership.

Just having these delineated for me by Pat inspired me to constantly pursue the formation of high-performance teams. Pat's book *The Performance Factor: Unlocking the Secrets of Teamwork*[2] describes these in great detail. The six team characteristics described in his model have proven to be exceptionally effective in designing and training teams that consistently deliver exceptional results.[3]

The five key perspectives about teams and teamwork that Pat taught me to appreciate are:

1. Not every group is a team.
2. Not every team is equal.
3. Teams don't just happen.
4. Teamwork does *not* make your ministry easier.
5. Teamwork is more than an attitude.

Having a leader who understands these principles and the distinction between a work group and a team is important. There are many opportunities within ministries for people to work together in groups, but in actual fact there are few teams. Ministries use the term "team" frequently—pastoral team, worship team, youth leadership team, to name a few—but upon examination, these "teams" are usually work groups in function. A team is an intentional creation. Teams are put together with the idea that they will stay together to achieve a specific long-term objective.

Teams encourage differences of opinion and are not always easy to work in because of the potential for conflict. "Teamwork" requires work by every member of the team. Teams usually form by bringing together all the people whose work connects them together. I've always found it best to hold an off-site training session to launch a new team. Just being away from everyday pressures of work, such as ringing telephones, helps bring people together and build cohesiveness. If the organization is constrained by time or finances, then select a day when you can close the office and retreat together to a home and bring bag lunches. The time together is what is important, so don't try to make the team-building retreat too complicated.

## Leaders as Team Members

A difficulty leaders have in forming good teams is their understanding of themselves as actual members of the team. Many leaders get stuck here because their leadership style is highly independent.

Insecurities within leaders can emerge at this phase in the team-building process. Again, this reminds us why it is important not to skip phases in the mentoring matrix. If there is an area in the leader's life that is holding him back and making him feel insecure, it is unlikely he would be able to function within a high-performance team he is leading. Team building may in fact be used of God to surface new discoveries about the leader's life. It may require actually going back to the first two phases of the matrix.

> When mentoring a leader to be a better team member and team leader, it may also be necessary to review some of the basics in simply relating to people.

Following are some of the ways leaders can become better team members.

Be a better listener. I have watched many leaders sit in a room and not give their full attention or even be open to what is being said. Leaders need to focus on the opinions of other team members rather than thinking about their reply. This shows respect to their fellow team members. Other leaders have a tendency to constantly interrupt by either whispering or blatantly cutting people off.

Be honest and open. Today I believe it's hard to get by leading a Christian organization without showing some of your feelings. The team will never be encouraged to share honestly if the leader remains stoic or superficial.

Respond to other people's needs and desires. Some people are prone to judge motives when someone disagrees with them. This is especially true among insecure leaders.

Approach the team with an open mind. Try not to be negative by evaluating an idea before it has even had a chance to be fully developed. Leaders should develop the practice of looking for the positive aspects in every suggestion.

Address any areas of defensiveness. Good leaders will always see criticism as something they can learn from and build upon. Leaders must strive not to personalize every criticism that comes their way. Leaders will have critics. It's a sign of leadership.

Encourage every member of the team to take initiative in sharing ideas. We really benefit from our teammates when we hear their "aha" moments. These will never emerge if they feel intimidated by the leader.

Understand that not everyone communicates in the same manner. By watching facial expressions, tone of voice, gestures, and posture, you'll see that there is always much more being communicated than the words that are said.

Create team settings that feel safe for everyone, including you as a leader. You need to feel safe enough to take a risk, such as saying how you feel or even trying something brand-new.

Champion the uniqueness of each team member. Try to build relationships with team members and talk publicly about how unique they are and their specific contribution to the team.

Trust: Leaders must trust not only themselves but others within the team and the team process itself. Leaders who do not trust others are perceived as untrustworthy.

The leader is ultimately responsible for what happens with the team. No one else can ensure team success. If you as a leader are not fully invested in the team, you set a pattern that encourages others to act the same way.

## Having the *Right* Crew on Board

On our sailboat I have found that I am most comfortable when there are at least three of us on board for sailing. The boat is just large enough that you need several hands to help the day's journey be successful and without stress. Perhaps this will change as we get more experienced, for I watch a few of the seasoned veterans in our marina take similar-sized boats out alone. However, as I seek for two others to join me for a sail, it is important that they are the right two. For example, Brenda is a trained and certified skipper, while my sons are certified as competent crew. I know that when any two are on board, we have the right skills and training to take us wherever we want to go. During the time we've been sailing together, we have also learned the various strengths that each of us has to add to the journey. Brenda is amazing at taking the helm and flaking the sail; Jon is our grinder for trimming the sails; Jeremy has strengths in casting off; and I enjoy navigation.

If I would like us to visit one of the San Juan Islands just south of our marina, it requires crossing the Strait of Georgia, which is a significant passageway in the Pacific. Doing so requires crossing a major shipping lane for large cargo ships, and the winds can change direction throughout the course of the day. If I have the right crew on board, we can adjust our journey depending on the winds and sea conditions with ease. In fact, if we have the right crew, decision making is actually easier.

Jim Collins, in *Good to Great: Why Some Companies Make the Leap . . . and Others Don't*, makes the observation that great companies take the attitude of getting the right people on board first so they can be more responsive to a changing world. He found that their leaders were saying, "Look, I don't really know where we should take this bus. But I know this much: If we get the right people on the bus, the right people in the right seats, and the wrong people off the bus, then we'll figure out how to take it someplace great."[4]

Many ministry leaders do not fully understand this concept and are still stuck in rigid role descriptions that are usually derived from specific need areas where they are feeling pressured. Yes of course, there are some basic skill sets and training necessary for each role, such as the certification I like sailors to have. However, if you have the right person—he can be trained.

Barry Hawes shared something about hiring team members early on in my leadership, and it too became a sticky note in my Bible. It reads, "Hire for character. You can teach skills."

That one nugget of wisdom has been proven through my observations of great ministries around the globe. Character flaws will bring about demise quickly. If you get too focused on the skill set the person brings and neglect the character side, a breakdown may eventually occur.

Character flaws are not always easy to spot, as the individual has probably had years of experience in keeping them hidden—or the evil one is blinding you to them until such time that they can wreak havoc on a ministry. Look for them in the little things. Remember Jesus addressing this in the parable in Luke 16? "Whoever can be trusted with very little can also be trusted with much, and whoever is dishonest with very little will also be dishonest with much. So if you have not been trustworthy in handling worldly wealth, who will trust you with true riches? And if you have not been trustworthy with someone else's property, who will give you property of your own?" (vv. 10–12).

So a Christian leader who is evaluating a potential staff member should be encouraged to watch for little things. Is the individual constantly referring to "bending the rules"? Does the person practice honesty in paying taxes or submitting expense reports? Is the person truthful about education experience on his resume, or has it been "padded"? If the candidate is married, spend time with both together. Do you see in their marriage a reflection of what the candidate says he believes and practices?

Great vision without great people is wasted.

## Tips for Bringing on Team Members

Ensure that their faith in Jesus is solid. They do not have to be of the same denomination as you, but they should sense a call to be involved in the ministry due to their personal faith in Jesus.

Do not hire somebody just like yourself. Many leaders make the mistake of looking for others just like themselves—unsuccessfully, I might add. One of the things I look at first when visiting or consulting with another ministry is the diversity of the leadership team. Leaders need others who complement them, not clone them.

Hire for character and attitude rather than skill. Teaching skills is a snap compared with trying to do character or attitude transplants. With attitude, look especially for a great sense of optimism.

Look for core confidence and risk takers. In interviews, look in candidates' eyes to measure confidence level. Ask if they have ever been in trouble, and have them describe the situation. This will help you discern how cautious they are in their risk taking and give you a measure of their confidence level.

Hold out for character. When you are feeling tempted to hire based on skills, remember this. Never hire someone with good potential but questionable habits, thinking you can change the person. Basically, what you see now is what you are going to have.

Go for humor. A great sense of humor is a sign of intelligence. Team members who can't laugh easily, particularly at themselves, are not going to add much to the team and will probably be very rigid employees.

Mind the gap. This expression is used throughout the Tube, or subway in London, England. It refers to the gap between the platform and the train. When hiring new members, look carefully at the aggregate strengths and skill gaps of your team and go for the qualities and styles that are missing.

Don't be satisfied just with references. Remember that many of the most glowing references are given for people others are eager to dump. The Christian community, in particular, often tends to not speak critically of anyone. Ask to see actual expressions of their work. Use your network to see if anyone else you know well could provide an additional reference for the candidate.

Stock the bench. The very best baseball or hockey teams have a talent pipeline that is constantly driving the best people toward playing on their team. Keep an eye out for prospective team members before the need arises. Don't just wait until a vacancy occurs. Keep a list of potential employees handy and hire new talent when you can afford to.

Push for diversity. Make certain you are spreading your net wide enough to find those high-potential, but different, fish that generally don't swim in the waters near you.

Listen. Most Christian leaders talk way too much when interviewing. Listen to hear the story of the candidate's life at home, at church, and at work. It's been said that being a leader is like practicing psychiatry without a license. That may be truer in hiring team members than in any other part of the job.

Pray. Ask the Lord to give you insight, wisdom, and peace about the candidate. Give yourself time to pray about it—even if just overnight.

For key leadership positions in your ministry or organization, you may consider using a professional to assist you in the search. Bruce Dingman, president of Dingman and Associates in California, is a leader in the executive search field and has been very helpful to ministries in looking for new leadership, as has Stephen Robinson, president of the Robinson Fraser Group in Toronto. The value is found in their ability to check references, to interview properly, and even in maintaining a distance between the ministry and the individual to ensure that both are treated well in the process.

Bob Dingman, author of *In Search of a Leader*, offers these tips for those doing reference checks.[5] First, open the reference check with the assurance of absolute confidentiality within the search committee. You may say the reference's words will be shared "without attribution." That is, the reference's name will not be disclosed, even to the search committee, but only identified as "a board member," "a deacon," "a faculty member," or whatever. This assurance can help to loosen up a reluctant source. And be sure you honor your word when you promise confidentiality!

Second, you can remind the source that he is only one of a number of people you are checking with. In effect, you are saying that nothing the source says will by itself cause the candidate to be dropped. You ease the contact's sense of guilt in this manner.

Third, you can still activate a sense of prospective guilt in references by posing your questions in such a way that they would need to lie if they did not answer them honestly. While they may not want to damage the candidate's standing, they normally will choose to do that rather than lie to you. Awareness of this approach can be a useful insight.

Fourth, if significant negative information develops, get off that particular point as soon as you can and avoid judgmental reactions. Also, be sure to conclude the reference check on an upbeat note.

## The Emotive Side of the Search

It is rather straightforward to create a role description for a position on your team, but often there is an emotive side that does not get reflected. When we at Arrow desired to hire a personal assistant to the president, we created a very accurate role description for the position. However, Dr. Jim Postlewaite, who was working with me at the time, asked me for a list of what I was looking for in an assistant beyond the actual tasks that needed to be accomplished (the feeling, emotive side of the search). A few days later I provided him a list of what I wanted in an executive assistant. I wanted someone who:

- anticipates my next move
- takes initiative
- is loyal to me and Arrow
- presents well on paper—both writing content and layout
- makes a great first impression
- is a problem solver
- is confident
- is at his best when I am at my worst
- has an "up" attitude
- gets along with the other team members
- has traveled and understands hotels and flights, etc.
- is secure when I am away from the office
- can produce when given a task—job delegated, job done!
- can make me look good
- is an encouragement to me—encouraging words and prayer support

- has a good memory—for people especially
- can handle multiple incoming projects
- has proven stress-coping mechanisms
- is well organized and can assist me in being organized without being obtrusive
- can handle long-range planning
- can see the big picture of my life—understands all my roles
- is professional yet warm
- puts first things first and knows what is first

## The Spiritual Side of Team Building

Remember that the spiritual forces of the evil one are tasked with the assignment of preventing the work of God from moving forward. When a leader enters into the team-building process, multiple layers may be attacked.

The leader may experience the evil one as the accuser. In trying to draw together people to join the team for the vision God has given, the accuser may dredge up from the past all relational difficulties the leader has experienced. Often leaders hear an inner voice saying, "Who are you to lead these people? What about your own sinfulness?" The purpose is to raise insecurity in the leader and thwart the forming of the right team.

Spiritual vulnerabilities are also found in each of the team members. A team is only as strong as its weakest link, and if a member of the team is particularly susceptible to the attacks of evil, this is where we can expect the intentional subversion of the team. It does not stop here, for if the team is strong and prayerfully protected, the spiritual warfare begins to be redirected toward family members and loved ones of the team. Anything that can cause a distraction to the team proceeding forward toward God's vision drains energy and resources, causing the team to lose focus.

It often takes teams and team leaders a while to notice what is happening. So it is incumbent on the leader to keep a wary eye on the activities of the evil one on each member of the team. Leaders should pray for their team members regularly, as well as all members of the team's households.

Another ploy of the evil one is to infiltrate the team with someone capable of creating dissension, disharmony, or disgrace to the things of God. This is why it is critical to discern carefully as you add staff to the ministry or organization. I have yet to meet a leader who has not made mistakes in adding team members. It is often very difficult to pick up the subtleties that should serve as warning signs. I've also observed that ministries often hire new staff during very busy seasons. We need to examine the nature of the busyness to determine whether it is legitimate or possibly a distraction being orchestrated at the spiritual level.

Christians are often shy about asking important questions when adding new members to their team. We do need to provide people with an "out" if they are not spiritually ready for this type of position or the responsibilities that come with the territory. Bob Dingman was doing a search for a Christian organization and spoke with a significant Christian leader. Everything was going well with the interview and then Bob said, in effect, Friend, if you have anything in your background that has the potential to blow up you and this ministry if it were revealed, I'm sure you don't want to discuss it with me. If by chance this is your situation, I implore you to use any reason you find convenient to withdraw from further consideration.

The next morning Bob received a note from the leader stating that he had to attend to some things before he could consider a leadership position. So Bob's question actually helped this leader address some issues in his life, and he was a wise enough man to do so.

## Pride

Another subtle form of team disruption occurs when very gifted and talented members of the team are affected by pride or jealousy. Gifted team members may begin to jockey for position and power. They begin to hold sidebar meetings with others on the team, trying to win them over to their leadership. This undermines the leader and often other members of the team. If not addressed in an open and timely manner, it sets back progress toward the vision and usually causes the team to dismantle.

This pattern of spiritual attack exists at other levels of leadership as well. The same criteria apply. However, a team that gathers together solely under the powerful influence of leadership, exchanges information, and works hard to produce results without keeping a vigilant eye on the spiritual interactions will experience cracks and eventually break apart.

# 8

# Budgeting Time and Resources

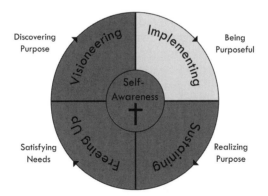

Are you the type of leader who plans ahead? Or instead, do you find yourself disorganized, chaotic, and unsystematic—never making progress on your most important goals? What are your priorities?

All leaders have something in common. We have only twenty-four hours in a day. Time is arguably the most valuable thing we have on this earth.

Our family was planning a trip to Thailand to celebrate Christmas with my brother and family who were living and working there. As it

When mentoring leaders, the issue of time and priorities comes up frequently. Therefore, understanding some basic time management strategies is important for all leaders. There are a multitude of systems and procedures that are recommended. Mentors can help leaders find a system that works for them and will help bring about renewed balance and increased productivity to their lives. The two must be tied together.

turned out, the only time we could leave North America was on December 24. Our youngest son, Jon, was quite intrigued by all of this because it meant crossing over the international date line. He was worried that we were going to miss Christmas altogether, for we would arrive in Thailand on December 26. It started a very interesting discussion about time at our dinner table. What would the impact be of losing a day—especially one that is such a major celebration for Christians?

Leaders lose days and weeks and sometimes months all the time—not due to crossing a date line but through the misuse of time in their day-to-day work. We all go through different stages or seasons as leaders, and each stage has its own time challenges. Sometimes we have to work too hard—the days are long and perhaps the travel schedule taxing. And sometimes time seems to drag on and the days seem long. Leaders are affected by workload, fatigue, and emotional and spiritual drains that cause our perception of time to be altered.

## God Bless Dr. Duncan

In 1989 I served as a volunteer for the Winter Olympics in Calgary. Years prior to the games, training events were held to assist those serving during the games, and one was on time management. We were encouraged to utilize a system to help us plan our time efficiently in order to give all that we could to the success of the Olympics. I had never heard such teaching before and began to reorder my use of time based on this system.

It was extremely effective, and I found that I was able to increase my "output" by at least 60 percent through practicing the disciplines of their time management system. All seemed great, and the years that followed the Olympics remained productive due to my continued practice of time management. In the ministry I accomplished more than many would think possible, but something was missing. I was not leading a balanced life. Years later this caught up to me, and it was our family physician who alerted me to the fact that I could not continue to live in this manner and ignore caring for my health.

I had actually gone to see Dr. Duncan because of our son Jeremy. Both Brenda and I had been sick for quite a while—along with all of the boys. After Dr. Duncan examined Jeremy, she asked me how I was doing. Suddenly, seemingly out of nowhere, I began to sob in her office. As the tears flowed, Jeremy, who was only four at the time, was looking at his dad with great concern. Dr. Duncan consoled Jeremy and told him everything was going to be all right and she just let me cry.

I tried to apologize, saying, "I don't know where that came from," but it took a while to get that out amidst the full-body crying I was doing. You know how it feels when you are crying loud and the tears and mucous are flowing? Your body undergoes involuntary shudders while you breathe deep and are gasping for air. I experienced a physical sense of pressure and pain in the chest area, which was both propelling the tears and being relieved by them at the same time. It was obvious that this cry was not being directed or controlled by my brain. She let me cry myself out that day and then asked me to come and see her again, making an appointment for the end of the following day.

The next day I felt fine and thought it silly to use up a doctor's valuable time with my appointment, so I called her office to cancel. The receptionist said, "Dr. Duncan thought you might call to try and cancel, and I was instructed to tell you that you must keep this appointment and that she will see you at 4:00 p.m."

I felt awkward when I arrived at the clinic again—twice in two days—and this time I did not even have the security of having Jeremy with me. I sat in her office and waited for her to finish with the patient just before me. When she entered, she was all smiles—proud of her ability to anticipate my attempt at canceling the appointment and pleased that I had shown up.

As a wise physician should, she asked me a whole series of questions about my life and ministry. She was of a different faith persuasion and admitted to me, "I don't understand this 'clergy thing,' but as your physician I can tell you that you are doing too much."

She continued, "When I finish this appointment with you, I am going home. I work in a clinic where every sixth week I do have to go on call twenty-four hours a day—but then I have five weeks where I do not. As I have been with your family and watched you over several years, I see that you are on call all the time."

My immediate response was to think that she really didn't understand what the ministry was like and to brush off her comments. Then she asked me, "Do you keep a to-do list of any sort?"

*Do I!* I thought. *Wait until I show you how disciplined I am with my time.*

I handed her my planner book, and she flipped through my daily to-do lists. Dr. Duncan looked at it more carefully and then exclaimed, "There are over thirty items on your list for today!"

"Yes, I know," I replied, feeling a little proud that I was so busy.

She told me she thought I was suffering from a mild form of depression and reached for her prescription pad.

"Wait, I don't want to be taking medicine for depression," I said in a startled manner. After all, I was feeling pretty good and had come to see her only because I was not able to maintain my productivity at the level it had been just months earlier. She kept writing and didn't even look up.

Now I was feeling sick. What would this mean? I'd heard about terrible side effects with some forms of depression medication. What was I going to do?

She then tore the page from her pad, and as she handed it to me she said, "Carson, I am not prescribing medication. I'd like you to take this to your church and give it to the senior pastor or board chair or whoever is appropriate." When I glanced down at the note on the pad, I saw the doctor was ordering me to take a two-week leave from the church and to rest.

Dr. Duncan then began writing on a separate sheet from the pad, and this was a note asking me to promise that when I returned to work in two weeks, I was not to put more than ten things on my to-do list for a day. "Ten? Only ten? What if I finish them all by 11:00 a.m.?"

"Then I want you to go home, rest, and be with your family," she responded.

I did take the medical leave and actually found that I slept a great deal of the time. Two weeks later, I did not feel picture-perfect but was certainly ready to get back to work. However, I still had the ten-item limit that I had promised Dr. Duncan.

The first day back was easy because I observed that while I had been away, things had continued without me (first lesson), and second, because I had yet to create my list for the rest of the week's days. When I was briefed on all the ministry demands that had piled up, I began to create a master list of all the action items—there were close to sixty. But I had given her my word I would limit my list to ten per day, so I began to go over the list and chose the critical and time-sensitive items first—there were still nineteen of these. So back over the list of nineteen I went, creating a list of my top ten for the following day.

The next morning I explained to my assistant that this was going to be my new regimen and that I was seeking her support. I arrived at the office just after 8:00 a.m. and focused on the items at hand. By 10:30 I had finished!

I thought it was strange to be heading home; however, I was still feeling tired and looked forward to having a nap in the afternoon. So I took a half hour to begin planning my next day. And so it went for the next several weeks. After a month back on the job, I was beginning to feel better, my productivity was excellent, and I was enjoying more time at home with Brenda and the boys.

What I learned in this valuable time is that although the Olympic period had taught me how to squeeze the maximum amount of time out of each day, I was not balanced in how I managed my time.

My two life friends, Bob Kuhn and David Bentall, and I attended a seminar hosted by Stephen Covey called "First Things First." The seminar began with a historical review of how people have approached time management in the last fifty years. I saw the system I had been trained on explained as a daily schedule, and as the speakers talked about its strengths, I could fully concur. Then they shared the shadow side of this system—that increasingly long to-do lists simply got shifted from one day to the next. They proposed a next generation of planners that was unique by looking at planning a week at a time. Taking a half hour or so each week to begin preparing for the following week was for me a novel idea at the time. However, there was a twist. They sought for us to build balance into our calendar by putting the most important things in our life into our calendar first rather than trying to squeeze them in around everything else.

God wants leaders to live life to the fullest and to live in a balanced manner. Life becomes more meaningful if we can expand our view beyond just our work hours and build in time for relationships, emotional and spiritual health, and leisure. It does require that we distribute our twenty-four hours a day and our seven days a week differently, but it also awakens us to what is missing in life.

If our lives as leaders are to have some sense of balance, we must have time for more than just work. Life should contain time for the following:

*Spiritual Well-Being and Nurture.* Christian leaders often starve themselves by always giving and never receiving spiritual food. Many leaders spend time in Scripture only when they are preparing a message. Prayer life can become nothing more than perfunctory statements made while working or over the meal table.

*Work.* Establish a reasonable number of hours necessary for the calling. Time expectations that leaders have in their heads are internal, not external. Leaders are often harder on themselves than others are. The two weeks I was away from the church and the days I went home by noon—no one even spoke to me about them. Why? Because the job requirements were still getting done.

*Relationships.* Our family, friends, and loved ones do not take away from us. In fact, they give nourishment to the lives of leaders. However, this category is often the first to be sacrificed when the pressure is on. I also include here long-distance relationships. It does not take very much time to write a note or pick up the phone and encourage friends from your past, colleagues in ministry in other regions, and friends of your parents you knew as a child. A television ad for a telephone company used to repeat the refrain, "Reach out and touch someone."

*Health.* Both emotional and physical health need to be tended by setting time aside intentionally for restoration. Holidays are very important, as are breaks in between heavy seasons of ministry. Physical exercise in the form of walking, workouts at the gym, or playing a sport can invigorate leaders as well as provide time for social interaction with others we may never meet any other way. Emotional health can also be achieved through a support therapist. Mine is Dr. Mitch Whitman. He assesses leaders for us at Arrow, but I first met him going for counseling support. You do not have to do it frequently, but allowing someone else into your life who can hold you accountable for emotional health and encourage you with new insights is a wonderful gift. There are particular times when a therapist or counselor should be sought out, such as when you are grieving, under great stress, or want perspective on a very heavy workload.

*Adventure and Crazy Fun.* Many leaders allow fun to slip out of their lives. They seldom embark on adventures like they did in earlier years. Road trips, camping, or even curiosity explorations to find out how something works slip away from their lives. I once went with our realtor friend Gregg Griffiths on a harbor pilot boat and boarded an ocean freighter from Brazil that was entering Vancouver harbor. We had to climb a rope ladder forty feet from the pilot boat to the deck of the freighter. We then watched as the pilot guided the captain to safe moorage. It was an amazing adventure that still makes me smile with a sense of restoration. Sometimes leaders begin to feel too sophisticated for adventures, practical jokes, and the like, but these activities can pump life back into their hardworking lives.

*Building into Others.* I believe that every Christian leader needs to be involved with what we call "normal people": those who are outside the church and do not know Jesus yet. This is the reason why we are in ministry. When you break it all down, our calling is to see others come into the kingdom of God through a saving knowledge of Jesus Christ. However, most leaders do not have time for this because they are too busy doing the "work of the Lord." Build into your neighbors, friends of your children, extended family—even those who service your home regularly. Brenda has established a great relationship with the family that owns the dry cleaners we visit. They are Muslim, and yet Brenda talks with them, laughs with them, encourages them, and prays for them. These are people whom she is building into. Whenever I go in to pick up shirts, they know who I am and call me Mr. Brenda! It makes me smile every time.

Many leaders I meet with are out of balance. I'm out of balance, and as my friend Bob jokes, "We are probably never in balance! We're like the pendulum on your grandfather clock—the only time we are in balance is for that moment as it ticks through the swing from one extreme to the other." It is important, however, to make an effort and avoid lives that look like this:

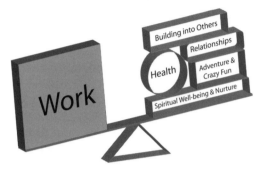

In mentoring leaders toward a more balanced life and use of their time, we can ask them questions such as: Where might your life be out of balance? What and who gets the majority of your time and attention? Are there areas of your life that you neglect or constantly put on hold? If this were your last week on earth, would you be pleased with how you have used your time? How much of your time is spent caring for others versus yourself? Are you involved in too many activities?

Leaders need to understand that when the Lord gave us twenty-four hours in a day, he gave us all the time we need to do what he is calling us to do. So if you as a leader are frazzled by busyness, it is time to examine closely the priorities of your life. If Jesus gives us enough time to do his will, then being overly busy is suspect.

> There is a time for everything,
> and a season for every activity under heaven.
>
> Ecclesiastes 3:1

Mentors can encourage leaders to take an afternoon alone in a quiet place and begin to reevaluate their priorities based on their calling and vision. Leaders must be good stewards of the time they have been given to lead, and far too many Christian leaders burn out due to poor time management and living unbalanced lives.

How leaders spend time is a revelation of their true priorities. Yet most leaders do not accurately track how their time is used. The only way you can understand time use is to keep a twenty-four-hour-a-day log for about three weeks. Record when you sleep, how many hours you spend eating, how long you spend on personal hygiene—everything. When recording work hours, keep track of exactly how those hours or minutes are used. How much time is spent on the phone, writing, meeting with staff, and preparing sermons? This is usually quite a revealing exercise, and it is helpful to go over the log with a mentor to gain perspective and talk about your stewardship of time.

Journaling is helpful in this process. Consider journaling answers to questions such as:

• In this season of life, what is most important to you?
• Where would you like to spend more of your time?
• If you could do anything and money was not a problem, what would you like to do?
• Are there specific areas that you recognize as needing more of your time and attention?
• Do you have dreams that have been in the back of your mind for a long time that you would like to explore? What are they?
• Are there items in your time log that you need to give less attention and time? Any that need more attention?

Stephen Covey in his "First Things First" approach taught that we should have a greater "yes" within us that allows us to say no to other wonderful opportunities. There are always going to be needs presented to leaders, and most of them are very worthy causes. However, we cannot respond to everything, therefore we need to create a yes list, and I suggest we write it out on cards that we can carry with us at all times.

Mentors can serve as a powerful encouragement to leaders by giving them permission to pursue these priorities toward a balanced life. I have even said to younger leaders, "I want to give you permission to reconstruct your life around those things that are most important to you." I also have presented leaders with scenarios such as this: "Let's pretend that next week you receive another invitation to speak at such and such a ministry conference. Practice with me how you are going to say no to this invitation" (understand that this was one of the areas they had identified as needing to give up in order to reorient their life). The rule of thumb is that leaders should say no to everything that is not on their yes list, unless God moves in them in a special way urging them to accept this as his will.

Let me add: many leaders who struggle in this area are quick to spiritualize such invitations as being from God—so the mentor's role is to pursue why the leader views everything in this way and why he spiritualizes it, thereby making it impossible to say no to anything.

## Hobbit House and Eric

When I was the community minister at First Baptist Vancouver, I had a recurring difficulty every morning for several weeks. My office was outside the church, above Hobbit House, an outreach center of the church so named long before the resurgence of *Lord of the Rings* on the big screen. Hobbit House offered English language training, international student ministry, weekend coffeehouse nights, and inexpensive meals served to those in need in the downtown community. It was a connecting place for people in need and has been a miraculous ministry for decades.

Eric was one of our regulars, and for several weeks I came to my office in the morning and found him asleep on the porch right outside my door. I would wake him up and help him get on his way for the day, which consumed about an hour of my time.

I was sharing this with Dr. Bruce Milne, then senior pastor, and he said something I have thought of for years since. He told me that sometimes it is okay to step over the Erics in life to get on with the work. He told me that often we are tempted to misuse time, with the evil one usually being behind it. That hour spent trying to assist the Erics in life perhaps was keeping me from something that was going to have a significant impact for the kingdom of God. He told me to keep in mind that there are other people who could care for Eric.

He was not saying that Eric was not important but rather that Eric was not solely my responsibility. It is helpful to point out that leaders can find other people to take care of needy people, and it is all right to pursue their yes list.

## Practical Planning

Each leader I meet has a different style, but if what God has set before us is really important, all leaders must put some time into planning. Realistically, I know I will not accomplish everything in my daily plans, but I find that I can sit down once a week to restate the important goals for the week ahead, and once a month to write out objectives.

What works best for the leader? Is it a summer planning marathon? Are monthly planning days better? I do encourage nightly reviews of what you accomplished that day and hope to accomplish the next. I encourage nothing too formal for the daily review so as to not get dragged back into the daily planning routine. Keep your eyes on the weeklong block.

## Annual Planning

Bobb Biehl coached Brenda and me on the importance of annual planning. If you want to have any chance of balancing life as a leader, you have to begin planning a year in advance. In between Christmas and New Year, we put substantial time into planning for the twelve months to come. The entire family is involved in the process, and it enables us to make sure that I am not traveling when it is important for Brenda or the boys to have me at home. For example, Jon wants to make sure I am here for the football championships; Jeremy may want me here for his band's concert; Jason for my help as he prepares to speak at a conference. Brenda and I also have traditions in our marriage such as our anniversary or our annual time each summer for coastal cruising and sailing with friends. By stopping to consider these important things annually, it gives us a fighting chance to live a somewhat balanced, though busy, life.

The change of the calendar year is an excellent time for us to plan for the next twelve months—personally, as a family, and organizationally. In our ministry we are also gathering as a core team to examine the "must do's" for the coming year and then setting objectives for each month. This gives shape and purpose to the coming year.

This is the time to take off your watch and pick up a compass—reidentifying your direction and those things that make up the best use of your hours, days, and weeks. As leaders we are usually driven by time and therefore try to control our effective use of each minute in the day. However, if we plan only our time rather than our priorities, we can suddenly find ourselves having completed our schedule of events yet completely unsatisfied because we have sacrificed the things that matter most.

Many leaders I relate to admit to not taking the time to do this kind of "compass" planning. Why is that? It seems easier for them to make an appointment with someone else than to book an appointment with themselves to revisit those things that are "best." Taking the time to do compass planning requires a mature sense of knowing who you are and assumes that you have some forward motion.

All leaders are caught in this battle between those things that are good and those things that are best. When we take the time to plan with a compass, we create an antidote for the "frantic" ruling our lives. As we lead out of the direction of the compass, we might make changes to our schedule out of a renewed sense of knowing what to do and what not to do.

There is also a dark side to this preoccupation with time and "the watch." I observe that leaders who like to control their time, money, and things also tend to try to control people. They express more concern about efficiency than calling, purpose, or relationships, which in the long run ends up being very ineffective and unsatisfying.

Remember, it's not about getting more things done—it is about getting the right things done.

## The Spiritual Side of Time Management

There are three primary areas of ministry to leaders concerning time.

First, fear is often at the center of leaders having trouble saying no. Christian leaders do not want to hurt anyone, and saying no can conjure up feelings of disappointment.

Second, fear may also be instilled in leaders by the thought that perhaps saying no to this opportunity is a mistake. Fear used in this way virtually paralyzes leaders, or throws them into a harried lifestyle that drains them of energy and causes them to lose focus. Leaders need to be reminded of Jesus's words about the coming of the Holy Spirit: "Peace I leave with you; my peace I give you. I do not give to you as the world gives. Do not let your hearts be troubled and do not be afraid" (John 14:27).

Third, leaders can also be tempted by pride, and this begins to corrupt their use of time. A common example is when a leader is really beginning to emerge, especially as a communicator, and invitations arrive to speak at various ministry events. Just the invitation alone begins to stroke the ego of the leader, and at the same time the evil one begins whispering in his ear, "Yeah, you are getting really popular. You are *the* one who can speak here. They had a really 'big name' speaking here last year."

A mentor can prayerfully work with the leader to discern God's desire from his own inner needs. As you pray together, review the yes list and accurately reflect on priorities with the leader. This may also be a time to reflect on inner needs that may have been pushed to the surface at this time.

## Budgeting Resources

Every vision requires resources—both financial and human. For leaders to implement their vision, they must have capabilities in the area of budgeting. However, many Christian organizations are led by leaders who have never had any formal training in this area and are often in need of help.

Churches usually have someone other than the leader assisting with the finances—and that is a good thing. I cannot tell you how many pastors I have met who do not have their personal finances in order, let alone can guide a church in this area. However, these same ministers often ensure that resources in the ministry are better attended to than those in their own homes.

I think many ministry leaders see the creation of a detailed budget as an annoyance rather than as a way to define their priorities for the coming year or period of time. I actually find it to be a spiritual experience every year I engage in the process.

As leaders, we need to take what God has given us in terms of our life history, our money, our time, our talents, our abilities, our opportunities, and use them in an effective way for the kingdom of God. We are to be stewards of all these for the sake of the kingdom.

We are also to be good stewards of the human resources that are under our care as leaders. So how do we assist a leader to develop a budgeting mind-set?

Aklilu Mulat, a CMA (Certified Management Accountant) who serves with me at Arrow, is an amazing leader. Born in Ethiopia, the son of a Christian leader in Africa, he was educated in Canada. Aklilu has managed to retain a unique perspective on the budgeting process. I have had the privilege of learning a great deal through his process of taking my ideas and visions and putting them into a spreadsheet that makes them fiscally understandable.

What is unique is that Aklilu is able to guide us as a ministry through this process while maintaining a mind-set that empowers rather than stifles vision. Our board comments frequently on the wonderful complementary gift mix we share. There have been times during board meetings when I excitedly shared a vision for a ministry extension in response to which the board (almost to a person) then cast a gaze toward Aklilu to have him explain how this could or could not work.

Now, in practice, we would not even be discussing it at the board level if there was not a financial model that made sense, or without a very strong calling from God for us to move forward on something and needing the board's direction in figuring out if this is indeed God's calling for us as a ministry.

Getting into someone's head and understanding how he thinks is not an easy task, so I asked Aklilu to reflect on what makes the budgeting process an empowering experience within ministries. Here is what he has to say:

> Understanding the place and purpose of budgeting is at the crux of effective organizational leadership and management. Often, ministries view budgets as constraints imposed by their respective boards, and their boards, in turn, use the budget as the only yardstick by which the performance of management is measured. Both treat budgets as stand-alone phenomena with little connection to the organization's mission. This results in a corporate culture that is focused on meeting the budgetary goals rather than the organization's mission.

Aklilu identifies five common misconceptions that lead to this incoherent approach to the planning and implementation of budgets. Ministries that have successful planning processes avoid most of these misconceptions in their operation.

Here are Aklilu Mulat's five common misconceptions of budgeting.

### Misconception 1: The Strategic and Tactical Plans Follow the Budget

It is often the case where the first step in the planning process undertaken by ministries is that of putting together the budget. This is the most common of the misconceptions, which leads ministries to engage in a budgeting process that is counterproductive. A classic instance of goal incongruity results when the long- and short-term operational plans of the organization do not dictate the budget.

The budget in this type of scenario is usually drafted based on the previous period (usually the previous year) by adding a subjective percentage. Sometimes the CEO sets an arbitrary budgetary goal based on purposes that have nothing to do with ministry objectives. This goal is often not reconciled with a coherent plan that would reflect the consumption of resources to generate the revenues required to deliver programs.

The outcome of such processes is that the budget ends up determining what the programs should look like. Those responsible for carrying out the ministry's programs often look to the finance office to see what they can and cannot do. In essence, the purposes or mission of the organization end up being driven by capricious decisions.

The resulting goal incongruity causes a reckless battle between organizational mission and budgetary objectives. Organizational effectiveness in meeting its goals and its stewardship in using its resources wisely, suffer a great deal.

### Misconception 2: Budgeting Is Solely the Finance Department's Function

Related to the first misconception, many ministries assign the function of budgeting to the finance department with limited interdepartmental dialogue. In essence, viewing budgeting as a stand-alone function causes the leadership to leave it up to the accountants to come up with the budget for the ministry. In the most extreme cases, the accountants are sent away to work on the budget and not allowed to come back until they have completed it. They are not to be interrupted as they complete this task. The budget process, hence, becomes a purely technical exercise carried out by the finance people.

In this situation, the budget often fails to consider what is happening with the various departments. It is usually based on the historical transactions of the ministry. The finance department is asked to prepare a budget based on some generic guideline such as "a 5 percent increase over last year" or "keep it the same as last year." However, strategic and operational moves planned by the various departments may not be considered in the budgeting process.

The second difficulty this would create is one of viewing the finance department as a menace that introduces unnecessary roadblocks in the path of progress for the ministry. For example, a department within a particular ministry had a vision to hire staff to expand an aspect of their work. The plan included incurring costs in the first couple of years but becoming self-funding and generating a surplus in years four and five. This plan received amazing support from the ministry's board. However, by the time the plan was approved, the budget, which did not include this department's plan, was already under implementation. This meant that a plan the board was very excited about had to be deferred for another year. Had the finance department been working along with the other departments as it was putting together the budget, this unnecessary disruption would not have occurred. Needless to say, the relationship between the particular department and the finance people was not helped by the outcome.

This can easily be avoided by making the budgeting process very inclusive. In fact, the finance department should coordinate and facilitate a budgeting process in which department heads are active participants. The finance department would help in creating a budget that takes into account other aspects of the planning process from all divisions.

Leaders should always remember that the budget planning process should be inclusive—not a function of the finance department only.

### Misconception 3: Budgeting Is an End in Itself

The natural outcome of misconceptions 1 and 2 is to consider the budget an end in itself. If a leader does not tie the budget to other plans nor coordinate across departments, the budget becomes an isolated phenomenon.

A typical example of this is when ministry leaders say, "We just completed putting together our budget. It is now time to start planning our operations." Another example is where the budgeting process is taken as a discipline carried out every year and, after approval, shelved somewhere, not to be referred to until the end of the year for purposes of reporting to the board. Furthermore, it is important for the ministry to be able to implement these programs within the budgetary framework. For these reasons, the budget has to be designed and used as a tool to help the ministry realize its mission. The budget is a custom-designed recipe that shows the resource requirement and allocation formula for efficient accomplishment of the ministry's mission.

The best way to accomplish this is to treat the budget as an integral part of the planning process from beginning to end. As such, the budget becomes not an isolated but an inclusive procedure, involving all departments and every step of the planning process. It is like a bridge that helps take the ministry from where it is today to where it could be in the future.

### Misconception 4: Budget Performance Analysis Is about the Budget Itself

Ministry leaders often assume that the periodic budget analysis reports, which compare actual results with budgets, are about the budget itself. In essence, they do not associate the budgetary variances with operational issues.

Ministries with sophisticated budgetary reporting systems would use various MIS (management information system) type reports that offer the leadership highly summarized indicative reports. These reports often select critical information from the budget and provide analysis of important variances. When these types of reporting methods are utilized, the process itself may lead to analysis of the budget in view of operational issues.

In many cases, however, if the ministry meets its budget, the operational variances are ignored. For instance, a ministry may set a given amount as its revenue target for the year. It may also identify certain sources that would total this revenue target as it sets its annual budget. At the end of the year, it may have met its total revenue goal. However, the sources it identified at the time the budget was set may not be the ones with which it ended up. Many budgetary performance reports would not show this important variance.

In this case, what the reports fail to measure is ministry effectiveness. The ministry set out to accomplish certain specific goals (that is, specific sources of revenue) but did not really accomplish them. The measurement tool (the budget variance report) fails to indicate that. This may be the case with expenditures as well. The ministry may be staying within its total budget but may not have accomplished its specific operational goals. For example, the annual program budget of a relief agency for a particular region may be one million dollars. This may have been based on providing food supplements for ten thousand individuals for the year. At the end of the year the ministry's budgetary performance report may show that it remained within budget (one million). However, the fact that it provided food supplements to only six thousand individuals is not indicated. An incorrect view of budgetary targets would lead some leaders to conclude that they have met their budgets when in fact they have not.

Budgets should help an organization measure its effectiveness. Failing to tie operational results with budgetary ones is not only an indication of poor planning but will also be detrimental to the ministry. It prevents a ministry from taking appropriate corrective measures because problems are not being identified by the performance report. It also leads to very poor decisions because the right things are not being measured. It may be an unusual occurrence that has led to a dip in income or an increase in expenses for the current year. Future planning has to take this into account. It may be that the assumed sources for revenue are based on historical factors that no longer apply. The fact that total revenue has been met does not mean these sources continue to be valid. The results of decisions based on an incorrect budget analysis report could be disastrous. The solution for ensuring that budgetary reports are used to measure organizational effectiveness is tying operational results with the budgetary results. In essence, including information about output in budgetary reports in various forms would accomplish this. Such things as budget and actual figures on the number of individuals who received food supplements, the number of full-time employees, and sources of funds alongside the budgetary figures provide information that is useful in determining ministry effectiveness.

### Misconception 5: Budgets Are Inflexible, Rigid Plans

In many ways, once the budget proposed by the management of a ministry has been approved by the governing body, it becomes the standard by which the organization must operate. Ministry leaders often feel that once the budget is approved, even if subsequent developments demonstrate that the budget was based on wrong premises, they have no choice but to live with it for the year. This view that the budget is somehow an inflexible, rigid plan is a misconception that would render a leader ineffective in guiding the ministry toward its mission.

Flexibility in the budgeting process should be built in right at the planning stage. Leaders often assume that this is a luxury in which they do not dare dream of indulging, when in fact their boards and their management team would welcome a measure of flexibility built into the budget.

Boards would like to see flexibility built into the budget especially when management presents a growth budget. In this case, the board would like to encourage growth but wants to ensure that certain conditions are met before they approve the budget. The most common of these conditions is that of the ministry meeting the increased revenue objectives. In this case, the board would give conditional approval of the budget. Hence, what would occur is that two budgets are approved—one in the event of accomplishing revenue objectives, and the other a reduced budget if management fails to meet its growth objectives.

This gives the board peace of mind that the ministry is not going to go out and spend money before securing the funds it has set out in its revenue goals. On the other hand, it offers management an ability to propose and receive approval for growth. It is a cautious approach to growth that offers comfort to the board while offering a level of conditional freedom to management.

The key to success in building flexibility within the budget is to accomplish it at an early stage. Management and the board should understand this clearly as the budget is being prepared and approved. For the leader, such an approach could be very useful at a time of ministry growth. Otherwise, the budget will become a cage that will not only stunt organizational growth but might contribute to its death.

In summary, the critical issues the leader of a ministry should understand about budgeting are related to integration. The leader must facilitate a process by which the budget is not isolated but is an integral part of planning—be it strategic or operational. In addition, the budget should be a function of all departments and its measurement should reflect their respective performances. Last but not least, the leader should view the budget as a flexible tool that must be designed in such a way as to help the ministry accomplish its mission.

## It Is Not Just a Piece of Paper

For several years I worked in our family business. It was in the interior design and home furnishings field. Emblazoned in my memory are my father's words: "It is not just a piece of paper!" He was usually referring to an order for a customer, and what he was instilling in me was that the paper represented people. We were to think of the paper in accordance with the people it represented. You would not normally set aside a person and leave him there for the day unattended to. So we were not to allow customer order paperwork to pile up or be treated flippantly.

Similarly, budgets are not just pieces of paper. They represent the ministry of the Lord that will reach out to serve people. There is a human side to budgeting. It is not just some business practice that we must do to comply with regulations or requirements.

Budgets affect every person working with you, and every person you minister to. Every program is fueled by the resources outlined in the budget. So getting it right is extremely important. Every budget line item is someone's sincere request, wrapped in our mission and tied with the person's hopes and dreams.

## Praying about the Budget

When mentoring leaders about financial matters, ask them if they have prayed about the budget.

Even within Christian organizations and ministries, the prayer of the finance department or committee can be absent from the process. I am not talking about token gestures of prayer but about being thirsty and hungering after the Lord's desires for the coming year. A prayerfully prepared budget is one in which every line item is committed to God's purposes and is not simply a repeat of last year's budget with an increase slightly above the cost of living.

### Twenty-five Dollars' Worth

Any leader who has pastored a congregation knows the kinds of issues and battles that can arise at church meetings over financial matters.

I smile as I think about a lunch meal at an Arrow seminar where six American pastors were gathered at a table, talking about their church finances. George was heard above the crowd, exclaiming in disbelief, "You mean as the pastor you do not know how much your people give?"

George comes from a denomination and culture where the pastor is aware of his congregation's giving—and where every member has an accountable relationship with the church to tithe 10 percent of his annual income.

He went on to tell a story about a church meeting where the budget was being discussed, and a woman was being very argumentative with the elders and the pastors about what she thought were expenses they could do without. George finally had enough of her verbal lashing toward his elder, and knowing her personal giving history, he stood and said, "Mrs. Smith, sit down. You have used up your twenty-five dollars' worth."

Laughter burst forth from all listening—myself included. Admittedly, some of it was nervous laughter as we wondered if it was right for him to know such details, yet those of us from other church tribes where this is not practiced sometimes wish we had access to that kind of information to use in such a time as he described.

Leaders during the budget preparation and presentation months may face strong opposition and attack. Most mentors can help leaders prior to the budget preparation months by seeing that the leader is prepared. How can a leader prepare?

Develop budgeting skills. There are community continuing education courses available for leaders on budgeting and fund accounting. Perhaps an introductory accounting course is appropriate.

Begin an intentional prayer process for the budget preparation. Try to include as many people as possible and use it as a time to encourage staff and congregation to seek God's vision for the new budget.

Ensure that the household budget is in good shape. I believe that God desires to see our personal finances in good order prior to blessing the ministries we lead.

Remember the "people aspect" of budget planning. If the leader suspects there will be difficulty with a particular person over the budget, then pray specifically for that individual. You know the ones I mean. It is not hard to figure out whom, since the person has caused difficulties in the past at annual meetings. Well, instead of dreading the interaction, or simply brushing the person off as a nuisance, I encourage leaders to meet with the person well in advance of the budget preparation. Identify that you are aware that the budget is something that is very important to the person and seek his input as you begin to undertake the budget process. Listen to the person, and then prior to presenting the budget at the meeting, let the person know where everything settled out. Remember, people support what they help to create.

### Revenue versus Expenses

Early in my ministry life as a youth pastor, I became adept at figuring out an event budget that would break even or be at very little cost. I did this by estimating how much the families of the youth in the group could afford for a special event and then making absolutely sure that my expenses were below that by cutting costs as necessary. Little did I know that this would begin a pattern in my life that would not be helpful later in ministry.

One meeting I was leading on the budget for Insight for Living was a breakthrough moment for me. Steve Boehmer, a business leader from Toronto and member of the Insight for Living Ministries board, said to me, "Carson, we have a revenue problem, not an issue with expenses. We need to concentrate on the revenue side of the budget."

What a concept! Focus on revenue and keep your expenses under control. I had become quite adept at watching and managing expenses but had little or no training in building the revenue side of the budget.

Over the years I have learned that one of the attributes of a leader is the ability to raise the financial resources necessary for the ministry to continue. Most of us in Christian ministry did not start down this road thinking, "Yahoo! I get to be a fund-raiser!" But speak to any pastor who has been through a building campaign, or self-supported missionaries from ministries such as Campus Crusade for Christ or Youth for Christ, and you will hear stories of how much of their time has to be put into raising the resources to make the ministry vision possible.

One time I watched the color drain from a young leader's face while he was telling me all about the new regional role he had just been promoted to. The face lost its color because I had pointed out that he was also now responsible for raising the support for the entire ministry. His face told the story—one I have experienced again and again. Christian leaders want to avoid having to increase the revenue line on the budget. They often just want to "do ministry" and not spend time fund-raising.

This phenomenon manifests itself in the local church through pastors seldom talking about money in the church. It is defensively argued that it will "scare people off," and that you do not want them to have this experience in church.

I have heard it said that the unchurched think the church is only interested in money. In actual fact, their concern about the church asking for money is quite far down the list of reasons for not being connected with a local church. Relevance, children's programs (or the lack thereof), commitment to the community, and a nonwelcoming atmosphere are bigger issues than concern about being asked for money.

When I talk to "normal" people attending church, I've had many actually ask me about how the church is funded. "Where does the money come from to pay for all the programs and pastors?" That is a legitimate question deserving accurate information—and I think it is helpful to do that in an unapologetic manner from the front of the church.

Money is spoken about in the Bible more than most other subjects—yet we avoid discussing it publicly. What is that all about? Perhaps our fear of speaking about money is a ploy of the evil one to underresource the Lord's work and therefore slow the growth of the kingdom here on earth.

## A Lunchtime Conversation

While several Arrow leaders were enjoying lunch at a round table overlooking the beautiful Pacific Ocean at Barnabas Family Ministries conference center, the discussion turned to finance and ministry. The observation was made that Christian leaders get bewildered by the conflicting messages of dissimilar approaches such as John Maxwell's stewardship ministry approach to raising money for capital campaigns and the testimonies of ministry saints and missionaries like George Müeller who "never asked anyone for money, and never lacked for anything."

Kirk Goodman, a leader from Guelph, Ontario, started with, "I'm not happy with thinking we would be building doctrine around either of those experiences. How we often approach raising money for our ministry is to look at how other people have done it and then we try to implement that as opposed to the approach that says, 'What does God want us to do?'"

Jerry Clonch, a pastor from Lancaster, Pennsylvania, agreed. "My foundation is a dependence upon God, but I think there comes a time when God wants to partner with me to raise resources. I have been in church situations when I would pray and say, 'God, I just need to know that you are taking care of us.' We moved to Calgary and didn't have money to buy a house, and without asking, the down payment arrived from two complete strangers. We didn't have to ask for a cent; we just prayed, 'God, please provide.'

"But there did come a time when God was saying to me, 'Jerry, you have got to develop your skills to be able to effectively train in stewardship to share the vision.' This is the partnership I am describing. God wanted to show me there was another way he could provide."

A pastor from the Stony Plain Alliance Church, Graham English, was listening to the conversation through the ears of a local church pastor. Graham said, "We need to continue to teach people about stewardship, and that is the responsibility of the teaching pastor or senior pastor. We also need to continually teach people about generosity and work that into our development of people as disciples so that it just becomes a part of the culture of the church." Graham added that he felt it was important for the church to give people the opportunity to give.

Graham's emphasis on giving people an opportunity to give even within the church setting reminded me of a conversation with a financial supporter of our ministry who told me that his church seldom gave its members the opportunity to give beyond their tithe. "You see, Carson, we have the spiritual gift of giving, and if a pastor does not ask us to give, then you are denying me (and others) the opportunity to exercise our spiritual gift."

As I heard his words my mind went to Romans 12:6–8, and I prayed seeking God's forgiveness. I realized that in my pastoral ministry I had been guilty of not allowing people to exercise their gift of giving while I had made great efforts to see that all other types of gifts had expression in the church. Here is what Paul wrote to the Romans: "We have different gifts, according to the grace given us. If a man's gift is prophesying, let him use it in proportion to his faith. If it is serving, let him serve; if it is teaching, let him teach; if it is encouraging, let him encourage; if it is contributing to the needs of others, let him give generously; if it is leadership, let him govern diligently; if it is showing mercy, let him do it cheerfully" (Rom. 12:6–8).

> As a mentor you can provide a safe environment for the leader to discuss theology, fears, and strategies for resourcing ministry.

Leaders need to work through their theology and establish a level of comfort regarding the importance of gathering financial resources to fuel the ministry of the kingdom of God.

## Leaders Also Need to Be Taught
## How to Teach about Giving

Graham English agrees. "I believe that people really want to give but they need to be taught how to give. I really see it as a part of our teaching and a part of our ongoing process of making disciples. Rather than bringing in a company to do special fund-raising drives, I believe that teaching is an effective way to raise support. I preach in series throughout the year, and I consistently do a series once a year on stewardship and then raise the topic again throughout the year in various passages in other series. We have seen giving increase over the past couple of years, and it has been through teaching on a consistent basis."

Gary Klassen, a leader with World Vision Canada, provides another perspective on how we approach finances as leaders. He says, "I think sometimes we enter the discussion about finances with a poverty mind-set. It is a scarcity model that is driving the discussion, so it comes across as though you 'should' be doing this, as opposed to 'we get to' do this. This change of model can transform the discussion around giving. People also find finances such a personal topic, 'How can you tell me how to spend my money?' It is like an idol for them."

# Measuring People and Outcomes

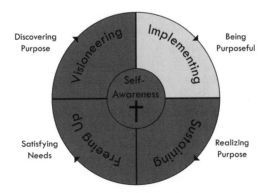

For every ten leaders I encounter who know how to budget financially for ministry, I meet forty who are unable to manage the budgeting of human resources properly. Unfortunately, most leaders learn about this the hard way.

## George

Over the years I have been greatly aided in my leadership by working with various executive assistants. One assistant was named George. Well, that was not her real name. It was Val. But to me she was George.

One day I was working at my desk on a project and I walked out to Val's desk only to find it empty. Something was pressing on my mind, and I tracked her down in Aklilu's office, where the two of them were working on something. I walked right in like a man on a mission—which I was.

"George, can you tell me where I might find the other part of this report?" I asked.

Val looked at me with a quizzical expression. "Did you just call me George?"

"No."

"Yes, you did," she insisted.

"No, I'm sure I didn't," I persisted, firmly believing that I had done no such thing.

"Yes, you did," Aklilu said, laughing like an older brother getting a younger brother in trouble. "You called her George!"

I stared at Aklilu, perplexed and feeling a bit betrayed by the brotherhood. Then I gazed back at Val, who continued, "You looked me right in the eye and called me George. I am so not a George!"

Well, that part was true; she did not look at all like any George I have ever known. Still without my answer, I retreated to my office with the two of them laughing at my mistake.

Later that afternoon I received an email from Val, and as I read to the end of it, I smiled. She had signed it . . . George! That did it; she became George from that moment on.

## Losing George

George and I had worked together for three years and had just reached our stride together as leader and assistant. Together we had done some speaking to Arrow leaders about the role of an assistant to a leader. Many other ministries and offices would come to us asking about how we functioned and worked so efficiently together. So imagine how hard it was to lose George, but that eventually happened.

Arrow had been going through a very difficult time. Finances were at a critical stage, and we had to eventually lay off half of our staff. George stayed with us and doubled her efforts, taking on tasks that were outside of her normal portfolio. I knew the ministry would eventually come out the other side of this and that it was going to be a taxing time for us all.

While I was watching the workload George was carrying at the office, I failed to factor in the load she was carrying at home. Val was the primary caregiver for her husband, who was on disability at home; she was a new grandmother and under a great deal of stress both at home and now at the office.

Eventually her doctor recommended that she reduce stress, and that meant making a decision about work. She ended up accepting a receptionist position with significantly less responsibility at an accounting firm nearby. Her loss to our team was a significant one, and it set me back several months in productivity. However, I understood her situation and wanted her health restored—even at Arrow's loss.

One of the lessons I learned through George's departure is the importance of leaders budgeting human resources and the importance of focusing on maintaining your staff team.

Human resources have often been an area of lesser concern among leaders. Leaders overlook it because their ministry is often small and either does not have employees or thinks it has too few "workers" to deal with specific needs.

The management of human resources is another discipline leaders need to be concerned with. Human resource management is like accounting for the "human currency" aspects of our organizations. Think about your staff employees as the intellectual capital that helps your ministry function effectively. You need people as much or more than financial resources.

However, human resource management is a new concept for many ministries. Every day it seems like the labor laws are being adjusted, so much so that a leader of even a small ministry cannot afford to be without employee policies and procedures documented and in force. As Christians, we should be leading the way in employee treatment through policy and practice.

A human resources orientation is as important to a ministry as its ministry service orientation. Most churches or ministries are focused on taking care of people or reaching out to those outside of the organization, whereas human resource management is the ministry that is directed inward. It shows we value our people as something more than just laborers.

## Inexpensive Employee Benefits

To retain your team, you will need to provide them with benefits and perks. Otherwise over time you will lose them to higher-paying jobs or to work environments where there is greater flexibility. Benefits are expensive, so the creative leader will offer highly perceived value to employees while keeping costs in line. Here are potential rewards you can offer to your employees that are inexpensive.

- Work from home
- Flexible hours

- Training
- Child-care provisions
- Floating holidays
- Being understanding about family roles
- Company outings or luncheons
- Recognition in front of peers
- Days off

### Sailboat Batteries

Our sailboat has two banks of batteries. One bank is used for starting the motor and the other provides house power—the lights and pumps within the boat itself. On the electrical panel is a sensitive meter that indicates whether the batteries are discharging or charging. If I were to leave the boat with the battery switch and an interior light on, the discharge would eventually run the batteries down and they would need to be charged.

Dr. James Postlewaite is a friend and colleague who is very gifted in the area of team ministry. We have ministered together both in church ministry and at Arrow. Jim talks about the importance of a staff team having a mixture of gainers and drainers in their work portfolios. He describes the need for the meter to not always be indicating a discharge. No matter what our role is, some aspects of the job are going to be draining. These are appropriately called drainers. If there are a disproportionate number of drainers, then the battery has a constant discharge and eventually we lose all energy for the work and mission and often become angry in the process. Here is how Jim describes it:

### "Gainers and Drainers," by James Postlewaite, D.Ed.

In my years of experience in working with ministry staffs and teams, I have often found discussing "gainers and drainers" with staff/team members a helpful developmental tool. By "gainers and drainers" I am referring to the aspects of a ministry position, which either give a leader encouragement or create stress of various degrees. A leader will often be able to handle the "drainers" of a ministry position if they are outnumbered by the "gainers" or joys of the work. If the "drainers" become too dominant, the leader will probably experience greater frustration in the work or ministry, which can lead to bitterness, ministry fatigue, and may even lead to burnout.

In a team setting I will often lead a discussion of gainers and drainers in the context of an assessment tool such as the MBTI (Myers-Briggs Type Indicator), which creates an atmosphere for discussing differences. As the team discussion takes place, it becomes obvious that team members have different gainers and drainers. This discovery creates (1) a basis for understanding each other's similarities and differences, and (2) an opportunity for team building, which may include the actual exchanging of some job functions. One person's drainer may be another person's gainer and vice versa. Thus, the team becomes strengthened through both understanding and team job sharing.

In an individual setting, I will often use the gainer-drainer discussion to assist a person in deciding about their acceptance of a ministry leadership role or change in a role. When investigating drainers it can often help to investigate whether the drainer can be reduced or changed through further education or training. For example, it may be difficult to help a drainer if it involves working with people, but training may help the person whose drainer is working with computers if the drainer is really caused by a lack of knowledge of computer use.

The gainers-drainers tool can be an easy and positive way to assist both individuals and teams in understanding and dealing with various ministry stresses.

So you can see that if team members have a mixture of gainers and drainers, the gainers can serve much like a trickle charge for my battery on the sailboat—restoring energy and giving satisfaction.

## Inspiration in the Workplace

We need people, resources, and events that will inspire you, lift you to a higher standard, and motivate you.

When you come into the office and love the people you are working with, it gives you a great sense of lift. Leaders need to watch for this when hiring. Does the individual have the personality and attitude that will lift the entire organization? Does the person have a sense of humor? Is the candidate bright and inspiring with thoughts and ideas?

If you are well equipped with the resources you need to carry out the mission, you are also encouraged. I remember a story told to me by Dr. Gary Nelson, general secretary of Canadian Baptist Ministries, of a time when he was being called to pastor a church, and as he was being toured through the building, they showed him a room with a large duplicating machine with a crank handle on the side.

"What is that?" Gary asked.

"Oh, that is the machine you will use to duplicate the church bulletin," the elder replied.

I cannot remember the exact response that Gary had, but I can picture what his face may have revealed as he communicated that this piece of equipment was going to have to go. He didn't even know how to use it, as this was the age of photocopiers.

So many ministries require their people to limp along with poor equipment and resources. These staffs don't benefit from the inspiration gained from having efficient tools to work with.

When you hold a public event that has tremendous impact for the ministry and you are able to see lives changed—this motivates your people to keep going. Leaders should plan to have each of their team members get close to the front lines of the relationships involved with the mission. There is nothing more inspiring than seeing the fruits of your labor, especially when you have a support role.

While leading Insight for Living Ministries, I remember the joy and "lift" provided by a special supper for the entire staff and their spouses while Chuck Swindoll was in town. Being able to sit with Chuck and listen to him tell stories of God at work and share how important their contribution was to the ministry was very meaningful. Even greater was the inspiration provided by attendance at one of the celebration events, where they met thousands of listeners to the radio broadcast and heard Chuck preach in person. They returned to the office the following week with a new spring in their step.

## Nourishment from God's Word

Christian leaders ironically often neglect the power and inspiration of God's Word. Staff members can be encouraged to be in the Word on a daily basis. Leaders themselves can model this by referencing Scripture that they are reading in their conversations with the staff.

Use the Bible during your team times together. Help to show them the connection between the mission of the organization or church and the Word of God. We each need the daily strength that reading the Bible brings.

There are many email devotionals as well as Scripture-reading guides available. Leaders can find one that is appropriate for the ministry they serve and encourage the staff to use the same materials so as to create a language and focus for the entire team. This may be difficult, given the wide variety of styles people prefer, but your team might be willing to participate if it is a short Scripture per day and a paragraph thought.

## Spiritual Side of Budgeting

The tactics used by the evil one during the budgeting process usually follow one of two routes. First, the evil one might discourage the leader, prompting him to worry about where the funds are going to come from or using the realities of finance to throw cold water on dreams and vision.

I have also seen the evil one distract leaders: the leader allows the dreaming process to get out of hand and is no longer bound by any practical parameters.

Remember to be prayerful during this process and refuse to engage in things that are meaningless. Determine which activities really count, and then work on a way to resource them.

## Evaluating Progress

As we continue around the mentoring matrix and examine the phase of implementing the vision, a leader may stumble into the new area of evaluating progress. It emerges by simply asking the question, "How am I able to evaluate the progress I'm making toward the vision?"

If as a leader you have determined your personal goals and those of your organization, then you need to manage these goals well. You cannot manage what you don't measure. I might carry it a step further and say that if you don't measure, you don't really care.

I come across ministry after ministry that has no means of accurately measuring its progress toward its mission. This is especially true of ministries that have been around for a while. Church planters are much more careful about progress measurement because it is often a "live or die" situation.

So why do many Christian leaders fail to have a means for measuring their progress? Is it that they don't care? No, I don't think that's the case. I have come to see that many leaders don't know how to measure, or don't make time for it.

Most leaders have a love-hate relationship with evaluation and measurement. One part of them wants to know if they are making progress toward their goal. The other part is fearful of finding out the truth. Most ministry leaders are so busy that they can retreat into a highly protected, make-believe world. They are constantly surrounded by their own people, who get caught up in wanting to maintain the ignorance about how they're really doing.

When Dr. Roy Bell was first mentoring me in church ministry, he said to me, "Let's not believe our own press releases." Since those years I've come into contact with dozens and dozens of ministries that do just that. Their only way of evaluating how they're doing comes from the press releases—the church newsletters, church announcements, and full-color brochures they themselves are producing. Without some way of accurately grounding our organizations and ourselves to reality, leaders are left with no means of knowing if they are being good stewards of their time or their resources.

Lack of accurate feedback and evaluation can also lead to extremely stressful situations.

## Dashboard Report

When we drive a car, there is a dashboard of instruments that gives us a continuous readout of how the car is doing. Usually the largest instrument is the speedometer, which tells us how fast we're going. Beside it is the fuel gauge, with an F for full and an E for empty, along with a red zone just prior to the E that reminds us to fill up with gas. Then there are the instrument lights, such as the dreaded oil light.

Leaders often recognize that there is a significant gap between their strategy or plan and their ability to execute it. Many leaders try to address the problem without having the right information in front of them. The creation of a tool such as a dashboard report can give leaders the insight they need to address the strategic plans and modify them if needed to obtain the desired results.

While dashboard reports give accurate information in a quick, easy-to-read format, they do not indicate the cause-and-effect linkages between what they are measuring and the daily activities of those working for the ministry in striving to achieve those measurements. I mention this only as a caveat to the temptation some leaders can have to feel that because they have a dashboard report, everything will succeed.

An effective leadership report for a ministry organization should correctly identify the key performance drivers, both financial and nonfinancial; you need to measure in order to grasp an overview of the organization's ministry performance.

A dashboard report for a local church might include such key performance measurements as:

Attendance of adults at worship services

Attendance of children at weekend church services

Number of people attending the small groups of the church

Tithes and offerings on a weekly, quarterly, and year-to-date basis

Number of missionaries supported by the church

Number of junior and senior high youth being ministered to by the church

Number of baptisms

Number of people who have formally entered into the membership of the church

Total population of the parish or community where the church is
located

Number of children attending Sunday school or being ministered to
by the church on a weekend

Now I know that any pastoral leader reading this will inwardly be
arguing that the church is much more than what is captured in this measurable list. I totally understand and agree. However, these are some of
the things that can be measured that do provide insight into the overall
health of the church as an organization.

The Evangelical Free Church has established a survey they use to examine their churches for overall health.[1] The list is inclusive of some of
the softer but critically important measures of ministry. Here are some
specific areas included in their survey that serve as examples of what can
be measured within churches. With the addition of some scriptural references, this resembles a missional statement for a local church.

## Centrality of God's Word

"All Scripture is God-breathed and is useful . . . so that the man of God
may be thoroughly equipped for every good work." (2 Tim. 3:16–17)

- The Bible is the focal point of our church's decision-making, teaching, and preaching.
- We do not simply teach and preach about the Bible, we strive for
  ongoing life transformation.
- Our people are equipped and growing in their ability to use the Bible
  for themselves.

## Passionate Spirituality

"Be filled with the Spirit . . . be strong in the Lord and in His mighty
power . . ." "Put on the full armor of God . . . And pray in the Spirit on
all occasions with all kinds of prayers and requests . . ." (Eph. 5:18–21;
6:10–18)

- Our congregation emphasizes in practical ways the presence and power
  of the Holy Spirit to enable us to live transformed, obedient lives.
- Prayer in our church reflects a deep dependence on God.
- In every area of church life, we seek to experience God and follow
  him according to his Word.

### Fruitful Evangelism

"The Son of Man came to seek and to save what was lost." (Luke 9:10)

- We are driven to reach our neighbors with the gospel of Christ.
- The budgets, programs, and leaders of our church reflect a high commitment to outreach and evangelism, both locally and worldwide.
- We expect significant conversion growth in our church.

### High-Impact Worship

"Shout for joy . . . Worship the Lord . . . Enter His gates with thanksgiving . . ." (Ps. 100)

- Inspiring worship that glorifies God and engages the heart, mind, and emotions of people with God is a hallmark of our public worship.
- We are committed to meeting the worship needs of the various generations attending our church.
- Our worship is characterized by a spirit of joy.

### Mission and Vision Driven

"Therefore go . . ." (Matt. 28:19–20)

- Our congregation has a clear sense of God's mission and a compelling vision for the future.
- We regularly and systematically measure all areas of our church's effectiveness—leadership, ministries, and organizational structure—based on our mission and vision.
- We are willing to change and take risks to fulfill our God-given mission.

### Leadership Development

"Entrust to reliable men . . ." (2 Tim. 2:2; 1 Tim. 3:1–13; 1 Peter 5:1–11)

- We are committed to intentional leadership development and the exercise of the leadership gifts.

- We desire that trained, godly individuals who are spiritually mature lead our congregation.
- We regularly see mature leaders deployed in full-time vocational ministry.

## Church Planting

". . . in Jerusalem, and in all Judea and Samaria, and to the ends of the earth." (Acts 1:8; Acts 13–28)

- Church planting is one of our core values as a congregation.
- We have a measurable commitment to "reproduction" as a church.
- We have a vision for the planting of churches in our community, district, and the world.

## Financial Stewardship

"Command . . . neither to be arrogant nor to put their hope in wealth . . . but to put their hope in God . . . Command them to do good . . . and to be generous and willing to share . . ." (1 Tim. 6:17–19)

- Faithful stewardship of all our resources—including possessions and money—is systematically modeled and taught in our church in biblical, practical ways.
- People in our congregation are challenged to make a sacrificial investment in eternity through regular and special financial gifts.
- A mark of discipleship in our church is the willingness to be generous and share.

## Intentional Disciple Making

"Therefore go and make disciples . . ." (Matt. 28:19–20)

- Our church measures its disciple-making effectiveness by the Great Commission and the Great Commandment.
- We have a clear picture of the disciple-making process—from new life to spiritual maturity—that is built into the fabric of our church.
- We have a commitment to see each member of our congregation using their spiritual gift(s) in the context of the church.

*Loving Relationships*

"By this all men will know that you are My disciples, if you love one another." (John 13:35)

- We know our neighbors and we know how to love them.
- Our church helps people grow in their ability to love and connect with one another.
- As a congregation, we model and provide a meaningful experience of "community"—especially through small groups.

You can see how a church functioning with this set of statements could give itself some kind of rating on how it is doing in each of the areas. A different set of measurements, from Natural Church Development, also allows church ministries to get a read on how they are doing and areas where they will need attention if they are to grow in impact.[2]

# Regular Reviews

Among Christian leaders I have worked with over the years, probably the least understood aspect of evaluation is performance appraisals of staff and key volunteers. Yes, some larger organizations do fill out a form annually that they call a review. However, many routinely fill them out to fulfill some kind of organizational need or perhaps to justify an increase in salary. Most leaders find this to be an unwanted task on their to-do list. Yet I would argue that done well, performance appraisals of key people actually embody the very elements of disciple making and spurring one another on to good works.

As Christian leaders we should see performance appraisal times as an opportunity for developing people. My personal experience with them when I was in pastoral ministry was "hit-and-miss." Often they were used as times for the board, or governing body, to correct an employee for something they didn't like. At its very best, the performance appraisal is an opportunity to get people together and talk about work-related issues with the goal of developing the skills necessary to improve.

No matter how large the organization, Christian leaders need to find a way to evaluate their employees and their key volunteers in a fair manner.

We have just begun a new performance appraisal process at Arrow. As Aklilu Mulat and I were developing this for our team here, we considered these important issues:

We believe that everyone wants feedback on how he is doing. It is important for all staff and volunteers to know and hear from those they look up to that their participation on the team is acceptable, that their work behavior is okay, and that they are a contributing part of the ministry. We believe that even if it is not okay, people still want to hear what the standards of acceptability are so that they can work toward a greater contribution in the future.

People are actually accustomed to having to measure up to standards. If we have done any schooling at all, we are familiar with report cards and final exams. We believe that in ministry people want this feedback also, and too frequently it is avoided.

Appraisal is a method of being able to distinguish between the high achievers and those who are ordinary. We want to reward outstanding work, and without some means of appraising performance, there is no clear way for us to know when that has been achieved.

Without evaluation, ministries can function with little or no communication. Members of the team do not know where they stand with the senior leader or with the board, and over time they begin to "hide out." This pattern of behavior as an organization reduces its ability to be effective and actually lowers the results in ministry productivity.

Arrow is in the ministry of developing leaders. One of the most important jobs we can have with our staff is helping to develop them. In the same way that we measure the performance and growth of the leaders we are working with, we want to provide our staff with regular sessions of evaluation of service/work. By pausing to have a performance appraisal, we are able to provide a summary of these activities and establish patterns for growth in the next period.

We did not want the appraisal form or tool to confine people in boxes. We are a very fluid organization, and on the form we use, we provide several blank areas where we ask the employee to write in longhand.

Before we began the appraisal process, we agreed that the top rating, or "excellent," would mean there is no room for improvement. Christian leaders frequently overrate employees to avoid dealing with the realities or causing them to feel hurt.

If within Christian ministries we were more serious about the development of people as an ongoing process, we would hardly need a formal appraisal time. However, in the business of ministries, many leaders simply won't do anything unless it is a required part of the organizational structure. Encouraging leaders to have a formal appraisal process helps turn them into people developers. The process also assures a point of communication. We have both the supervisor and the employee sign the form after the performance appraisal, and this symbolically shows a hearing of each other. Appraisal times are also important because they align an organization or ministry with its vision and goals. They also treat all the team members in the same manner.

### Tips on Evaluating Team Members

When mentoring a leader on evaluating team members, I find that the following guidelines are very helpful in setting the parameters for this to be a very effective and meaningful contribution to the leader's building of a team.

Do not be satisfied with simply an annual review. Try to meet with your staff team often, keeping in touch with them and talking about their area of ministry. If we do this effectively, the annual review becomes simply a continuation of the discussion that has been taking place throughout the year. There should be absolutely no surprises for the team member.

Make sure you schedule ample evaluation time. You may find that what you thought you could do in thirty minutes takes sixty because of the excellent level of dialogue and conversation that comes from the review meeting. Also, ensure that your time is exclusively your team member's by turning off cell phones and two-way pagers.

Keep yourself in a position to pastor and care for the individual, especially when the feedback is negative. If the team member is not able to meet the standards of the job, then the leader needs to make a decision. Do you retain the person, believing the person can change his behavior—or release the person to move on to what God may be calling him to do and has uniquely gifted him to undertake? Leaders need to understand that it is possible to leave people feeling good about the negative feedback they have received as long as they feel you care for them. We owe them a careful explanation of their performance, correctly administered, and accompanied by lots of love.

A significant point of growth for all leaders occurs when an appraisal becomes a two-way conversation. Try asking the team member how he perceives you and how your relationship could improve. Ask how you can help the team member achieve his goals. If you are able to create an open enough environment to listen and have a meaningful conversation with most of your employees, your people will grow, you will grow, and you will have taken on the trait of a great leader.

Prior to the review meeting, ask yourself, "What is the desired outcome for this team member?" At the time of the meeting communicate these expectations thoughtfully, and then regularly remind the team member of them throughout the year. This precludes misunderstanding as you work together.

Guard yourself from the temptation to rate people very highly. This often emerges from our desire for people to like us, and giving people high ratings does not in any way assist the team in growing. Keep the actual performance criteria limited to team members' work accomplishments and contribution to the team.

As a Christian leader working with those in ministries, take the opportunity to pray with your team members at the end of the review and even ask questions about their spiritual walk with the Lord at that time.

### Introducing Evaluation and Celebration to Ministries

In the beginning, there is an understandable degree of discomfort to the evaluation of ministry. Boards can find it difficult to sit down with a senior pastor and tell it like it is. The lead pastor or organizational leader—while understanding it's a wonderful way to develop people—feels uneasy about meeting with the staff team. Part of this is simply the Christian culture. In North America there is a very strong desire to make everything seem "nice." Not only do I believe this is unhealthy, but I believe it has also frightened off some of the stronger leaders from involvement in the church and weakened the fiber of the church considerably. Christian leaders need to understand that they will have times in their leadership when maintaining harmonious human relations is simply not possible. Trying to be "nice" leaves people not really knowing where they stand. Not confronting or giving feedback to those we work with in ministry allows them to keep making the same mistakes—something that is not helpful to them or the ministry.

Ironically, Christian ministries are also very poor at celebrating good performance. When I was leading Insight for Living in Canada, a young team member named Mike worked in the warehouse and distribution area. One day he appeared in my office to talk about an idea he had. As he worked at packaging and shipping resources across the country, he had begun to envision a new way of organizing the warehouse to make it more efficient.

I walked with him down to the warehouse where he shared with me a plan of moving the shelving to a different orientation and storing the product in a more efficient manner.

To be honest, I would never have generated that idea. Mike worked with these materials all the time, and because he felt like a member of the team, and able to contribute ideas, the ministry benefited greatly. We were able to store more of our most popular biblical resources, which decreased our shipping costs. The new design of the warehouse also enabled us to speed up our service to people, providing a twenty-four-hour return on most orders.

Within two weeks the warehouse was converted, and at a subsequent staff meeting I presented Mike with a "WOW" award. I think it was something as simple as a T-shirt, but it sent a strong signal throughout the team as we celebrated this new accomplishment. All leaders should take the time to celebrate more, giving credit to their staff and volunteers liberally.

Prior to initiating evaluation within Christian ministries, it is a good idea to talk about it with your team. The leader has the opportunity to set the tone by letting the team know the following in advance:

- This is really about talking with each other—not at each other. We want to listen to each other so that we can both grow and have a clear understanding of expectations.
- It is all about being more effective in our ministry.
- We are all part of the same team and we need to work together.
- Performance reviews are not punishment. We are going to have a straight discussion, but that does not mean hurting or putting anyone down.
- We are not perfect and this will probably not be a perfect process, but we really want to improve communications, see how we are doing today, and see what we can do better as we move into the future.

## The Spiritual Side of Evaluation

Spiritually and psychologically, being evaluated can rattle people. The evil one often takes advantage of this by instilling fear and self-doubt even among very capable people. I know of a Christian worker who actually would resign from a ministry and move on rather than be evaluated.

Evaluation within the context of Christian ministry can force individuals to face the enemy within. Done well, it gives each of us an indication of where "self" has a strong hold on us. These are strongholds that prevent our spiritual progress, and it is not uncommon through a time of evaluation to learn of areas of deep-seated concern. The stronghold may be a person from our past, or a bad experience, a place or situation, a predicament, a problem that hinders us or even holds us in its grip as it seeks to destroy our potential for serving Christ.

The ministry side of evaluation is helping leaders face the enemy within. In 2 Corinthians Paul says, "The weapons we fight with are not the weapons of the world. On the contrary, they have divine power to demolish strongholds. We demolish arguments and every pretension that sets itself up against the knowledge of God, and we take captive every thought to make it obedient to Christ" (2 Cor. 10:4–5).

Paul reminds us that the enemy does lurk and prowl around within our own mind and hearts.

Regarding the Christian worker I mentioned who would leave prior to any evaluation, I believe that kind of behavior is not biblical. It's not right for Christians to run away from the problems of life when the love and power of Jesus is waiting to heal them. The irony is that we cannot run away from ourselves. For wherever we go, "self" is there with us. The worker I'm talking about followed this same pattern through three or four ministries. To hear him talk about the situations, there was always something wrong with the organization. Well, I know these organizations too—all of them—and they are led by good people with good leadership abilities. They are very different ministries with different styles of leaders. The only thing in common was the individual himself, who chose to "run away" rather than stay and learn.

Jesus came to this world to meet the problem of sin face-on. He did that so that we can face the reality of our opposing nature.

Prior to engaging in evaluation, bathe it in prayer, asking God to give you his insights and to prevent the evil one from mucking about with the team or the individuals involved.

PHASE FIVE

Sustaining

# Sustaining in Leadership

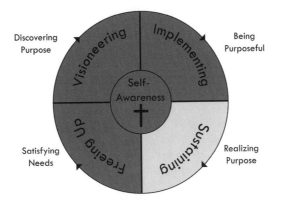

Learning to sustain yourself in leadership and in your ministry is one of the most challenging phases of the mentoring matrix. It is the nature of leaders to always be moving forward, but as their organizations mature, an "unsettledness" begins to grow.

Sustaining an organization or ministry that is achieving its vision is more difficult than one might expect. It usually requires adding new team members with different capabilities. Some team members need to leave. The gifts and skills that brought you to this point may not be what are needed to maintain the good work that has been established.

Actually, ministries are never fully at the sustaining stage, since our world is constantly changing. Therefore, leaders must constantly be reading the culture, economics, and demographics and prayerfully assessing if there is still a need for the ministry. And if there is, how will you have to change your ministry or your leadership to sustain the momentum?

As leaders mature in their leadership, they also have different needs and pressures spiritually. The evil one discourages and distracts leaders during this phase to thwart the ongoing work of the kingdom of God. Prayerfulness and wisdom are required at every turn.

This phase of the mentoring matrix is all about realizing purpose, and the effects of mentoring here are on the external environment while the focus of attention is on the inner life of the leader.

## Reorganizing the Team and Keeping Up with Change

Ministries go through different stages as they develop and engage in fulfilling their mission. The changes that take place during this process require that leaders look at their team composition again.

Reorganizing for sustainability and future growth should go far beyond simply altering processes; leaders should take a blank piece of paper and imagine afresh how the ministry should now operate.

The three areas of focus during this reevaluation are:

1. staff and their roles
2. method of ministry
3. systems that can improve capacity to fulfill the calling

Checking motivations in leaders' lives is an important role for mentors at these decision-making points for leaders and the organizations they lead.

Leaders can have a strong desire to downsize the organization or ministry through such an evaluation, thinking that creating a leaner infrastructure and reducing expenses will somehow ensure the ministry sustaining itself. Unfortunately, to do so means missing the opportunity to propel the ministry to a whole new level.

I overheard a board chair of a significant ministry organization wonder aloud if their CEO was trying to downsize the ministry to make it manageable for his leadership style. This could be the case and the leader may not even be aware of it—meaning it is not a conscious decision.

## Sigmoid Curve

My colleague Aklilu Mulat shared with me the principle of the sigmoid curve. This graphic curve takes its name from its resemblance to the lowercase

Greek letter sigma. It is one of the most useful tools in understanding the natural life cycle of an organization, a church, or even a relationship.

There are three phases of the sigmoid curve: introductory, growth, and decline. Try to picture where your ministry or organization is on the curve. Knowing where your organization is on the sigmoid curve and leading renewal at point A is a core leadership responsibility.

**Sigmoid Curve Illustration**

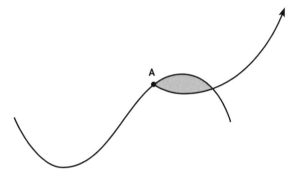

The secret to constant growth is to start a new S curve before the previous one ends, and the right place to start is at point A when there is the time, energy, and resources to get the new curve through its initial stages before it plateaus and declines. The sigmoid curve is a graphic way of portraying the point at which a ministry needs to reinvent itself, either building off the existing platform or risking the start of a decline and shortening its life span.

The shaded area is the end of the old and the barest beginning of the new: a mix of old practices and new ideas; a place of confusion, uncertainty, fear, and anxiety; a place of no rules; and a place of conflict. Leaders feel overwhelmed and frustrated during this period and are often tempted to seek a quick-fix solution.

## Three Ministry Development Stages

Let me place this concept into a ministry context. Arrow Leadership International Ministries has been on a journey as a ministry organization over the past thirteen years, and I can identify three distinct phases:

1. Ministry Founding and Early Growth
2. Ministry Midlife
3. Ministry Maturity

## Ministry Founding and Early Growth

Arrow actually had two iterations of this phase. It was founded by Leighton Ford in 1992 with the original vision and shaped by Tom Hawkes into what became the Arrow Leadership Program. However, at the time the founder stepped down and transitioned the ministry to my leadership, 92 percent of the financial support fell away and none of the previous staff continued except Irv Chambers and his wife, Marilyn, who volunteered as on-site mentors for our leadership residential seminars.

The rebirth occurred a year into my leadership when I had an epiphany moment and realized that Arrow was one year old again. We were starting over. I began to ask myself, "If I was starting from scratch, what would I do differently?" That one question opened my mind to an infusion of new ideas and a recommitment to the vision.

The founder, who is seen as the glue that holds the vision, formation, and identity together, dominates this first stage of a ministry's life. The vision is constantly being protected, refined, and implemented.

## Ministry Midlife

By this time, usually about ten years into the ministry's history, the original vision is likely to be diluted as things have been changing around it and new ministries have emerged. The church plant that was started in a new neighborhood ten years earlier and was the only church present is now surrounded by six others. At this stage there is an opportunity for realignment, revisioning, and changing.

During midlife for Arrow, we attempted to start a new leadership development process for eighteen- to twenty-four-year-olds. Although this endeavor did not work out for us, we learned a great deal through the experience and now are able to launch a new Executive Arrow program for those responsible for the business aspects of a ministry, such as CEOs, potential successors, and those Christian leaders who have been working in the marketplace but are exploring a call into leadership for a Christian not-for-profit organization. Arrow is currently at the midlife stage of ministry.

## Ministry Maturity

From seventeen to twenty years old, a ministry enters what I call the "sentimental" stage. The people who minister there have developed an addiction for how things used to be done and an unwillingness to even contemplate change. It is in this stage that the ministry is at its most vulnerable.

After the financial downturn that occurred following 9/11, I read a report that listed 178 ministries in North America that were on the verge of closing due to severe financial difficulties. Many of these did disappear, and several that did were "mature ministries" that had functioned for years on the understanding that the world, their world, had not really changed all that much. Well, the world certainly changed that day.

Founder leaders still lead many organizations that enter the ministry maturity stage. This subject could fill an entire book, but suffice it to say that holding on to control at this stage can mark the end of a ministry. And that's actually okay, for the Lord will raise up new leaders and new ministries to tend to their generation.

### Leadership Action

To propel the ministry forward and lift it to the next level, a leader must know where the ministry is on the sigmoid curve and prepare and plan the launch of a new ministry prior to the decline of its effectiveness. Identifying where the organization is on the curve requires input from others. Ask your team members and particularly the governing board for their input.

This is a window of opportunity for fundamental rethinking and what may seem like radical redesign of the ministry. Many leaders miss the opening because they're caught up in the day-to-day operations or lost in the fog of fatigue.

True reorganization of the team at this window is a recipe for a revolution in ministry effectiveness as you recognize that the past is history that you can build on and the future is there waiting to be engaged by the team taking on a new, optimal shape.

Part of the problem Christian leaders experience is their failure to impose changes to their existing team in order to achieve a new launch. Instead they focus on tearing down old programs while leaving the roles and responsibilities intact—despite the fact that the existing staff team may not have the skills, gifts, or desire to begin something new.

In mentoring leaders, I have found that some jump at this thought with great enthusiasm because of the excitement of creating a new enterprise and the adrenaline rush it creates. In doing so they can forget that leaders have a ministry to staff people as well.

Those we work with in Christian ministry organizations are there because of the calling God has on their lives to minister for his kingdom, so leaders must be encouraged to continually put a premium on the individuals involved and engage them in the process for the sake of the kingdom.

## Angie's Story

I worked with a very gifted woman leader at Insight for Living named Angie. I enjoyed working with her and saw incredible potential for her growth in ministry leadership. However, right when I was going through a leadership process of evaluating where the ministry should be heading in the next six to twelve months, I realized that Angie may not have the skill set that would enable her to adapt her role to get us there. What was I to do?

I opted to bring Angie into the discussion early on. I showed her on paper the pertinent facts about our current situation and how I saw us fulfilling the vision we had embarked on. With the resources I had available for the staff team, I explained that she would have to take on several new tasks and leave others behind. In a very open time of discussing this, we also talked about how these new areas were not her strengths.

Could she learn them? Absolutely.

Was there time for her to learn the skills? No.

Was she gifted enough to carry them out—yes, of course. But should she?

I knew it was not an area she would be passionate about, but I wanted to work with her in sorting this through for her sake and for the sake of the ministry. After taking time to think it over, Angie came back to me and said she could see that this is where the ministry needed to go, but that she was not the best person to take it there.

I expressed my appreciation for the thoughtfulness and prayer she had put into thinking this through. If we had been a larger organization, we could have found another role for her, but there were no leadership positions well suited for her. So we agreed on a plan whereby she would help us transition and I would assist her in seeking a new ministry position, even to the point of contacting other ministries on her behalf and letting them know that this decision was made for the sake of the ministry, that she had been a part of the decision, and that I fully supported and recommended her for other positions.

Angie moved on to a new ministry role. We parted by celebrating her contribution to the Lord's work in the ministry and prayed as we released her to do what God would have in his plans for her future. To this day we have a great relationship. She telephones to share how she is growing in her faith and also to direct my attention to leadership articles or issues that she thinks Arrow might be interested in. She refers to me as one of her mentors, and we have a friendship that has endured the pain of being "transitioned out," which most people inwardly translate as being "let go."

I have had to transition out twelve people during my leadership. Every leader must be able to do two things very well—hire and fire. Both must be done as before God and without crippling people through poor handling at either end of their employment. I feel that I have done ten of the twelve transitions well—and the two that were learning experiences for me perhaps went as well as they could have, given the circumstances.

### You're Fired!

The recent television-viewing obsession with Donald Trump's *The Apprentice* is a curious thing to me. Millions of people watch weekly to see which person Donald will turn to and coldheartedly and often rudely say, "You're fired." It must create some anxiety among workers even in Christian organizations who think that is how it always happens. I am sure it affects how people experience a performance review or even minor correction. So as Christian leaders, we should take the transitioning of people to a much higher level.

Bobb Biehl has the best process for releasing people that I have come across, and we ask him to teach this to leaders in the Arrow Leadership Program. He begins this process by explaining to the individual being released, "I care for you far too much to not be honest with you . . . ," and then leads the person through a process of truth telling about how the person does not fit in the current circumstances, acknowledging the person's strengths, then pointing out that the person is probably feeling stress over this (or is causing stress), and ending by releasing the person to do the Lord's work where he will fit better.

### Round Pegs in Round Holes

Dr. Ted Engstrom, who established a benchmark in Christian leadership in his roles with Youth for Christ and World Vision, told me that the secret to handling staff is putting round pegs in round holes. His words reminded me of the children's toy that has various shapes of pegs and a box with different-sized holes in it. Young children can be amused for hours trying to match the shape of the peg with the hole. Occasionally a peg can fit in the wrong hole, but it usually requires pounding to make it fit or it slips right through. It is all about getting the fit right. Whenever we evaluate a staff team for the future of the organization, we need to remember—it is all about round pegs in round holes.

## Gifts: Mixing It Up

After working with a team for a period of time, leaders become aware of the gifts represented in that team. Another form of reorganizing a team is to move people into different roles that suit their gifts and allow for new challenges for them.

When I was an associate pastor working with youth, I was sitting in my office one day preparing for the weekend activities when my phone rang. It was the church secretary informing me that a couple in the lobby wanted to make a counseling appointment with me. Although married, this couple had no children old enough to be in youth activities at the church. What could they possibly want in seeing me?

I complained, telling the secretary that there must be some mistake. Compromised by the couple standing right in front of her, she cryptically asked me once again to see the couple, and I complied.

A few days later they arrived promptly on time and began to share with me why they had wanted to speak to a pastor. The wife sat looking both angry and nervous at the same time. The husband was fidgeting and seemed quite uncomfortable with having to be in this place at this time.

I tried to break the ice quickly by getting us into the reason why they were there and asking, "So, why are you here?" The husband began to respond and then said something that launched his wife into her exegesis of their problem.

Waiting for a break in their story, I interrupted and told them that after hearing just the introduction, I thought they may be better off speaking to Dr. Roy Bell, the senior minister, who held degrees in theology and counseling and had always displayed incredible wisdom in helping couples in marital situations.

"It was Dr. Bell that sent us to see you!" the husband shared. "He told us that your gifts in this area were much better suited to assisting us than his own."

Inwardly, you could have picked me up off the floor, but on the outside I was unflustered by this obviously gratuitous statement. I managed to act as though it happened all the time.

Hearing Roy's words caused me to do an attitude check and give all my attention to this couple and their challenge at the time. After all, if Roy believed I could be of help, then I at least needed to try.

Roy's referral to me remains to this day one of the markers I look back on as wind beneath my leadership wings as I was learning to fly. On the basis of gifts he had discerned in me, he pushed me beyond my role description.

This was the same mentor in my life who would place magazine articles in my mailbox in the church office with a note clipped to them asking what I thought were the implications for the church in the pieces, or what were the theological rebuttals to the articles.

Roy also shared the pulpit at the church, allowing his associates to grow in their preaching gifts and skills. He also encouraged development of a television series on a local cable company that tapped into other gifts and skills within our team and pulled us out of any routines we had become accustomed to.

Through Roy's leadership I learned that there is another way to reorganize the team in less formal ways than letting someone go or rewriting the person's job description.

To reorganize a ministry, the leader must engage in the following activities:

1. Identify who is being ministered to and their needs.
2. Develop a message and method for responding to those needs.
3. Develop a process, system, and team that is able to produce transformational impact in the community they are called to minister to.

### Warning about High-Level Hires

A temptation for leaders reorganizing their team is to hire new high-level team members. My experience is that executives tend to make work for each other, and that most ministries would benefit from hiring more support staff. An example that is repeated again and again is a local church of around two hundred people moving to a multiple staff situation by hiring a new pastor for a specific area while still having only a part-time secretary or administrative assistant. Pastors and churches are almost always better off hiring a full-time assistant or perhaps two to facilitate the engagement of more volunteers within the congregation. Pastors unskilled in team leadership can find overseeing a multiple part-time staff a daunting experience, but the horsepower provided by this type of team would surpass most dual-pastor staffing.

## The Spiritual Side of Reorganizing the Team

If Screwtape and Wormwood wanted another way to slow down or destroy a person's or ministry's ability to further the kingdom of God, they would act very strategically at the time of a reorganization. It is a season ripe for misunderstanding, hard feelings, and relational hardship, during which an exorbitant number of hours are consumed in meetings that get bogged down in non–vision-driven discussion. They will make every attempt right at this point to pull ministries and leaders off of God's track.

One of the more subtle spiritual diversions that I observe occurs in a pattern that goes something like this: The leaders begin to think and process how the ministry might be reorganized, and when they look at their team members, they observe that some of them are not very passionate about their faith and the ministry. In a very short period of time, they work themselves up into quite a frenzy about this—neglecting to accept any responsibility for the spiritual state of their co-workers, even though they've worked together for however long.

In a response, the leaders try to get their co-workers active and busy with ministry—an attempt to "smarten them up."

This is a mistake. As A. W. Tozer says, "That would be but to take them out of one error and into another. What we need is a zealous hunger for God; an avid thirst after righteousness, a pain-filled longing to be Christlike and holy. We need a zeal that is loving, self-effacing and lowly. No other kind will do."[1]

This raises another approach to reorganizing the team, and that is to spiritually nurture them toward having a zealous hunger for God. It is interesting to contemplate what God might do if we were to throw ourselves into developing co-workers for the sake of bringing them into a closer relationship with Jesus.

## Keeping Up with Change

It goes without saying that we live in a time of unprecedented change, and leaders must be able to manage change. Despite what many say, I no longer believe there are any overall guiding rules concerning change in ministries. Our global environment is currently so chaotic that previous experiences with change may no longer be a good teacher. Yet, leaders are expected to handle the emerging issues that are important to the people under their care. What do members of your congregation or organization expect from you? Primarily, I believe they watch leaders to see how they manage and live their own lives in the context of change and at the same time direct and lead the organization.

Change is a foundational reality to organizational life, and no ministry or leader is immune from it. During intensified moments of change or uncertainty, people look for leaders to react quickly to problems by doing the following:

- Predicting changes to mission—constraints or objectives
- Finding contingent solutions

- Refining solutions as more of the problem is revealed
- Sequential problem solving
- Interactive problem solving
- Wisdom in the face of change
- Calling them to faith
- Comparing the techniques used by similar ministries to solve similar problems

The expectations are as overwhelming as the buffeting winds of change. The pace and overriding tempo of leaders' lives are often predicated on how well they are able to deal with change. We as leaders can respond to change in one of two ways:

1. To undertake extensive planning and try to use change to our advantage.
2. To do nothing, muddle along, and risk being overwhelmed by the effects of change.

Studies have shown that too much change can actually overload our systems as leaders, leading to physical and emotional problems. I would argue that the culprit is not change but rather our ability to adjust or adapt to that change.

Most leaders we work with view themselves as being ready to accept change. They're able to cite how they've moved from one ministry setting to another, or even the various job responsibility changes they have made. But too often these same leaders, when challenged with a new situation in their ministry involving organizational change, react with proven formulas rather than creativity.

When mentoring leaders in the phase of the mentoring matrix where they are learning to sustain themselves and their ministry, it is interesting to note that even younger leaders begin to display traits of being change resistant. This is a pattern we have observed among church planters.

## Zane's Church Plant Vision

Zane Grant is a church planter who embraces a vision of building a church with leaders who have recently become Christians themselves. Zane is passionate about this vision; however, as a leader he is realizing the realities behind achieving this goal. Listen in on a Web conversation that took place in our Arrow Leadership Forum:

Zane Grant: Okay let's be vulnerable again . . . lol (laugh out loud). I must really trust Arrow people or something. Anyway, here is the situation: I chose to start a church . . . pioneering style—i.e., reaching "normal" people with no core team so that they become the core team and then we build the church from there. It has really only been two years this past week so we are actually doing quite well. But my first set of goals saw us being self-sustaining by the end of three years . . . which just isn't going to happen.

Tim Brown: I would take some time (which it seems you are doing) and reevaluate the goal, the situation, and other possible avenues for accomplishing the same goal.

Zane Grant: But now I have to, as Tim says, reevaluate. The challenge is, from my estimation, this is going to take between five to seven years to become self-sustaining, which is fine. But, that will also mean sacrifice on my part . . . more so than ever before. I will need to move to a tent making model and have been looking into policing as a source of income but I don't really think I can see myself as a cop for the next 25 years of my life.

So, my goal of having the church self-sustaining by now isn't a reality etc. I am in a much better place mentally concerning this issue than I was a few months ago but am now in the place of reevaluation.

Doug Balzer: They say (whoever "they" are—the guys in black helicopters) that 80 percent of corporate goals are never reached but that should not discourage us. Goals propel us in a positive direction that otherwise would never have seen the light of day. We may not end up where we hoped but we will seldom remain where we were.

Zane Grant: And to be honest I like Doug's words on this topic as well . . . I feel this is where God wanted me and wants me.

In mentoring a leader like Zane, one of the most effective things we can do is to help him endure. Mentors can also help leaders take the time to plan for all the different actions that must be taken to navigate successfully through challenging changes.

This discussion will continue, no doubt, but what Doug was conveying is that often our vision or goals are used to move us as leaders into new places—places we never could have dreamed up before we began. Leaders can get stuck for a period between the original vision and how it actually rolls out.

The challenge of changing the original idea or vision has the propensity to make one feel almost sick inside—it can feel like failure. The key to minimizing the impact of these types of changes—vision changes—appears to be resiliency. Leaders need to have the ability to bounce back effectively when faced with challenges.

The most effective way for a leader to deal with change is to minimize it through planning. My mentors have helped me a great deal by pointing me to others who have gone down the path before. It is a good idea to list in a notebook or Palm Pilot strategies tried by proven leaders. Leaders need to be encouraged to see change within an appropriate time frame so that the entire task is not quite so daunting. The more leaders understand changes that are coming, the less negative impact they will have on them.

Leaders also need to realize that they are not wholly at the mercy of change. If a leader can anticipate the potentially positive results from a change, this "future orientation" will allow the leader to put up with temporary hassles and hardship.

If leaders are going to be effective in dealing with change, they must change their thinking processes. Most of the problems associated with change among leaders stem from fear and the inability to develop a strategic plan of attack. When we as leaders are uncertain of what will happen, we have a greater tendency to exaggerate the negative impact of situations. Whenever I establish a plan of attack, it has provided me with a foundation of hope and the ability to face another day.

When leaders are in the sustaining phase of the mentoring matrix, it's important as they anticipate change to get the facts right. Leaders should become as familiar as possible with the problem and develop and stick to a plan of action.

Change is not all bad, but it is inevitable. It is another of the constants in the daily life of a leader. Leaders can't change that, but they can change their outlook toward it. That, I believe, is the best way to start when handling change. Despite what we are told about viewing change as an opportunity rather than a problem, most leaders deeply dislike being forced to deal with change. Mitch, our psychologist here at Arrow, put it this way: "If you are someone who enjoys having your life suddenly and unexpectedly turned upside down, you are probably sick and should consider seeking professional help." This statement is invariably followed by laughter.

There are three reasons why leaders inwardly struggle with change.

1. We fear the unknown.
2. We fear we are going to lose something that we currently enjoy because of it.
3. The change creates a new possibility of failure for us.

## The Positive Side of Change

When ministries are in a growth stage, change occurs at a very rapid rate. Many leaders have greater difficulty leading during a time of growth than when things are difficult. I believe it is because the number of options for what can be done expand greatly during times of growth. Growth also awakens people who are fundamentally opposed to change, and leaders can find themselves against barriers that become exhausting.

## Leading through Change

"People support what they help to create." Dr. Gerald Fisher said that to me thirty years ago at the Baptist Leadership Training School, and I have found it very helpful when leading a team through change.

Give your team what they need today. Some leaders are too involved in planning for the future. Many leaders have a future orientation that is so strong they forget the past and neglect the present. Take care of your people today.

Anticipate ripple effects. Leaders need to be encouraged to anticipate the side effects of introducing change. An example would be to add one more senior team member and then find that you need to build new offices to accommodate him. Many people and the ministry budget will be affected.

Know everything you can about your ministry. In hindsight, one of the best things that happened to me as a leader was the downturn of the finances for Arrow, because there was a season when I had to be involved in every aspect of the ministry. I mean every aspect! For several months Arrow existed with just Brenda and me carrying the ministry load for three Arrow classes. That season acquainted me with aspects of Arrow I "knew" but didn't "know."

Do your work with the "old guard" in advance of the change. Dr. Roy Bell taught me how important it is to engage the people who have been part of the tradition and history of the ministry when you want to introduce change. Most often I found these people to have been the change agents at previous points in history. So, calming their fears about changes you are planning to implement will increase your chances of success.

Review the relational aspect of the change. We as leaders can often get caught up with a paper plan that outlines the change process. However, our boxes and flowcharts seldom take into account the relational impact the change will have on the team and constituency. Leaders need to be encouraged to carefully consider people along with the plan.

Articulate a very clear understanding of how the change is going to be implemented and back it up with homework. Allow your people to see that you have done careful homework behind the scenes in order to show them that this is not just an idea but a well-thought-out plan. Again, let me reiterate my preference for incremental steps. As you share your plan for change, show it to the team in graduated steps that include markers toward progress.

Find someone who will support your idea. There is not a lonelier person in the world than a leader with no support for his change ideas. It may be that you do not have such supporters on your staff team, so during the thinking and planning stages of growth change, find other like-minded people who will stimulate your ideas and help you flush them out.

Watch out for wackos! Ministries and organizations that are growing and functioning with innovative ideas attract people. Some of the people are terrific team members who can help you go from point A to point B. However, these seasons of growth also attract people who distort, bend, and twist your original intentions and plans. Leaders spend so much time trying to combat this misalignment that it can actually paralyze ministries. A catch here is that it is often hard to discern between the creative innovator and the needy, neurotic wacko. Look for certified, card-carrying change agents—not those trying to fill their own inner needs or who are perhaps spiritually being used by the evil one to distract your attention as a leader and as a ministry.

Don't overpromise. Many leaders get caught up in the "every challenge is an opportunity" motto and are not realistic about current realities. Make sure your team's expectations are realistic and yet optimistic. The leader's entire team should be able to clearly see the gap between vision and reality, and feel that under God's power and authority the reality is reachable.

## The Spiritual Side of Change

For those days when the wind is not blowing, our sailboat is powered by an inboard diesel engine. The sailboat has been my first experience in working with a diesel engine. I find the mechanics of the whole thing very interesting.

To start the engine, I begin by holding down the button for the glow plug. This tiny glow plug is nothing more than an electrical element that heats up until it is glowing white. When the glow plug is hot enough, I then engage the starter. If all goes well, the engine will sputter for one or two revolutions and then come to life with a rhythmic roar.

In the spiritual realm, life is a little like that for leaders. The evil one uses times of change to heat up the inner "glow plug" that ignites fear. Fear is the common foundation of spiritual attack on leaders during seasons of change. Many Christian leaders cover the fear in their lives with a smooth and shiny veneer that allows them to continue in ministry and leadership without public awareness of the fear or insecurity. Behind closed doors most leaders will admit to me their fear in different areas of their life. A significant part of our ministry at Arrow Leadership is to help leaders identify the core, or root, of fearfulness in their life. The Scriptures are quite clear in proclaiming to us as Christians and as leaders that we are to "fear not."

Paul and Christa Schoeber have been engaged in a prayer ministry for a couple decades now, and over the years they have prayed with many leaders concerning fear. I personally have borne witness to the absolute transformation of the lives of leaders they have prayed with concerning fear. Hear their counsel on ministering to those who are experiencing fear.

## Leaders and Fear: Paul and Christa Schoeber

*Where do you see fear being a factor in Christian leaders today?*

Paul: Our experience is that fear is mostly hidden beneath the surface. It comes out in various other forms and it comes out more by accident rather than as an issue that is being raised voluntarily. It comes when you deal with other issues.

Christa: For example, a young leader comes with a difficulty of actually leading. He has difficulty asserting, difficulty presenting his vision of the changes that ought to be happening in the church, difficulty leading others in the church. As these things emerge, you ask some questions and soon it becomes apparent to the leader and us that he is afraid. Then we begin to see that their fear is not just in the area that they presented at first. It turns out that they have fears in relationships, fears of being adequate to do the job at all, fear of conflict or addressing something that needs to be addressed. Their fear is often not just in one area; it spreads through everything.

Paul: I also believe that more often than not . . . we start out dealing with an anger issue. The anger is an outcome of fear—fear drives the anger. Anger is often the symptom. We actually have to tenderly search for the roots of that anger—very often the Lord reveals that fear underlies anger.

*What are some of the other ways that fear paralyzes leaders?*

Christa: The whole area of fear of intimacy is a big one. Leaders can't believe they can have deep relationships. They tend to hold people at arm's length, frightened of getting into a relationship with others or letting people get too close to them. There is also the fear of even looking at what's really at the bottom of their fear. The fear of even facing their fear and overcoming it also paralyzes them. Fear is a huge barrier for leaders.

*How does fear have this ability to prevent leaders from even investigating or seeking the Lord's healing in this area of their lives?*

Paul: The Lord said in Deuteronomy 30:19, "This day I call heaven and earth as witnesses against you that I have set before you life and death, blessings and curses. Now choose life." God has given us a choice. When we deal with people that cannot make a choice, then we start praying toward the root. What is the root that prevents them from making good choices? Often it is fear, often hidden, and this fear disables them from approaching God. There are multitudes of fears. I think there is a whole army of spiritual fear.

*If you are meeting with a young leader who is filled with fear and afraid, what do you do?*

Christa: Well, we carefully point out if you are afraid to that degree, it is having a major impact on their life. They are usually aware of this and we usually then just ask them, "Well, do you trust God?" They are usually quite startled when they finally connect these two! Almost all the time they agree, saying, "If fear rules me to the degree that I'm affected by it, then no, I don't trust God." So, we suggest that they need to ask God's forgiveness for letting fear have such an effect on their lives. Next, we encourage them to surrender the fear to the Lord, and we have to be very insistent that they do not ask the Lord to take it. You see, it must be given to him; it must be surrendered to him as an act of the will. He will not take it. When fear is such a major factor and we point out to them that it is a lack of trust, they almost all the time acknowledge it and don't want to stay there. They then struggle to first make the choice to surrender the fear, ask forgiveness for having allowed it, and then choose to surrender it and ask for forgiveness. We then encourage them to declare, "Lord, I choose to trust you. Now show me how this works in my life."

Paul: An important point to make clear to every young leader that we meet is that this will reoccur repeatedly. They will have to go through that process every time. The stronghold of fear can only be broken if it's demolished totally. It is not a onetime event and then it's done with. Once we face the issue that caused the fear to rise, it will happen again. So we let them know that they will need to deal with it again, but we teach them how to pray and they can move on.

*Many people pray, saying, "Lord, take this fear from me." However, you are saying no, you have to give it to him. Help us understand what you mean.*

Christa: Well, in Scripture how many times does it say, "Do not fear"? In the New Testament how often does Jesus say, "Do not be afraid"? It appears repeatedly. To me, this means we have a responsibility, a choice. Therefore, whenever we say to God "take it," we give the responsibility to God, while Scripture states that we have a part to play in that. Once we are willing, and say "I surrender," God will remove fear from us. When we say, "Take it," we are still holding on to it.

Paul: It may actually be that fear is preventing us from surrendering it.

Christa: So there has to be a willingness to make the choice to surrender and to give it to the Lord, otherwise it's not gone. And God will not take it when he tells us, "Do not fear." We must willingly do our part in it. He will help after we've made the choice, and it's amazing how much he helps leaders.

*What are the main areas of fear you see emerging in leaders' lives?*

Paul: Fear of rejection is huge. It reveals a fear of man, which opposes the fear of God. We always prefer to be accepted by other people, our peers, so fear of rejection is very big. Fear of failure is also prevalent in young leaders. Also fear of confrontation or conflict resolution is very common among leaders.

There is another point we need to make. Often fear combines with pride. It often affects those with a very high level of intellect. When leaders have that kind of combination, it is difficult to get near the fear because they explain everything away. Pride prevents them from facing what the fear alone would probably allow. If fear and pride combine, it is a huge, huge barrier.

*What about family background and/or denominational background? Are these historical roots or causes of fear?*

Paul: I do believe it enters in, in a big way. I think that we come back to this concept of choosing. If we cannot choose well, often, there are several reasons for it. Either we are living with unconfessed sin and the devil has a hold on us, or we are under the influences of generational patterns that have not been dealt with. Again, the generational sin is unconfessed, and sometimes it is even unknown as the person may not really be aware of this entire area until you start raising the issues. For example, unforgiveness can be a block to many leaders and often it goes back generations and can be at an unconscious level to the individual.

Paul and Christa have given spiritual insight into what takes place when we encounter fear in our leadership and how to address it. However, the first step is knowing that you are afraid, and as Paul pointed out, the fear is often hidden.

## Hidden Fear Checklist

Do you have problems with loving God, yourself, and others? If so, fear is present. Here are some questions to help you get beneath the surface on the subject of fear, along with some Scripture passages that speak into that specific fear.

- Do you feel anxious when there is nothing to fear?—Psalm 53:5: "There they were, overwhelmed with dread, where there was nothing to dread."

- Are you afraid of something suddenly happening to you?—Proverbs 3:25–26: "Have no fear of sudden disaster or of the ruin that overtakes the wicked, for the LORD will be your confidence and will keep your foot from being snared."
- Do you feel trapped or snared?—Proverbs 29:25: "Fear of man will prove to be a snare, but whoever trusts in the LORD is kept safe."
- Do you have problems resting?—Isaiah 30:15: "This is what the Sovereign LORD, the Holy One of Israel, says: 'In repentance and rest is your salvation, in quietness and trust is your strength, but you would have none of it.'"
- Do you lack peace?—Jeremiah 30:5: "This is what the LORD says: 'Cries of fear are heard—terror, not peace.'"
- Do you cry out a lot?—Matthew 14:26: "When the disciples saw him walking on the lake, they were terrified. 'It's a ghost,' they said, and cried out in fear."
- Do you know that there is a fear of death that makes you subject to bondage? Hebrews 2:14–15: "Since the children have flesh and blood, he too shared in their humanity so that by his death he might destroy him who holds the power of death—that is, the devil—and free those who all their lives were held in slavery by their fear of death."
- Do you know that fear is often associated with shame? Job 11:15: "Then you will lift up your face without shame; you will stand firm and without fear."
- Do you know that fear is a characteristic of "no faith"? Mark 4:41: "They were terrified and asked each other, 'Who is this? Even the wind and the waves obey him!'"
- Do you understand that fear hinders your ability to love? 1 John 4:18: "There is no fear in love. But perfect love drives out fear, because fear has to do with punishment. The one who fears is not made perfect in love."

# Fear, Loneliness, and Other Challenges

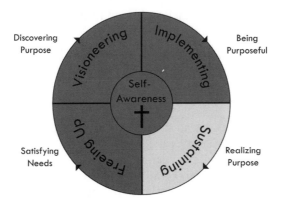

## Strong and Courageous? Yeah, Right!

All leaders need mentoring and help in dealing with challenges. Have you ever stopped to think about how you personally handle challenges that come your way as a leader? Have you compared your normal response to challenges with the instruction and counsel of the Scriptures? How you respond will affect how you lead others during times of challenge.

There are several times when it is important for a leader to be strong— during times of challenge is one such occasion. God created our physical bodies to respond to challenge. The scientist refers to this response as the fight-or-flight reaction. We want either to face up to the challenge and "duke it out" or to run away as fast as we can. In the Scriptures, there are passages that encourage us, or tell us to be strong and courageous, like Deuteronomy 31:6: "Be strong and courageous. Do not be afraid or terrified because of them, for the LORD your God goes with you; he will never leave you nor forsake you." Or 1 Chronicles 28:20, where David says to Solomon his son, "Be strong and courageous, and do the work. Do not be afraid or discouraged, for the LORD God, my God, is with you."

Other Scriptures describe situations when God deemed it appropriate for leaders to "run away." I think of Paul in Acts 9:25 being lowered down in a basket to escape his enemies, and the Gospels of Matthew, Mark, and Luke telling of Jesus instructing the disciples to shake the dust off their sandals and walk away from those who were unresponsive (Matt. 10:14; Mark 6:11; Luke 9:5).

God will call Christian leaders to face challenges sometimes by standing up and fighting, and sometimes by walking away. Both responses are equally difficult. I've met many young leaders who are bold, scrappy, and ready to go head-to-head with anyone who would challenge the forward movement of the gospel. These are few in contrast to the many leaders I meet who are averse to conflict and would rather be silent, do nothing, and slowly slip away. It is important to seek God for the wisest response when facing a challenge.

## Perseverance

Facing challenges as a leader develops an indispensable trait I see in all successful leaders—perseverance.

Dr. Perry Bowers is the president of Focused Living Ministries in Columbia, South Carolina. Perry and I have been friends for years, and I have watched him practice several disciplines, which I in turn have tried to emulate in my own life. One such discipline is choosing a passage of Scripture and a focus word for each year.

Every year at the beginning of Advent, I begin to pray and ask the Lord to help me choose a word and a passage of Scripture that will help lead and guide me for the following calendar year. These words and passages do not come easily, and I find that often I have to persevere in my prayer until at last they come together. I formalize the process by writing them down in my journal. I wish I could forget the two years in a row when God inspired me to write down the word "persevere" as my focus word.

My journal records the focus on perseverance beginning January 2, 2001. When I wrote down the word in my journal, my focus was on my need to continue moving forward in obedience with the ministry to which God had called me, even though I was still dealing inwardly with the death of my father the year before. I was still missing Dad and his influence and encouragement in my life—especially on Sunday evenings.

Every Sunday night over the past twelve years, with few exceptions, my father had called me, or I had called him, to talk about what the Lord had been doing in our lives over the week prior. Dad had a signature sign-off at the end of each phone conversation. No matter what we had been discussing and no matter how I might have been feeling on that particular day, my father would end each call by saying, "Remember, you've got to walk by faith, boy." The tone of that particular phrase still resonates in my mind. Especially the word "faith," for it was always said with a hint of the influence of his Irish bloodline.

Persevere. That's what I had to do to keep going without those Sunday night phone calls. It seemed like the right word to write in my journal for that year—"persevere." Little did I know how prophetic that word would become, for what followed was the financial downturn for the ministry of Arrow following the tragedy of September 11, 2001, and the World Trade Center disaster. The financial support of Arrow ministry from the United States completely dried up for more than three months. This occurred during the busiest season of our ministry, and our greatest time of expenditures. There was a rapid downward trend line on our financial statements, which led to the most difficult time in my leadership to date. It resulted in me having to make the leadership decision to lay off half of our staff. These were not just casual relationships but dear friends who were deeply committed to the ministry of Arrow. Brenda and I also had to cut our salaries and at the same time increase our work hours per week to double what most people would consider normal.

Persevere. Why had I chosen that word? It almost haunted me as I thought about the ongoing list of challenges through which I had to persevere. With every ounce of creativity I could muster, we continued to minister to the seventy-five leaders we were working with across North America. Through the help of over a dozen volunteers and a very committed board, we continued with only slight interruptions to our schedule. However, there was a high price to pay for this, and within a year I found that I had begun to slide into a depression that was hindering my ability to function. The ministry at this time needed more of me, and yet physically, emotionally, and even spiritually, I had little to give.

Persevere. In the midst of all this our neighbors called saying they had a collection of discount coupons for the grand opening of a new restaurant in our community. They invited our family to join with them in the savings. While we were eating together and enjoying the fellowship, Brenda's cell phone rang with another life-altering phone call.

"No! Is this a joke?" Brenda then handed the phone to me and began to cry. As I took the phone a Royal Canadian Mounted Police officer sensitively shared with me that my mother had been found dead in her home of an apparent heart attack.

Persevere. How was I possibly going to get through this? I can look back now and understand how I was able to continue to do the work of the Lord. It was because of my close relationship to Jesus Christ and the work of his Holy Spirit in and through all the circumstances.

Jesus was very evident through the love and support of our extended family. During times like this the Pue clan responds quickly by circling the wagons and being there. Jesus was also evident through the pastor of the church where my parents had been worshiping for many years. Dr. Axel Schoeber ministered to us deeply through his prayers and also his attention to so many of the details related to the memorial services for both my mother and father. Jesus also appeared during this time of challenge through the entire board of Arrow Leadership International Ministries. A special board meeting was called at that time, and I was fully willing to step down from my role as the president in order to allow the great work of Arrow to continue. I knew it was a critical time for the ministry, but I also knew I was unable to give any more. Jesus also appeared to me through my mentor Barry and his wife, Sharon. Their compassion and their listening allowed me to express my feelings in a place that felt safe.

> Mentors are often used by God as one of the most significant means of assisting leaders during times of challenge.

## What Hinders God's Leaders?

There are so many different ways in which Christian leaders are hindered from doing the work of the Lord. Some leaders are hindered by:

- Lack of capability or the skills necessary for their role or position
- Lack of time, or improper use of time
- Lack of financial resources
- Fatigue
- Physical limitations or ailments

- Wayward or rebellious children
- A spouse who is unenthusiastic to the things of the Lord
- An uncooperative spouse
- A difficult deacon or elder
- A senior pastor or supervisor who is threatened, insecure, or consistently negative

Of course, the list could go on and on, and for some, especially gifted leaders, several of these challenges often seem to converge at a single point in their lives. When you as a leader face challenges like these, it is helpful to sit down with a trusted mentor who can help you to:

1. Understand that recurring problems are not your fault.
2. Ask for specific help.
3. Communicate often and honestly—something that can be difficult for "heroic" leaders during a time of crisis.
4. Engage in some form of stress management—it is particularly important for Christian leaders to try to find something outside their normal routine.
5. Encourage patience with themselves, their board, and their staff.
6. Regularly take time to reflect and learn, particularly about the value of serving others for Christ.

> Mentors can also help leaders focus on persevering and seeing the value of that. Leaders who focus only on failures and on problems will not be able to hang in there for the long haul. Barry would often ask me to share things that were going extremely well, and then we would take time to thank God for those things. Those prayers over a period of time created a practice of remembering to give thanks.

Doing the work of the Lord is not an easy task. Yes, there is joy and pleasure in serving God, but there is the shadow side of ministry to contend with. This is the reality of the deployment of Satan's elite guard, whose primary assignment is to discourage you to the point of giving up. Perseverance is a key trait underlying any leader's success.

## Overwhelmed

Today's young leaders often shoulder incredible loads of leadership, which equals huge responsibility. Many oversee teams of staff and/or volunteers that number in the hundreds. Others are solo pastors who handle multiple roles, often single-handedly, while managing a hundred or more people. Others lead large parachurch ministries, with heavy demands and responsibilities. Despite leadership articles like Bill Hybels's "Watching the Gauges" or books like Eugene Peterson's *The Contemplative Pastor*, most of the young leaders we work with are overwhelmed by the load of responsibility they carry and the demands of nurturing growing families at the same time. It doesn't take rocket science to realize that they will be challenged trying to balance it all.

For many Christian leaders, days off have morphed into another form of a regular workday. These leaders are often on call seven days per week. Even when there is an occasional day off, they can be tracked down through the technology of cell phones and pagers. Not even watching their child's basketball game or eating a meal out as a family is off-limits anymore. When they get home, they fire up their computers to answer email and continue writing sermons, presentations, or reports.

### The 24/7 Syndrome

Many leaders functionally live life with no days off for many reasons, such as internal pressure, external expectations, perfectionism, drivenness, and technology, to name a few. What does it take to help a leader break this cycle? Although there are many practical tools that will make a difference, there must be an overarching reason for trying to work through the issue of balance. I believe that God's example of resting and finding joy in creation is a good place to start.

That is recorded in Genesis 2:1–3: "Thus the heavens and the earth were completed in all their vast array. By the seventh day God had finished the work he had been doing; so on the seventh day he rested from all his work. And God blessed the seventh day and made it holy, because on it he rested from all the work of creating that he had done."

### My Son Jon

A close second is thinking about legacy. What would you like your family—your spouse and your children—to say about you at your retirement party? We've all felt guilty when passing the framing or poster stores in the shopping mall and seeing the beautiful photos with pithy little sayings at the bottom. One of them I wrote into my PDA (personal digital assistant) and personalized for our son Jonathan:

> One hundred years from now it will not matter
> what my bank account was, the sort of house I lived in,
> how many leaders I taught, or if I was the president of Arrow.

But the world may be a better place because of time spent
with my son Jon.

## Twelve Steps toward Balance

Sometimes working back from a desired dream gives us perspective
for the present. Following are twelve practical steps to getting your life
back:

1. Set boundaries . . . If you don't set boundaries, other people will
   set them for you. Establish ones that are healthy for you and your
   family without taking advantage of the ministry God has called you
   to.
2. Watch, ask, and listen . . . Observe other leaders and talk with a
   mentor about managing the demands of ministry, marriage, and
   family life.
3. Work smarter, not harder . . . Often people default to do what is
   easiest first, rather than those things that are most important.
4. Make appointments . . . Entries in our day planner should reflect
   what's important to us, such as family, reading times, time for
   neighbors and friends, etc. Write them in!
5. Begin small . . . Give yourself the gift of a couple of hours of freedom. Then expand it to a half-day block of time.
6. Leave work at the office . . . Or it can ruin your days off, cause feelings of guilt, consume emotional energy; turn off your cell phone,
   BlackBerry, etc.
7. Teach yourself to grow into your leisure time . . . It takes practice,
   but it's fun. Develop a healthy theology of leisure.
8. Find other ways to get all the work done . . . Keep chipping away
   at the tasks and delegate.
9. Let people know when you are "off" . . . Keep staff informed and
   set boundaries.
10. Find ways to clear your mind of your work . . . Take an hour every
    Friday to organize your next week; it helps to unclutter your mind
    for the weekend.
11. Create more space around activities . . . Resist packing more into
    each day, and instead build a little margin into your activities.
12. Learn to not overschedule errands . . . Avoid pushing all your per-
    sonal errands onto your days off.

## Threats to Ministry Marriages

Brenda, my wife and partner in ministry for almost thirty years, has been observing Christian leaders and their marriages for over a decade. We began to ask specific questions of the Arrow leaders we are mentoring.

When young leaders first arrive at Arrow, we often see physical, mental, and emotional weariness, even though they are excited about the journey. They often bring the heavy load of responsibility they carry with them. We ask every Arrow applicant's spouse (if the applicant is married) to comment on the strengths and weaknesses of family life. We also survey leaders and spouses from time to time on the Arrow website. Brenda observes, "The responses are fascinating, in that they often reflect the stress and weariness we observe as those same leaders walk through the door."

When we compiled the results of the issues identified in ministry marriages, the number one issue was finding balance between ministry demands and family life. Before Brenda and I comment further about this, you may be interested to read the other issues that were seen as threats to ministry marriages:

- Inability to balance family life and ministry
- Leaders more concerned about calling than marriage covenant
- Failing to facilitate partner's dreams—not helping one another grow
- Failing to have fun
- Alternative confidant found outside marriage
- Money problems
- Ministry makes spouse live like a single parent/widow/widower
- Unfulfilled expectations
- Admiration sought from someone other than partner
- Isolation

Although the order of ministry marriage issues may differ somewhat from class to class, the first one is always clearly at the top of the list. Note how the second, "Leaders more concerned about calling than marriage covenant," links to the first. Trying to stay balanced as a leader is challenging. For that reason, it is prudent to spend time on this subject.

## Other Professions

The ministry is not the only profession forced to deal with the balance issue. Doctors, lawyers, entrepreneurs, and politicians also face this challenge. Of those professions, politicians come the closest to the ministry due to the pressures of public life. Nonetheless, all the professions carry a great deal of responsibility, and there is much to be gained by seeking out other professionals to find out how they handle the pressures of leadership and responsibility. Words of caution here . . . don't compare the ministry too closely to other professions, because there are vast differences in spite of some similarities. For example, finances are one such area. Some professionals can afford to hire extra help to relieve pressure points on the home front. The ministry is a high calling, even though your bank account may not reflect that. Remember that there are many things money can't buy, and remember to keep a godly perspective.

## It's Not All Bad

Please note that ministry marriages can exhibit many wonderful strengths, like good communication, flexible hours, sharing faith together, rich family times, commitment to each other, and good conflict resolution. I suspect that many people from other professions or occupations secretly desire to have the level of intimacy and joy that many ministry marriages possess. We now circle back to the issue of how to manage the demands of ministry with the demands of family. How do we carve out time to protect the intimacy and joy that many ministry marriages enjoy?

## Steps to a Healthy Ministry and Marriage

Gail Johnsen is married to Rev. Darrel Johnsen, a senior pastor in Pasco, Washington. Gail is also the mother of four children, and she works as a writer. She offers her perspective, as a ministry spouse, on some principles and practices that help them with the juggling of schedules and the building of a healthy marriage. She writes:

> *Learn to Pause.* I call it downtime, time alone, time away. It's hard to see when you are on the move. Perspective is lost and priorities compromised. So often when the demands of ministry become overwhelming, the first thing we eliminate is the thing we need the most: quiet, reflective time. Take time to think, refocus, and contemplate on what's working and what's not.

Not only will you see the changes that are needed, but you will have the emotional and physical strength to carry them out.

*Remember That There Are Seasons in Life and in Ministry.* When my children were young, they were my main focus. Although my passion for ministry never waned, I purposely focused my energies into nurturing them. I knew they would not be small forever. As they have grown and seasons have changed, I have had opportunities to expand into other areas of ministry, refocusing and adjusting in the pursuit for balance.

*Build a Hedge around Your Marriage.* Ministry can become all-consuming. Make a plan of action to protect your marriage. Schedule a date night (or day) once a week or at least once a month. Get a babysitter if necessary. Write it on your calendar and guard it tenaciously. Protect your days off and spend them together.

*Recognize Your Own Strengths and Weaknesses.* My tendency is to do it all. If something needs to be done and nobody else will do it, I will. At least I used to. I have finally come to realize I can only do so much. I tend to be task-oriented and must constantly fight the temptation to put the work of ministry over my family. However, each time I have given in to that temptation, I have wandered into imbalance.

Brenda and I affirm these things in our marriage and ministry life. We believe that next to our personal relationship with God, the spousal relationship is *the* most important relationship at a human level. The parent-child relationship, as well as extended family relationships and other friendships, build on it. Our faith in God is the foundation on which all else rests. If that is in order, a healthy marriage, healthy family, and healthy interpersonal relationships will follow. If that order becomes confused, the foundation crumbles and usually much pain will ensue. This is illustrated with a triangle that Brenda uses in mentoring to show our foundation and subsequent relational priorities.

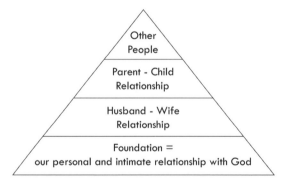

Once the proper foundation has been laid, you can focus on more practical tools that will make marriage and ministry more satisfying.

One such tool has to do with time management. Our family is learning a rhythm of enabling ministry (Arrow), church life, and home life to hang together, although it has taken us twenty-nine years of experimenting to get there.

I'll let Brenda explain. "Our Arrow seminar schedule is laid out at least three years in advance. This forces us to plan the rest of our lives one to two years in advance. We start planning about a year ahead for our family get-togethers and holidays. We often plan speaking engagements a year or so out. One of the things we had to work through, as a family, was becoming less spontaneous than we have been in the past. Often friends will invite us over, or our church will host an event that we would love to participate in, but if it falls within the time frame of an Arrow seminar week, or other Arrow travel, we simply have to bow out gracefully. Sometimes it's hard, but for the sake of our calling, we have learned to sacrifice spontaneity. Knowing our schedule, well in advance, makes this task much easier."

### Planning Like Clockwork

Following a method shared by our friend Bobb Biehl, we now plan our activities a year in advance, with some of our ministry commitments booked three to five years in advance.

Here is how we approach it. I use a dinner plate to trace a circle on a large piece of paper. Starting at the top on the outside of the circle, I write "12." Then continue around the circle with numbers 1 through 11 creating the face of a clock. With this clock face the numbers actually represent the months of the year. As a family we then write, and shade in, on the paper any prebooked events such as our Arrow seminar weeks or family reunions—those things that require more than a year to prepare for. Then we discuss other family events and holidays as a different kind of nonnegotiable. Let me have Brenda illustrate this. "An example of this would be our son Jeremy stating that this is his senior year and he definitely wants Dad around for all the graduation festivities. Jon thinks his football team will likely make the playoffs this year, so he gives us the dates and asks that Dad be in town. We also make plans for Christmas and New Year and our summer holidays a year in advance. We write all these on the circle, and it becomes covered with markings around the twelve months of the year."

Everything else that ends up on our calendar follows after these important events have been scheduled. This way, ministry opportunities do not control the show or overwhelm family plans.

It's important to realize that since relationships are fluid, we never "arrive." We will never achieve perfection in balancing ministry and marriage and other relationships, at least not this side of heaven. However, it is a worthwhile pursuit for the leader you are mentoring . . . one that God himself will bless and nurture through all the challenges and seasons of life. Sometimes it is hard work and slow going, and other times you will experience turning a corner and feel the pure joy of accomplishment. May God bless you as you journey alongside other leaders, helping to give them perspective in the area of balance between ministry and marriage.

This system works very well for our family. We usually plan this annually at a family gathering between Christmas and New Year, fondly referred to as the AGM, or Annual General Meeting. We plan a nice breakfast and then meet to review and discuss personal goals that were discussed the year before. Each member of the family sets goals in five life areas: spiritual, intellectual, emotional, physical, and social. We also discuss household projects and dreams during this time. As the goals are shared, they are recorded by the "secretary," then typed out and emailed to each family member with a reminder email halfway through the year. During our meeting, we rate ourselves on a scale of 1 to 10 in the accomplishment of the aforementioned goals. It is primarily a time of encouragement and occasionally a time of realization of overzealous goal setting. We end our day by going out for dinner as a family and celebrating.

This is the most effective tool we have discovered for managing the demands of ministry and the challenges of family life. In addition, Brenda and I try to meet weekly as a couple to discuss the coming week, preferably over an early Saturday morning breakfast. In these ways we are able to keep on top of both long-range and short-range planning. Knowing the weekly demands we will be facing enables us to communicate clearly and cooperate with each other in managing those demands.

## Lonely Leaders

Part of the mission of Arrow Leadership in developing leaders is to network leaders together in relationships that can remain a resource for a lifetime of ministry. We discover that although we are working with the finest Christian leaders around the world, many of them are lonely. It could be that they are serving in a remote area, but I have actually found that many are more frequently lonely due to being misunderstood, out of sync with their denomination, or passionate among dispassionate people.

Some of the women leaders Brenda and I have spent time with have also discussed how lonely it can be ministering in a male-dominated area of service.

Most leaders confess a deep sense of loneliness, although most of us work hard at wallpapering over the cracks caused by loneliness. Behind closed doors in a session with two leaders, I heard again about the angst one leader had due to the loneliness in his life.

Years ago I was talking with Doug Moffat, then executive minister of the Baptist Union of Western Canada. Doug was telling me how lonely it was at times as a leader. As a younger leader at the time, I had trouble understanding just how deep those words could possibly go. It was not until my leadership responsibilities grew in later years, when difficult decisions had to be made, when personal agendas and goals would be sacrificed for the sake of the ministry, that I began to realize just how lonely it can feel.

## Doors of Loneliness

Over the years that followed in my own leadership, loneliness entered through many doorways. I'll list a few:

- At the completion of a big ministry project—it was done, leaving me with an empty hole. Many pastors leave churches right after they complete a building project or launch a new service.
- The loss of key people in your life—family, friends, colleagues, other leaders—and key members of your congregation, by death, rejection, or moving away physically. I pastored at a church where about a third of the congregation seemed to move each year due to their involvement in the oil patch.
- Losing some of your main encouragers—the people who admired you and encouraged your heart up every time you were together.
- Serving with a work group that called itself a "team" yet nurtured a negative and often critical spirit.
- Conflict within the congregation that is out of control.
- Loss of respect for an individual you once looked up to.
- Dramatic changes to your personal health.
- Spiritual crises that overwhelm you and remind you how far away you are from the vision of where you want to be.

Leaders are often able to keep their inner loneliness under control until these types of experiences come their way.

"It's lonely at the top." This often-quoted leadership motto is true to some extent, because while a good leader can delegate tasks to others, the burden of responsibility ultimately falls on his shoulders. Others have quipped that it is only lonely at the top because you haven't taken anyone with you—promoting a team approach.

I have also heard it said that "leadership begins with loneliness"; however, this is suspect, to say the least. Many younger leaders that I have worked with who are engaged in significant leadership have not yet hit the point where loneliness sets in. But those of us who have experienced the loneliness I am referring to know that as a result of feeling lonely, our leadership changes, which in that way may mean that our emergence as a leader is just beginning.

Loneliness often kicks in during this sustaining phase of the mentoring matrix. Although loneliness rears its head at earlier moments, it seems that when we as leaders move into this stage our focus changes. The previous stages have been extremely busy in comparison. Usually the role of the leader changes and other staff members handle more and more of the administrative responsibilities, causing some leaders to lose a sense of purpose.

Christian leaders need to be reminded that even Jesus experienced loneliness. Isaiah 53:3 prophesied that he would be rejected, and in the Gospels we see that this was fulfilled. "And they all forsook him, and fled" (Mark 14:50 RSV). "My God, my God, why hast thou forsaken me?" (Matt. 27:46 RSV). Jesus was an outcast because he was different. He knew what it was like to be alone.

Oftentimes that's why leaders feel lonely. We're different! And if we are following Christ's lead, we may be making decisions that will cause people to fall away, to forsake us. When this occurs, what we need to remember is that we are always loved and valued by God and that we are not alone.

I love the story in Exodus 18 of how Jethro's daughter told him about how out of control her husband was. He responded by visiting Moses to observe the situation firsthand. What he found was a Moses who was burned-out, tired, and lonely. Jethro's spiritual wisdom needs to be heard by many Christian leaders today.

> Moses' father-in-law replied, "What you are doing is not good. You and these people who come to you will only wear yourselves out. The work is too heavy for you; you cannot handle it alone. Listen now to me and I will give you some advice, and may God be with you. You must be the people's representative before God and bring their disputes to him. Teach them the decrees and laws, and show them the way to live and the duties they are to perform. But select capable men from all the people—men who fear God, trustworthy men who hate dishonest gain—and appoint them as officials over thousands, hundreds, fifties and tens. Have them serve as judges for the people at all times, but have them bring every difficult case to you; the simple cases they can decide themselves. That will make your load lighter, because they will share it with you. If you do this and God so commands, you will be able to stand the strain, and all these people will go

home satisfied." Moses listened to his father-in-law and did everything he said. He chose capable men from all Israel and made them leaders of the people, officials over thousands, hundreds, fifties and tens. They served as judges for the people at all times. The difficult cases they brought to Moses, but the simple ones they decided themselves.

Exodus 18:17–26

Jethro was mentoring Moses by pointing out that he was not able to control everything, and if he continued to try and do so, it would eventually break him. Whatever took place in those discussions, the end result was that Moses was able to find capable, competent people around him to undertake much of the responsibility. He was not all alone.

It was loneliness that brought this "control freak" into a spiritual transformation that allowed him to receive relief from loneliness.

### The Experience of Loneliness

Loneliness is a very painful emotion and creates an environment that will either draw leaders closer to God or cause them to make personal decisions that can be devastating to the lives and ministries they serve. The foundation we have is Jesus. When we take our loneliness to God, he understands, cares, and will encourage us.

> It is very important that mentors know how to come alongside, and even pursue, leaders who are experiencing loneliness. Ask your mentee for permission to pursue him during times when you see him retreating or becoming reclusive.

### Effects of Loneliness

So what are we to do with all this loneliness among leaders? As I have observed and experienced the lonely lifestyle of leaders, I have discovered unforeseen results of loneliness.

Did you know that lonely people have impaired immune systems, making them more vulnerable to colds and other illnesses?

Lonely leaders turn to the Internet in increasing numbers, leading to problems with depression and online sex addictions.

Alcohol and drug abuse intensify feelings of loneliness.

Having many "functional" relationships at work also can distract us from pursuing healthy, intimate relationships. We can get our "fill" of people while at the office and then have little or nothing left to share when we get home.

Loneliness attacks the senses. Leaders feel isolated, rejected, and abandoned—like no one really understands. However, loneliness can

There are several ways mentors can assist lonely leaders. Just being with them is one of the most powerful. So demonstrate your love and concern by giving the invaluable gift of time.

build something into our character that few other experiences allow—that we all need love—that is, to give and receive love. "A person standing alone can be attacked and defeated, but two can stand back-to-back and conquer. Three are even better, for a triple-braided cord is not easily broken" (Eccles. 4:12 NLT).

## How Can a Mentor Help Guide a Lonely Leader?

Jethro gave us one approach to mentoring the lonely—assessing the realities and helping the leader find solutions that would break the patterns causing the loneliness. We can also mentor leaders by coming alongside to encourage them in many practical ways.

Encourage leaders to undertake an honest appraisal of their life by surveying the relationships of significance.

Ask them to share their thoughts and feelings with you. This is a time to be a friend.

Encourage them to pick up a pen or a paintbrush and dive into their creative side. Remember that many of the world's masterpieces came from the minds and hearts of those whose lives were plagued with loneliness.

Have them keep a journal. It can be very helpful to record our experiences of life, our thoughts, feelings, and relationships, and can give great insight and growth in self-understanding.

Help them realize that friendships and social bonds with others are a necessity for healthy living.

Encourage them to begin reaching out, as they are able. Writing letters is a start—talking to people on the phone is even better.

Television is the most prevalent passive activity in the Western world. Assess the amount and frequency of leaders' television viewing. Encourage a reduction, but don't eliminate television, for it is often the fodder for many discussions with people they know, such as their neighbors and those they work with.

Consider that leaders may have a "learning deficit" in forming friendships with others. Do they have any close friends? Have they learned how to form friendships? It startles me to meet so many Christian leaders who are functioning at a very important leadership level without any significant friendships in their lives.

Perhaps help start a "Lonely Hearts Club" for Christian leaders in your area—getting together occasionally with others who understand the loneliness of leadership.

Ask leaders to think about getting therapy as a way to acquire relational skills they may be lacking. A therapist can help them analyze what causes the loneliness, and the more they understand it, the less threatening it is.

Seek medical treatment for severe anxiety or depression brought on by loneliness. If the feelings of loneliness are such that leaders have difficulty eating, sleeping, working, or continuing relationships with the people with whom they ordinarily associate, the best course of action is to consult a psychiatric specialist. Many excellent medications are available that can be prescribed only by a doctor. Short-term medication to correct a chemical imbalance or clinical depression should definitely not be ruled out.

Encourage leaders to make the effort to join a small group for leisure, support, and fun. For example, my good friend J. John took a break from his demanding evangelism ministry to take a cooking course with his wife, Killy.

Limit use of the Internet as an anonymous source of interaction. Although convenient, the World Wide Web is no place to hang out if you are lonely. Although there are uses for those in remote places, much caution must be used, for the Internet causes a reclusiveness that is not healthy among leaders. Spending excessive hours in chat rooms visiting with virtual friends or engaging in fantasy or combat games and taking on idealized identities should be seen as warning signs.

Following the same routine day in and day out is a major contributor to loneliness. Encourage leaders to vary their daily activities.

Some leaders are most alert and efficient early in the day—"the morning people"—while others are far more effective late in the day—"the night owls." Evaluate with leaders how they might plan their most challenging activities for that point in the day when they are most efficient and effective.

> Leaders who are lonely need to be regrounded in their identity in Christ (the core of the mentoring matrix). Ask them about developing their spiritual life and building their relationship with God. Study the Bible for nourishment, not purpose, and pray and fellowship with other Christians. Becoming more God-conscious will help ease the problem of loneliness.

Ask them about someone they know who is in need and encourage them to reach out to help others.

## The Spiritual Side of Loneliness

The message of the gospel is specifically this: even in the most unimaginable, uncontrollable, hellacious scenarios, God is in control. As millions of people watched Mel Gibson's movie *The Passion of the Christ* in theaters, they were exposed to an image of the loneliness of the cross.

As Jesus hung there, he vicariously cried out for us, "My God! My God! Why have you forsaken me?" Jesus in the midst of loneliness submitted to the Father's control, releasing his spirit into the loving hands of the Almighty.

In the midst of his great moment of loneliness, it is important to note that Jesus did not try and take control—but he humbled himself "even unto death." I mention this to have us note the issue of control, for I believe that many leaders struggle with loneliness because of their inability to control their environments. Many are like Moses—control freaks who for years have denied it effectively. Those closest to them are aware, but it is often kept concealed through an unofficial social contract reminiscent of Hans Christian Andersen's story "The Emperor's New Clothes." Some very prominent Christian leaders do not have people close enough to them to let them know that their need to control is naked for all to see. Perhaps they need more children around.

> A child, however, who had no important job and could only see things as his eyes showed them to him, went up to the carriage.
>
> "The Emperor is naked," he said.
>
> "Fool!" his father reprimanded, running after him. "Don't talk non-sense!" He grabbed his child and took him away. But the boy's remark, which had been heard by the bystanders, was repeated over and over again until everyone cried:
>
> "The boy is right! The Emperor is naked! It's true!"
>
> The Emperor realized that the people were right but could not admit to that. He thought it better to continue the procession under the illusion that anyone who couldn't see his clothes was either stupid or incompetent. And he stood stiffly on his carriage, while behind him a page held his imaginary mantle.[1]

When leaders are confronted with their issues around control and the facade is shattered, the healing process begins. The immediate default is still loneliness, since it has been held at bay through discipline. Think for a moment of a leader you know who is quite controlling. If you can ever get close enough to that leader, you will find a lonely person. Perhaps you are that lonely leader. Getting to the place of honestly admitting loneliness, to oneself and to others, is the first step of a rewarding journey toward healthy relationships.

# 12

# Accountability

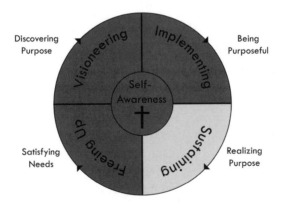

As iron sharpens iron, a friend sharpens a friend.
Proverbs 27:17 NLT

## Who Sharpens Leaders?

Over the recent past, the body of Christ has encountered many difficulties and scandals among its leadership. Unfortunately, these will continue if leaders continue down pathways with little or no accountability. Sexual misconduct, questionable practices, problematic pronouncements, and doctrinal deviations have all hurt the cause of Christ, giving "occasion to the enemies of the LORD to blaspheme" (2 Sam. 12:14 NKJV). Such highly visible departures from biblical Christian leadership have called into question the ability of most pastors and Christian leaders to carry out their duties in a manner consistent with biblical teaching and their own professional principles.

I am not going to cite examples of leaders who have fallen. When discussing this with any Christian leader, you will find hurt caused by failure in another leader's life. Often leaders have friends who have fallen. Mature leaders also know it is only by God's grace that they have not succumbed to falling too.

Christian leaders glide upward to some kind of invisible pedestal. Most are not seeking this upward position—although some do, and that is a different issue. The majority simply find themselves unprepared on the pedestal with power. Combine this with the "loneliness factor" of leadership, and we have a deadly cocktail—so to speak.

## Can Anything Be Done about It?

The Bible supports two types of accountability—external and internal. Dr. Mitch Whitman has been so helpful to me in understanding this. Mitch, whom I've referred to earlier, works as a therapist specializing in helping Christian leaders and pastors. Many leaders are referred to him after some sort of problem or breakdown in their life and ministry.

Over the years, Mitch has seen it all. I remember one conversation where we began to talk about accountability among Christian leaders and he introduced his opinion concerning internal and external locus of control.

Mitch referred to research that dates back to the 1960s. A psychologist named Julian Rotter developed an inventory to measure locus (location) of control. Since then, hundreds of studies have been done on this topic. In these studies, locus of control is the perceived source of control over our behavior. People with internal locus of control believe they control their own destiny. They tend to be convinced that their own skill, ability, and efforts determine most of their life experiences. In contrast, people with external locus of control believe their lives are determined mainly by sources outside themselves—fate, relationship dynamics, work situations, powerful people, or God's will.

## External Accountability

All leaders have some external accountability. For example, there are laws to which we must adhere. Leaders are not above the law. The denomination or church usually has policies and guidelines that must be followed.

One of the examples Mitch shared with me was the policy of many churches that a window must be built in the door of the pastoral or counseling offices. These boundaries are spelled out to protect leaders —and others.

This type of accountability is based in fear. "If I don't follow the rules or guidelines, I will be in trouble." Usually for church leaders, the problem is an addiction to work, sex, romance, self-abuse, power, or money. For leaders struggling with these issues, work, society, family, and friends do not create much fear of "making you change or else." In some cases, they actually encourage and benefit from your behavior. Addiction to work is encouraged in most ministry settings, even though the results are damaging.

Ministers of the gospel often see the results of their workaholism in the lives of their children and in their lack of friends. For those leaders who are parents, this woman's story should remind us again of our need to be accountable.

## One Minister's Adult Daughter Tells All

One day I picked up a book on adult children of alcoholics and was mesmerized. I couldn't put it down. There was no drinking in my family, but the dynamics described in that book were my family.

My dad was never home. He was always working. Even when he was home, he was "in the study" and we kids were not allowed to "disturb" him. His work was the most important thing in our family. If any of us complained about never seeing him, he always had the excuse that he was doing "the Lord's work" and working himself to death was justified.

Because he was always tired and overextended, he was always irritable. When I read the descriptions of the rages and mood swings of the alcoholic father, I realized that we had the same thing in our family. The entire family was always walking on eggs around him, and our lives were geared to his life and his moods. Nothing else mattered.

Because of his intensity about his work, his constant "cause," and his overwhelming obsession with money, my family was oriented toward crisis. We were always on the edge of some disaster.

He ran the church the same way. The only people who were worthy of his respect were those who were willing to "suffer for Christ." He was respected for being a hard worker, but he was never loved. Just as we kids always felt guilty and bad about ourselves in his presence, the parishioners were always uneasy and felt guilty in relation to him. No matter what they did, it was never enough.

Although he was always working and on the run, his actual productivity decreased. He recycled old sermons more and more often. He died in his late forties and no one ever knew him. I feel like I had a nonrecovering alcoholic for a father. He did not really serve Christ or the church. I now know he served his disease.

A fear-based accountability is only as helpful as the degree of fear perceived, and the focused direction of the fear. The minister in the above story was more fearful about how he was perceived at the church. Fear did not motivate this father. He did not even consider that his lifestyle addiction to work would damage his daughter. There were no external accountability structures in place to assist him.

Could there have been? Yes. Just a few people in his life may have made all the difference. A board of elders or deacons who actually knew of the lifestyle he was living could have created guidelines. Not that they could apply rules, but they would have been in relationship together and capable of holding him accountable for his daughter's well-being.

### David and Bob

If you visit me in my office, you will notice a photo on the wall of two men smiling and looking right at my desk. Bob Kuhn and David Bentall are two life friends I have that are close enough to me to make a difference. Our friendship has endured for decades now, and we fully intend to grow old together.

These two men have walked with me in my life since 1989. What any leader needs, to remain sharp, is another to whom he can be accountable—as iron sharpens iron. Instead of defaulting to adding better accountability structures, leaders must intentionally build more accountability relationships to keep that keen edge.

Over the years, we have met together regularly and have sought to be engaged in one another's lives in order to bring glory to the kingdom. There are lists of questions you can use when starting such a relationship. They circulate in various books, but I encourage you to develop questions specific to who you are. Try breaking life down into various sections and create questions for each section. Here are examples of such questions.

## Questions for Personal Accountability

### Physical

*Sleep*: Are you getting enough sleep each night? If not, how much are you getting? How do you plan to change?

*Exercise*: Are you exercising daily? If not, how often are you exercising? How do you plan to change?

*Eating*: Are you eating properly? If not, what are you eating/not eating? How do you plan to change?

*Substances*: Are you abusing harmful substances? If not, when and how often have you taken them? How do you plan to change?

### Spiritual

*Distractions*: Have you used anything other than God in an attempt to meet your emotional or spiritual needs this week? If so, what? What would help redirect you to Jesus?

*God's Word*: Have you been purposefully filling your mind with the knowledge of God's Word daily? If not, how often? How do you plan to change?

*Fasting*: Have you fasted and prayed in the last month? If not, when was the last time? When have you next scheduled these disciplines?

*Obedience*: Is your conscience clear? If not, why? How do you plan to attain a clear conscience?

### Actions

*Finances*: Where are you financially right now? Are things under control? Are you feeling anxious? Is there any great debt? How are you planning to proceed in this area of your life?

*Purity*: Have you kept your mind pure (thoughts of anger, bitterness, movies, magazines, Internet pornography, other)? If not, when did you fall? What temptations need to be removed or precautions taken to prevent it?

*Material Goods*: Do you have anything that is used for evil needing to be destroyed or removed? If so, what? When and how will you (we) destroy or remove them?

Mentors whose
leaders lack solid
accountability
relationships (where
this kind of dialogue
takes place) can do
several things to
encourage them.
Mentors can:

Pray for leaders to
develop an attitude of
accountability that will
help preserve their
"sharpness."

Find ways to
encourage them to
develop a relationship
or two where they
can get the kind of
interaction discussed
here.

Be open to being
that "iron" the
leader needs to stay
sharpened.

*Control*: Have you lost control either verbally or otherwise since we last met? If so, when? When and how will you do something to restore and correct your actions?

### Relationships

*Deposits*: Have you made positive emotional and spiritual deposits with your kids and your spouse? If not, why? What might you be able to do to make this a natural response?

*Family*: Have you offended any family member since we last met? If so, when? When and how will you restore and correct your actions?

*Truthfulness*: Have you told the whole truth in your answers to the questions I have asked you? If not, what do you need to correct? What actions do we need to take to stay and remain accountable?

*Process*: Is the asking of these questions adequate for you? If not, what changes are needed? Who else needs to be a part of this process?

## The Company You Keep

In his book *The Company You Keep*, David Bentall writes about the transforming power of male friendship. He comments on the value of being engaged in close relationship. "The benefits I see aren't speculative or theoretical. . . . Over the course of the years, we have spurred each other on in making risky, yet highly positive career changes. We have helped each other to become better husbands and fathers, and have led each other to grow in friendship with God. We have held each other accountable for how we live our lives and encouraged one another for how we live our lives and encouraged one another into ratcheting up our fitness levels. Carson, Bob and I are, in every sense of the word, true soul mates."[1]

The accountability friendship David is speaking about is based on eight principles.[2] We actually took the time to write these out in detail. I have a one-page document that can be carried in my day planner or wallet for easy reference.

The principles in summary are:

1. To affirm one another
2. To be available to one another[3]
3. To pray with and for one another
4. To be open with one another
5. To be honest with one another
6. To treat one another sensitively
7. To keep our discussions confidential
8. To be accountable to one another

David and Bob are leaders, and we recognize that our friendship is unique. Isolated and unconnected, leaders may not make the opportunity for this much-needed personal sharpening process. We do, however, encourage leaders to engage in relationships of depth. It takes intentional effort on our parts to build into others and to have them build into us for a lifetime.

As I watch senior Christian leaders, I note three different ways they usually finish their season of ministry. Some have developed deep relationships of trust, a circle of friends around them who encourage them to go deeper in faith and in ministry while keeping their family and personal life balanced.

Others isolate themselves in their leadership and eventually slip into "Christian leadership paranoia" where they do not trust others. They will not work with others, not even for the enhancement of the kingdom.

A third variation of senior leader becomes passive and reclusive, often without anyone really close to him. These leaders speak about others as being their "friends," but most people around them understand friendship in a very different way.

When leaders are trying to protect their ego and image, they often withdraw from other people—cutting themselves off. They do not want to be open and vulnerable with others for fear of eroding or destroying the image or persona they have worked so hard, albeit subconsciously, to construct. They do not want others to see their inadequacies, and they mask these by finding ways to tell you repeatedly of their past successes. They may even come to consider themselves so important that they jeopardize the interests of the ministry through some of their decisions. This would certainly be part of the downfall of Christian leaders who have come to mind throughout this discussion of leadership failure.

Accountability is very, very important in this phase of mentoring leaders. Leaders are to be about sustaining ministry vision, and the evil one is far too aware of the strategic advantage of taking out a leader in this phase. If a leader is "dropped" during this stage of sustaining, the public erases all the blessings, leadership, and accomplishments that occurred during the years leading up to the fall. Disarray, discouragement, and anger emerge within the congregation or broader community.

The marketplace and government are rattled by the scandals of their own, and they have launched a new emphasis on accountability. Dr. Gerald Kraines, noted management consultant, Harvard faculty member, and CEO of the Levinson Institute, argues that "accountability is the key to leadership."[4] So how do we nurture greater accountability in leaders?

## The Bible and Accountability

The Bible is woven through with strong statements about our need to be accountable as Christians and as leaders. The Bible reminds us that there comes a day when each of us will have to give account before God for how we have lived our lives. Other verses emphasize that we are part of a community and that we have to be responsive to those in authority over us and accountable to those we live with and serve.

So then every one of us shall give account of himself to God.

Romans 14:12 KJV

For we must all appear before the judgment seat of Christ; that every one may receive the things done in his body, according to that he hath done, whether it be good or bad.

2 Corinthians 5:10 KJV

But I say unto you, that every idle word that men shall speak, they shall give account thereof in the day of judgment. For by thy words thou shalt be justified, and by thy words thou shalt be condemned.

Matthew 12:36–37 KJV

Obey them that have rule over you, and submit yourselves: for they watch for your souls, as they must give account.

Hebrews 13:17 KJV

For we are taking pains to do what is right, not only in the eyes of the Lord but also in the eyes of men.

2 Corinthians 8:21

And he said also unto his disciples, There was a certain rich man, which had a steward; and the same was accused unto him that he had wasted his goods. And he called him, and said unto him, How is it that I hear this of thee? give an account of thy stewardship.

Luke 16:1–2 KJV

When I say to the wicked, "O wicked man, you will surely die," and you do not speak out to dissuade him from his ways, that wicked man will die for his sin, and I will hold you accountable for his blood. But if you do warn the wicked man to turn from his ways and he does not do so, he will die for his sin, but you will have saved yourself.

Ezekiel 33:8–9

## Beware of Unaccountability

Occasionally you will encounter Christian leaders who believe they answer only to God and no one else. As a Christian leader, a pastor, or even a member of my church, I am always accountable to someone. I am accountable to the elders, the elders are accountable to the church, and the church is accountable to other churches within the denomination. Beware of secretive leaders who proclaim, "I am accountable only to God and I answer to no one else." No leader is above accountability. Receive the confrontation of friends and mentors and remind yourself that only observed behavior changes.

"An unexamined life is not worth living." Although Socrates, who is credited with that quotation, certainly lived with a different worldview than Christian, his pithy quote is worth remembering. To have our lives examined closely by those who live with us in community actually gives us a greater sense of life to live.

Currently the movement toward apostolic leadership raises another concern in the arena of accountability.

## Theological Accountability

Several young leaders within the Arrow Leadership Program have been interested in the promotion of a new movement dealing with apostolic leadership. Peter Wagner is widely known for his teaching and writing on church growth and spiritual warfare, and now is a catalyst for writings about apostolic leadership. Wagner says, "I needed a name. . . . For a couple of years I experimented with 'Post denominationalism.' The name I have settled on for the movement is the New Apostolic Reformation."[5]

Wagner is talking about the need for a new reformation of the church. The primary goal of the movement is to create "city churches" under the leadership of self-appointed "apostles" and undermining traditional denominational structures—bringing leaders from across various denominations under the authority of a network of "apostles."

In my lifetime, there is nothing new about this movement, although it is a well-promoted reappearance. There was a movement in the twentieth century called the New Order of the Latter Rain. The Latter Rain movement started in 1948 and influenced almost all Pentecostal churches and groups in the 1950s. The revival was short and did not produce the results its leaders had hoped, but it did give birth to numerous teachings such as the Manifested Sons of God heresy. The Assemblies of God eventually renounced this movement, which brought disorder, in 1949.

Today, however, there is a new emergence among leaders and churches that are longing for something more. Unfortunately, enthusiasts of new expressions may not know the history of movements prior to them—and just how similar they are. This is why I think younger leaders genuinely think they are unique. They would do well to know something of history before they make promises of establishing the "right" kind of church government and make promises of revival.

Leaders need to address this question: Why did others before us fail, whereas we will succeed now?

Dr. Irving Hexham was my supervisor during graduate school at the University of Calgary. As a friend and a mentor, Irving has taught me so much about the appreciation of history and its importance in giving leadership to today. I also turn to him when I need input on theological issues, especially those dealing with world religions.

> Mentors can be effective as research assistants, helping leaders explore new movements they are involved in—their history and meaning—to promote greater understanding and accountability. Encouraging the leaders to visit other ministries and arranging to introduce them to others in ministry are valuable mentoring activities.

None of us wishes to squash the movement of the Holy Spirit—especially on inspiring greater effectiveness in ministry—yet I find that many emerging leaders do not reflect on the theology underlying "new" movements. This is an area where a mentor can be of immense value.

Early on in my leadership development, I was deeply impacted by the mentoring of Dr. Sam, as I still call him to this day. Rev. Dr. Samuel Mikolaski was born in Serbia but raised in Canada since the age of four. He is a recognized and highly respected scholar in his field of theology and ethics, and is a graduate of Oxford University, where he received his D.Phil. Dr. Sam has served at several universities throughout North America, including the North America Baptist Theological Seminary and Atlantic Baptist University in Moncton, New Brunswick. However, God allowed our paths to cross when I was eighteen and a student at the Baptist Leadership Training School in Calgary, Alberta, where Dr. Sam was president.

What Dr. Sam helped me understand early on is that we must push to understand the theology beneath what we are expressing. As leaders, others will follow, and if we do not have it right, we can and will lead many people down wrong paths. Now interestingly, I don't think Dr. Sam ever used terminology like that. It would certainly sound far too boring for a young Christian in the 1970s. Nevertheless, the outcome of his mentoring was to bring about a desire in me to understand what it was I believed and to base everything on the Word of God.

Christian leaders should all be required to have theological mentors in their life. Today, I can still contact Dr. Sam should I have a question or visit his website where he has posted many of his papers.[6] I also work at Arrow with Rev. Gib Martin, who serves as an on-site mentor for leaders. Gib is a graduate of Dallas Theological Seminary and has been the pastor at the Trinity Evangelical Church in Seattle for over forty years.

Gib has served as the chairman of the Billy Graham Phone Center and the Jesus Video Project but is perhaps better known to younger leaders as senior mentor for Arrow and Mark Driscoll's father-in-law.[7] When Gib sits in the back row of one of our Arrow residential seminars, he functions like a theologian in residence, and I have learned a great deal from him in the process. Gib is also a resource that I turn to when I have a theological question, and I have always appreciated that he is thoughtful and reflective in his responses. He does not usually rattle off a simplistic response but desires that I actually understand—he wants me to "get it."

## What about Accountability in the Apostolic Movement?

One young pastoral leader asked me, "Who is an apostle accountable to?" As we begin to engage this next generation, mentors will have to be willing to assist Christian leaders in working through their accountability within new structures as they emerge. In this instance, he had put his finger on the very thing that may be the vulnerability of the apostle-based movement—accountability.

In his book *Churchquake!* Wagner raised his own concern about accountability within the apostolic movement.[8]

I wish I had a more definitive word. For local church pastors who are in apostolic networks, the accountability structure is relatively simple. They are accountable to their apostles, which in turn raises the question, to whom are the apostles accountable? I frequently raise the question of accountability to some of the top leaders of the New Apostolic Reformation (NAR), and I must say I have not received consistently clear answers.

Barney Coombs, in his fine book *Apostles Today*, does talk briefly about the problem. He says apostles are accountable in three directions: (1) to God, (2) to peers, and (3) to the local church that originally sent them out. In my opinion, the peer-level accountability is the one on which the future integrity of the NAR will undoubtedly stand or fall.

I do not mean to single out NAR specifically for Wagner's last sentence does apply to every ministry or organization we are leading. Accountability is what will sustain the future success or progress of the ministry and a leader's integrity.

Hence it is vital to have people in your life who know you well enough to know when you are not being honest. Even just one person who knows when you are pulling one over on everyone else and cares for you enough to confront you about it.

## Internal Accountability

So far we have been discussing external forms of accountability, but perhaps the most important measure for a leader is internal accountability. Mitch's contention is that all the external accountability structures in the world will not prevent someone who has no inner locus of control from slipping past the systems.

Inner accountability is based upon our will—our desire and commitment to be accountable—and the work of the Holy Spirit within us. Our Lord, who knit us together in our mother's womb, is able through the Spirit to examine our motives, our thoughts, and our behavior. We recognize that he knows us better than we know ourselves. Like King David in the Old Testament, we surrender to God our deepest needs, hopes, and dreams, and in submitting find provision for our souls.

One discipline that is helpful in nurturing inner accountability is regularly praying a prayer of "examen." "Examen" was developed by Saint Ignatius Loyola, who was a practical kind of person, which is reflected in this daily method of prayer he recommended to his brothers. They prayed it numerous times per day as part of their daily rhythm of life.

It is a time of reflection and personal assessment before God. Here we invite God to examine not only our behaviors but our thoughts, emotions, and spirits. Our goal for this prayer is that we will be in greater harmony with our Lord. The prayer of "examen" asks: "Search me, O God, and know my heart: try me, and know my thoughts: and see if there be any wicked way in me, and lead me in the way everlasting" (Ps. 139:23–24 KJV).

When we pray the prayer of "examen," we invite God to reveal where and how we sinned, erred, or stepped out of his will. Then we can confess and be forgiven.

### "Examen" Prayer Time

Before beginning this prayer time, try to be in a place where you are least likely to be disturbed, and where there is the least amount of external noise. I use my noise-canceling headphones if I am in our home with others around. Dr. Lon Alison, director of the Billy Graham Center in Wheaton, Illinois, showed me once how he uses a candle to change the lighting and to symbolize the start of his prayer activity and devotional times. Then sit comfortably and quiet yourself. Relax, be aware of how you are feeling, and then follow these five steps. It should take only about fifteen minutes.

Recall that you are in the presence of God. In John 15 Jesus says, "Abide in me and I will abide in you." Be still and know that you are with God.

Look at your day with gratitude—give thanks to God for his presence in the big and the small things of your life.

Ask help from the Holy Spirit—ask that God's Spirit might help you look at your actions and attitudes. Ask the Holy Spirit to help you understand the motivation of your heart.

Review your day—your entire day. Be sure to notice the details, the context of what happened, and how you acted. Examine how conscious you have been of God's presence and activity in your life. You may wish to ask yourself some of the following questions:

- When did I fail today and why?
- When did I give love today?
- Where did I receive love today?
- What habits and life patterns do I notice in my day?
- In what ways did I notice God in my day?
- When did I feel most alive? Most drained of life?
- When did I have the greatest sense of belonging? The least sense of belonging?
- When was I most free? Least free?
- When was I most creative? Least creative?
- When did I feel most fully myself? Least myself?
- When did I feel most whole? Most fragmented?

Reconcile and resolve—talk with Jesus about your day. You may feel led to seek forgiveness, ask for direction, share a concern, express gratitude, etc.

### Outcomes of the Prayer of Examen

Those who practice this discipline report a number of changes in their spiritual walk with God. Here are some outcomes you might expect from praying a prayer of "examen":[9]

- It brings an increased consciousness of God's presence in our daily lives and how we have responded to him.
- It leads to an uncovering of those areas in our lives that need cleansing, purifying, and healing.
- It facilitates a remembrance of God's deeds, both in our lives and throughout history.
- It creates an increase in self-knowledge.
- It allows an inward turning of "the deepest level of the self to God."
- It creates a desire and ability to begin journaling as part of your prayer time.

### Internally Guided Leaders

Over the years I have noticed characteristics among leaders who are guided by a security in who they are in Christ Jesus. The quiet steadiness surrounding internally guided leaders is telling. I can determine that they spend time with the Lord prior to exercising leadership.

Internally guided leaders:

1. are more likely to work for achievements, to tolerate delays in rewards, and to plan for long-term goals.
2. are better able to resist manipulation.
3. are more likely to learn about their surroundings and learn from their experiences.
4. are less prone to serious depression.
5. are better at tolerating ambiguous situations.
6. are more willing to work on self-improvement.
7. derive greater benefits from those people near to them.

## Spiritual Side of Accountability

In this phase of the mentoring matrix, our goal is to assist leaders in sustaining themselves in the ministry or organization in order to fulfill the mission. The evil one's strategy, as I have already mentioned, is to bring the leader down so as to thwart the ministry that is already effective and to discredit everything that had taken place before.

Accountability is one way to lessen the areas of vulnerability in our lives as leaders, and every leader should be expected to practice both external and internal accountability. First Timothy 3:2 says clearly that "the overseer must be above reproach."

Mentors can also come alongside and support leaders by suggesting a prayer support base for them.

There are a few people I communicate regular prayer concerns with via an electronic "Knee Mail." I can actually sense the support brought through their intercession on my behalf. When establishing such a group, make sure you keep the numbers relatively low and that the members are people you can count on to pray on your behalf. Some leaders are tempted to put everyone in their prayer group because they use it more as an information-sharing, or fund-raising, newsletter than a strategic army of prayer warriors.

# Epilogue

## CONTINUED GROWTH AND NEW VISION

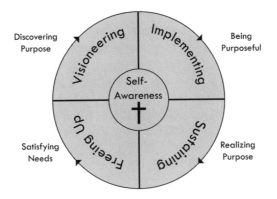

## So You Are a Leader

You've started to realize that you really are a leader. After all, others look to you for leadership. You have been a leader beyond the walls of your organization. All your reading and experience have combined to bring you to this place. You have poured yourself out into the ministry you lead. You have rolled out a vision and have led the way. The number of meetings you have attended, the speaking, preaching, and training you have done have shown great fruit for the kingdom. You are a leader. Now, would you like to stay one?

We have almost come full circle around this mentoring pattern. Yet for leaders there are always new challenges, and for those at this stage the great challenge is how to continue growing and stimulating new vision.

So what's your plan? Where do ministry leaders go, what do they do to further develop their leadership skills to stay sharp, focused, and effective? What will recharge your battery?

I'll begin by suggesting two sure winners:

Be a lifelong mentor: Stay involved with developing younger leaders.
Be a lifelong learner: Stay curious. Do research, writing, and study.

I am inspired when I am with senior leaders who still are on fire for Jesus, are learning and continuing to make new discoveries. You can see it in their eyes. And if you ask them how they stay so fresh, they affirm the above two points, which they exemplify in their own lives.

Dr. Eddie Gibbs is an example. When Eddie is with us training at an Arrow residential seminar, I find myself concerned for him given the pace and intensity of those weeks. As professor of church growth at Fuller Seminary in Pasadena and one well respected in the missions community, Eddie travels across North America and around the world teaching. His accent reveals his United Kingdom background, but his writings and his dialogue would never reveal his age.

Eddie stays young. He is such an inspiration to the leaders we work with as he shares their enthusiasm for the gospel and encourages them to step up to the plate. Dick Staub, radio host and founder of the Center for Faith and Culture, was interviewing Eddie and asked him what he might add to his book *Church Next* if he were to rewrite it now? Eddie replied, "It would address more closely the issue of leadership. I've learned a lot more by talking to young leaders. That's been a growing point in my own understanding."

When I heard that, it made me smile. It reminded me of a brief discussion Eddie and I had early in the year. I had been watching Eddie all day. He had been teaching all day at an Arrow residential seminar. The leaders were "soaking it up," as they later described the day. Eddie was animated, inspiring, and prophetic in his delivery.

Our leaders could hardly believe their ears as he shared with them his thoughts about the church and missions and evangelism challenges that they will be required to lead through. Few had ever been poured into by a leader like Eddie. They were so encouraged.

Brenda and I were keeping an eye on Eddie throughout the day, since he was unable to come to the previous seminar due to health concerns and surgery. He seemed to be doing extremely well, but when I found a moment, I asked him to check and make sure he was all right. He assured me he was, and he continued his teaching session well beyond what we had expected because the leaders were so engaged.

Now for those readers who teach, speak, or preach, you know how you feel after six hours of lecturing and interacting with a room filled with high-level leaders. You are usually exhausted—but not Eddie. I found him later that evening surrounded by several young leaders dreaming about the transformation of the church for the next generation.

I approached him, thinking he must be tired after such a long day, and he replied, "Carson, I love being here with these leaders. I learn so much from our time together." That is what he was referencing in the Dick Staub quote.

## Lifetime Development Phases

Eddie is a learner. What he is modeling is a leader who takes time to engage culture, mentor younger leaders, and remain open to learning. Evon and Jean Hedley, Michael Green, Irv and Marilyn Chambers, Leighton Ford, Ted Engstrom, Paul and Christa Schoeber, and Gib Martin have all modeled this in their leadership. They all share that it keeps them feeling young!

Each of these leaders has made personal leadership development a priority in life. They realize that we always can grow a little bit more. As they mentor others, they do give away a great deal—but in the process they are also learning from those they mentor.

Another way leaders can learn and give at the same time is through serving on the board of directors of other ministries. One has to be selective about this, for the opportunities to sit on boards far exceed most leaders' ability to respond. I will serve on a board only if I have a sincere interest in the ministry and can be supportive of the cause. I also want to know that I can contribute. Are my gifts going to advance the work of the board? Another reason I choose to serve on a few boards is that I learn. New people I might not otherwise meet can become new friends. I also learn about the leadership challenges and joys of other ministries.

When you reach the "I really am a leader" stage in your personal life, you realize that you do have experience and insights that can be used to further God's purpose, and sharing that through another ministry board is a wonderful way to share kingdom wisdom.

It is helpful to understand that there are three lifetime development phases: the age of learning, the age of contribution, and the age of investment. These are relatively simple constructs to assist you as a leader, or a mentor. We utilize them in our mentor training, and many can find themselves in the description of the various age groups. See if these seem to reflect your life.

## The Age of Learning (Eighteen to Thirty Years Old)

### KEY QUESTION: WHO AM I?

During this stage, we are trying to figure out who we are. We need models we can watch and observe safely. We want to develop understanding of who we are and how things work.

We welcome perspective, affirmation, and feedback to assist us on the journey. This stage also finds us dealing with inner life issues. We need accountability.

We know there are some very busy people in this age grouping, but there are relatively fewer external demands on our time in the age of learning than in the later stages; therefore we are actually less busy.

During this phase we are best helped by having an older mentor. Within Arrow we like to use mentors who are ten to fifteen years older as a guideline. This allows them to be further down life's road without being out of sight.

## The Age of Contribution (Thirty to Fifty Years Old)

### KEY QUESTION: WHAT DO I DO?

During this stage of life, we experience significantly more pressure. For those married with children, the household becomes very busy. It is the halftime season, and both men and women enter into a midlife reevaluation time as they have second thoughts about the first half of life and give more regard to the future.

During this phase of life, there is a danger of dabbling—trying one thing after another without making a significant contribution anywhere. We must also be careful that we do not plateau here. You must intentionally continue to strive for growth.

We need coaching and direction in this phase. It is an important time in life when we desire strongly to figure out our life purpose and find our voice.

A combination of senior mentors and peer mentors is most helpful in the age of contribution.

*The Age of Investment (Fifty Years and Older)*

KEY QUESTION: IN WHOM OR WHAT SHOULD I INVEST
MYSELF?

In this life phase, we will attend more funerals than weddings. Our focus turns toward "finishing well." There is a growing desire to leave a legacy.

Leaving a legacy means that something is remembered. But it doesn't happen by itself. It's something we have to work at. The legacy we leave behind is the imprint that lasts after we've retired or moved on. It is the lasting impact we've had on others throughout our careers.

Most people just live; they forget to learn. This can be a vibrant time of growth and learning, just as it is in the lives of those I mentioned earlier.

This season also brings with it a great deal of change. Aging parents and teenage children, moving or downsizing, friends and family moving or dying—each alters our world.

People in this stage are best helped through it with a peer mentor, one close to their age who will grow old with them.

## Maintaining Vision

Maintaining a vision that would have kept you awake at night with excitement twenty years earlier will begin to weigh you down. Maintenance of vision can be draining, and the search for something new in which you can invest yourself can provide a great deal of enjoyment and fulfillment.

I like to encourage leaders in this stage of life to understand this: "You are now the sage!" People look up to you. Many leaders have trouble transitioning into a sage and remain stuck in the contribution activity of the previous season.

Get behind the endeavors and dreams of a younger leader. Serve on a board of directors. Find something that interests you at life's sigmoid curve, and then invest in it for the kingdom's sake.

## Life Well Lived

Finding greater purpose and meaning in our lives transcends job titles and socioeconomic standards. In fact, I believe that the need for a deeper context for what we do every day is a basic human longing, which underscores our need for interpersonal connections.

As one reaches "retirement age" many things change, but living one's life to serve the Lord does not. A lifetime of walking with God enables us to relate the truths of God's Word in a personal, tangible way and shows how God has worked in our lives. The psalmist's prayer (Ps. 71:18) should guide us in this stage of life:

> Even when I am old and gray,
>     do not forsake me, O God,
> till I declare your power to the next generation,
>     your might to all who are to come.

Our elders ought to be treated with respect and to be learned from, especially when their lives have been lived for Christ. In like manner, as we age, we must focus on teaching those who walk behind us about Jesus so that they may be led more by Jesus, lead more like Jesus, and lead more to Jesus (Prov. 16:31).

# The Mentoring Matrix

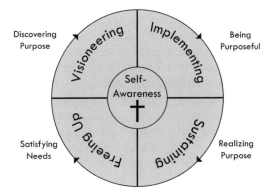

Together we have journeyed around the five phases of mentoring and growth for Christian leaders. I do hope the journey has given your spiritual and leadership legs a workout and that you have gained life-changing views along the way. Remember the five phases?

1. Self-Awareness—deep-seated understanding of who we are as children of God through Jesus Christ.
2. Freeing Up—disentangling ourselves from those things that hold us back and having our needs fully met by Jesus.
3. Visioneering—discovering God's purpose for our lives.
4. Implementing—being purposeful in how we live and lead.
5. Sustaining—learning how to realize our purpose and maintain zeal for ministry.

Notice how we can also look at the matrix diagram in sections—dividing the pie up into halves of varying emphases. The top half of the matrix requires mentoring that is primarily focused on engaging things that are out *there*. The bottom half requires mentoring that touches at things *in here* (I'm placing my hand on my heart as I type this).

Mentoring on the left side of the matrix will have an impact on the *mentee*, while the right side will impact the *environment* around the leader, his organizations, ministries, or staff.

## So You Think You're Finished?

There is nothing more exhilarating as a mentor than beginning to walk with a leader through the phases of mentoring once more. The leader and mentor have a much greater awareness of who they are —strengths and weaknesses—and are usually deeply committed to the enhancement of kingdom priorities.

Not so quick. There is one more observation I need to share with you.

Though we have taken a long, thoughtful look at a mentoring process for Christian leaders, the reality is that the journey is not over. Our experience is that once a leader is in the sustaining phase of the mentoring process, God often plants the seed of something new within.

Often the Lord points out something new about us and there is a new level of self-awareness that triggers new growth. The Holy Spirit also interjects himself into our lives at unpredictable moments—leading us into a deeper relationship with God and a renewed sense of calling. Mark Buchanan, when talking about his experience of walking through these phases, calls it a "holy ambush."

In typical God fashion, the flash point, spark, or ignition will be different for each of us as leaders, but what God wants to invite us to is a yet deeper understanding of who he is and our relationship to him as leaders.

And so the vision quest begins to either enhance or build the capacity of the existing vision, or to create something new.

Where are you in the mentoring process? I ask that personally, but also in terms of your mentoring of others. Can you see where you are in the matrix? Can you identify where younger leaders are in the matrix?

## Is Mentoring Leaders a Good Investment?

Absolutely! The conventional definition of effective ministry leadership is getting work done through people, but real leadership is developing people through ministry work.

So let me encourage you. Get a mentor—be a mentor. There is no better way for you to invest your time.

# Notes

## Chapter 2: Starting with New Awareness

1. Daniel Goleman, *Emotional Intelligence: Why It Can Matter More than IQ* (London, UK: Bloomsbury, 1996), 43.

2. Ibid., 48.

3. James Taylor, *In the Pocket*, Warner Brothers, 1976. Audio CD released 1990.

4. Bobb Biehl has not only been an amazing mentor to Brenda and me, but you can access his gift of wisdom through his website at www.masterplanninggroup.com. You will also find his book *Mentoring: How to Find a Mentor and How to Become One* (Lake Mary, FL: Aylen, 2005) a tremendous encouragement toward a lifetime of mentoring and filled with what Bobb is known for: "tomorrow morning practical" tips.

5. This conversation with Arch Hart took place while we were attending an African Enterprise conference for leaders in Pietermaritzburg, South Africa, 2003; however, much more detail is available in his book *Adrenalin and Stress: The Exciting New Breakthrough That Helps You Overcome Stress Damage* (Waco: Word Publishing, 1995).

6. This process is originally based on the writings of the early church fathers, and also of Teresa of Ávila, as outlined in Adolphe Tanquery, *The Spiritual Life* (Baltimore: St. Mary's Seminary, 1930). This chart is adapted from Benedict J. Groeschel, *Spiritual Passages: The Psychology of Spiritual Development* (New York: Crossroads, 1984). Used with permission.

7. Jim Bakker, as interviewed in *Servant Magazine*, Winter 1997, www.pbi.org.ca.

8. See D. M. Whitman, "The Effect of Ego Strength on Extramarital Involvement among Protestant Clergy" (Ph.D. diss., Seattle Pacific University, 2004).

9. Teresa of Ávila, *The Letters of St. Teresa Translated from the Spanish by The Rev. John Dalton* (London: Thomas Baker I, Soho Square, 1902), Letter 33, 179.

10. Charles Swindoll, *Come Before Winter* (Portland, OR: Multnomah, 1985), 178.

11. This Orphan / Child Perspectives chart has been used for years at Arrow Leadership International Ministries to teach the contrasting perspectives it displays. Original source is unknown.

## Chapter 3: Freeing Up

1. There are many variations of such a list available from multiple sources. The chart I have included here is adapted from Neil Anderson, *The Bondage Breaker*, 2nd ed. (Eugene, OR: Harvest House, 2000), 202–4.

2. Ed Dobson and Cal Thomas, *Blinded by Might* (Grand Rapids: Zondervan, 1999), 37.

## Chapter 4: Visioneering

1. See photos of the facilities (including the amazing view) and a description of the ministry of Barnabas Family Ministries at www.barnabasfm.org.

2. See www.listenuptv.com for more detail on this vision.

3. C. S. Lewis, *The Screwtape Letters* (New York: Macmillan, 1967), 27.

4. Bill Hybels, *Courageous Leadership* (Grand Rapids: Zondervan, 2002), 32.

5. J. Oswald Sanders, *Spiritual Leadership* (Chicago: Moody, 1980), 55.

6. Leighton Ford, *Transforming Leadership* (Downers Grove, IL: InterVarsity, 1991), 98.

7. J. Robert Clinton, *The Making of a Leader* (Colorado Springs: NavPress, 1988), 245.

8. Os Guinness, *The Call: Finding and Fulfilling the Central Purpose of Your Life* (Nashville: Word, 1998), 31.

9. Ibid., 47.

10. Ibid., 188.

11. John Maxwell, *The 21 Indispensable Qualities of a Leader* (Nashville: Nelson, 1999), 151.

12. Terry Fullam, as quoted in Leighton Ford, *Transforming Leadership* (Downers Grove, IL: InterVarsity, 1991), 104. When Fullam speaks about the burden that leaders often have we recognize that with special vision recipients, they didn't necessarily have a burden to know the will of God. God acted because of his agenda, not ours. It is a reminder that it is not about us—it is all about him.

## Chapter 5: Practical Vision Helps

1. George Barna, *The Power of Vision* (Ventura, CA: Regal, 1992), 47, www.barna.org.

2. Bobb Biehl offers a free online email called "Quick Wisdom" available from the website of Masterplanning Group at www.masterplanninggroup.com.

3. See Dave Phillips's website, www.courage4u.com, to see how purpose can make a difference in your life. He has some helpful downloads available on the subject of vision.

4. Thanks to Larry Brune, Kari Ylerenko, Rick and Donna Lamothe, and Chris and Andrea Stevens for such a stimulating spiritual discussion.

5. George Barna, *Building Effective Lay Leadership Teams* (Ventura, CA: Issachar Resources, 2001).

6. Karen Souffrant is founder and president of InsideOut International. To learn more about InsideOut and the services offered, visit www.insideoutinternational.org.

7. John Haggai, *Lead On* (Waco: Word, 1986), 21.

8. Psalm 46:10, *The Message: Psalms*, trans. Eugene H. Peterson (Colorado Springs: NavPress, 1994).

9. Charles Swindoll, *Intimacy with the Almighty* (Dallas: Word Publishing, 1996), 38.

## Chapter 6: Implementing the Vision

1. John Kotter, *The Leadership Factor* (New York: Free Press, 1988), 82.

2. Peter Senge, *The Fifth Discipline: The Art and Practice of the Learning Organization* (New York: Currency Publishers, 1994), 10. Senge is believed by many to be the father of the learning organization movement. Nevertheless, for further research interest, Senge's work is

built largely on ideas developed in 1984 by University of Lancaster's Peter Checkland and by Harvard professor Chris Argyris.

3. I have since stopped using the term "excellence," after a meaningful discussion with James Lawrence, director of Arrow in the United Kingdom. We were reflecting on how "excellence" can conjure up some motives that are not healthy in the long run. "Wholehearted" is a better word—and a biblical one at that: "Serve him with wholehearted devotion and with a willing mind, for the LORD searches every heart and understands every motive behind the thoughts" (1 Chron. 28:9).

### Chapter 7: Stepping Out Vision

1. President, "Special Message to the Congress on Urgent National Needs," *Public Papers of the Presidents* (May 25, 1961): 404, http://www.gpoaccess.gov/pubpapers/.

2. Pat MacMillan, *The Performance Factor: Unlocking the Secrets of Teamwork* (Nashville: Broadman & Holman, 2001).

3. Pat's "team wheel" and the chapters on the qualities of a high-performance team are worth the price of the book alone. If you are mentoring a leader, this would make a great gift for your mentee's resource shelf.

4. Jim Collins, *Good to Great: Why Some Companies Make the Leap . . . and Others Don't* (New York: HarperCollins, 2001), 41.

5. Robert W. Dingman, *In Search of a Leader: The Complete Search Committee Guidebook* (Westlake Village, CA: Lakeside Books, 1994), 158–59.

### Chapter 9: Measuring People and Outcomes

1. This survey by Jim Fann is available online at the Evangelical Free Church of America website at http://www.efca.org/health/checkup/health.html. The value of such a survey for church leaders is having a reliable benchmark that will enable you to zero in on decisive areas of church health.

2. For Natural Church Development resources, see www.ncd-international.org.

### Chapter 10: Sustaining in Leadership

1. A. W. Tozer, *The Size of the Soul* (Camp Hill, PA: Christian Publications Inc., 1992), 81.

### Chapter 11: Fear, Loneliness, and Other Challenges

1. Hans Christian Andersen, *The Emperor's New Clothes* (New York: P. F. Collier and Son, 1937), 238 (vernacular updated by author).

### Chapter 12: Accountability

1. David Bentall, *The Company You Keep* (Minneapolis: Augsburg, 2004), xii.

2. David deals with each of these at length in *The Company You Keep*.

3. Our availability to one another is always in proportion to our commitments to our marriage and family.

4. Accountability Leadership Seminar, 2004, the Levinson Institute, Inc.

5. C. Peter Wagner, *The New Apostolic Churches* (Ventura, CA: Regal, 1998), 18.

6. Dr. Sam Mikolaski's website is located at www.drsamstheology.org.

7. Mark Driscoll is the pastor of Mars Hill Church, one of the fastest-growing emerging churches in North America, located in Seattle, Washington, and also the author of *The Radical Reformission: Reaching Out without Selling Out* (Grand Rapids: Zondervan, 2004). Mark is

regarded by many (myself included) as being the Charles Spurgeon of this generation. See and hear more about this amazing leader at www.marshillchurch.org.

8. C. Peter Wagner, *Churchquake! The Explosive Dynamics of the New Apostolic Revolution* (Ventura, CA: Regal, 1999), as quoted on Wagner's Global Harvest website, www.globalharvest .org. For source of three points cited within this quotation, see Barney Coombs, *Apostles Today* (Tunbridge, Kent, England: Sovereign World, 1996), 212–13.

9. The "Prayer of Examen" is featured in Richard Foster, *Prayer: Finding the Heart's True Home* (New York: HarperCollins, 1992), 27–35.

**Carson Pue** is president of Arrow Leadership International Ministries, a ministry founded by Leighton Ford and committed to mentoring church and ministry leaders. An ordained Baptist minister, he has had a varied career in business, the pastorate, and parachurch ministry. He was executive director for Chuck Swindoll's Insight for Living radio ministry and has spent over twenty thousand hours mentoring Christian leaders over the past fifteen years.

### Other Resources

Arrow Leadership offers a free monthly e-letter written by Dr. Pue called "Mentoring Questions." As a resource for the files of every mentor, this e-letter shares proven and effective mentoring questions followed by sections on why you would ask the question; what to listen for in the response; and a biblical promise that speaks into the situation. Available at www.arrowleadership.org.

Arrow also offers a three-and-a-half-hour mentoring experience for churches or denominational gatherings to "encourage a mentoring heart" and provide essential resources to start mentoring relationships or strengthen existing ones. Contact Arrow Leadership toll-free in North America at 1-877-262-7769 for further information, or email us at mentoring@arrow leadership.org.